The Cambridge Handbooks of Liturgical Study

GENERAL EDITORS:
H. B. SWETE, D.D.
J. H. SRAWLEY, D.D.

THE OFFICES OF BAPTISM
AND CONFIRMATION

CAMBRIDGE UNIVERSITY PRESS
London: FETTER LANE, E.C.
C. F. CLAY, Manager

Edinburgh: 100, PRINCES STREET
Berlin: A. ASHER AND CO.
Leipzig: F. A. BROCKHAUS
New York: G. P. PUTNAM'S SONS
Bombay and Calcutta: MACMILLAN AND CO., Ltd.
Toronto: J. M. DENT AND SONS, Ltd.
Tokyo: THE MARUZEN-KABUSHIKI-KAISHA

THE OFFICES OF BAPTISM AND CONFIRMATION

BY

T. THOMPSON, M.A.,
of Saint Anselm's House, Cambridge

Cambridge :
at the University Press
1914

Cambridge:

PRINTED BY JOHN CLAY, M.A.

AT THE UNIVERSITY PRESS

NOTE BY THE EDITORS

THE purpose of *The Cambridge Handbooks of Liturgical Study* is to offer to students who are entering upon the study of Liturgies such help as may enable them to proceed with advantage to the use of the larger and more technical works upon the subject which are already at their service.

The series will treat of the history and rationale of the several rites and ceremonies which have found a place in Christian worship, with some account of the ancient liturgical books in which they are contained. Attention will also be called to the importance which liturgical forms possess as expressions of Christian conceptions and beliefs.

Each volume will provide a list or lists of the books in which the study of its subject may be pursued, and will contain a Table of Contents and an Index.

The editors do not hold themselves responsible for the opinions expressed in the several volumes of the series. While offering suggestions on points of detail, they have left each writer to treat his subject in his own way, regard being had to the general plan and purpose of the series.

H. B. S.
J. H. S.

PREFACE

THE aim of this handbook is to furnish an account of the liturgical history of baptism and confirmation. In pursuing this aim I have kept three objects in view: first, to trace the developements of the services, in early days in general outline, and later on in particular regions; secondly, to indicate, as far as is practicable, the relations of various rites to each other; thirdly, to provide some assistance to those who desire to study the services in the ancient liturgical books, in which the rites are usually either broken up and inserted at various points, or overlaid with ornamental additions.

The word 'confirmation' is used in this book for the rite which follows baptism, either immediately or after some interval. The word, however, dates only from the fifth century, and is confined to Western Europe. In earlier days and in the East other words, *e.g.* 'seal,' were used. It is important, therefore, not to read into the Eastern and earlier Western practice the implications of thought and custom which we

associate with 'confirmation,' but to remember
that the single term 'confirmation' covers a
diversity of usages, and that neither in the conceptions associated with it, nor in the manner
of its administration does it stand for a fixed
and uniform rite.

My debt to various works is acknowledged in
the Bibliography and notes. I have found particularly useful the articles in the *Dictionnaire d'archéologie chrétienne et de liturgie* and the valuable
collection of patristic materials in Dr Mason's
Relation of Confirmation to Baptism. I am also
indebted to the Rev. W. C. Bishop for reading
through the work in manuscript and for various
helpful suggestions. To the General Editors of
the series, Dr Swete and Dr Srawley, I owe more
than I can express. I am grateful to them for
unfailing patience, for criticisms and suggestions,
and, above all, for the inspiration and education
to which is due whatever may be of value in the
following pages. Lastly, I owe my best thanks
to the workmen and staff of the Cambridge
University Press.

T. T.

Feast of St Hugh, 1913

CONTENTS

PART I

PART II

ABBREVIATIONS

    A.C. = *Apostolic Constitutions.*
    C.Q.R. = *Church Quarterly Review.*
    C.W. = Duchesne, *Christian Worship.*
    D.A.C.L. = *Dictionnaire d'archéologie chrétienne et de liturgie.*
    J.Th.St. = *Journal of Theological Studies.*
    P.G. = Migne, *Patrologia Graeca.*
    P.L. = Migne, *Patrologia Latina.*

PART I

CHAPTER I

THE EARLY HISTORY

THE history of the Christian Church opens with the day of Pentecost, when the Holy Spirit descended on the Apostles. On that day St Peter preached to the multitudes assembled at Jerusalem, of whom we read[1] that three thousand, who received his message, were baptized and added to the small band of disciples. With this event the story of Christian baptism begins. As the Church expanded, new converts were made in Samaria[2], at Caesarea[3], and, further afield, at Philippi[4], at Corinth[5], and at Ephesus[6], and, on receiving the teaching of the Apostles, they were straightway baptized. That the laying on of hands was considered the completion of the initiation, may be gathered from the action of St Peter and St John at Samaria[7] and of St Paul at Ephesus[8].

The New Testament presents us with a bare record of the actual rite. Details we cannot expect

---

[1] Acts ii. 41.   [2] ib. viii. 12.   [3] ib. x. 48.
[4] ib. xvi. 15, 33.   [5] ib. xviii. 8.   [6] ib. xix. 5.
[7] ib. viii. 14—17.   [8] ib. xix. 6.

in such early writings, and in references generally
incidental; if a fuller account is attempted, a region
of conjecture and controversy is at once entered.
The evidence of the New Testament in regard to
various questions connected with baptism and confirmation—the 'form,' the minister, the 'matter,'
the age of reception—is stated and discussed in the
latter part of this book, in chapters specially dealing
with these matters.

A few words and phrases which bear on later baptismal usage may be noted here. The word 'catechize'
($\kappa\alpha\tau\eta\chi\epsilon\hat{\iota}\nu$ = 'to instruct orally') is used thrice[1], particularly
of instruction in the events of our Lord's life. A con-
fession of faith is contained in the Western text of
the account[2] of the baptism of the Ethiopian eunuch,
'I believe that Jesus Christ is the Son of God'; the attestation for this reading is as old as the second century.
When St Paul[3] writes that 'no one can say that "Jesus
is Lord" except in the Holy Spirit,' we have perhaps the
earliest Christian profession of belief, the nucleus of the
creeds.

Christian baptism is a new thing in virtue of the
new meaning attached to the rite and the new graces
flowing from it. But the custom of ceremonial
lustrations with water is of immemorial antiquity
and is found in most religions. As a part of the
ritual of purification from ceremonial impurity,

---

[1] Gal. vi. 6; Lk. i. 4; Acts xviii. 25.   [2] Acts viii. 37.
[3] 1 Cor. xii. 3.   For allusions to this 'confession' of the faith
cf. Rom. x. 9; 2 Cor. iv. 5; Phil. ii. 11; 1 Tim. vi. 12; some have
seen a similar reference in 1 Pet. iii. 20 (see Bigg in *International
Critical Commentary*).

washing was familiar to both Jews and Gentiles. From this practice easily arose an initiatory rite of baptism, when washing was used by a person entering a religious society or organization. Such initiatory baptisms were familiar in heathen mysteries[1]. A similar rite was probably in use among the Jews before the rise of Christianity. Certainly at a later date we find baptism practised by the Jews in the reception of proselytes, and, when we consider the deep and bitter hatred that was felt towards Christians by the Jews, we cannot conceive that the custom was borrowed from Christianity, or even adopted at a time when baptism was employed by the Church in a similar way for the same purpose[2].

If early evidence of Jewish proselyte baptism is lacking, it is otherwise with the baptism of John the Baptist, which is attested by the Gospels. The baptism of John was the symbol of a moral change ; it was a baptism of repentance and of preparation for the coming of the Messiah. Like the Jewish baptism of proselytes, it was the beginning of a new life; unlike it, it was applied to all who came, whether Jews or Gentiles. And it expressly differed from Christian baptism in that the latter was baptism 'with the Holy Ghost.' The baptism of John was a token of the change of heart in the person undergoing it. Christian baptism was more than this—it

[1] Tert., *de Bapt.* 5, nam et sacris quibusdam per lauacrum initiantur, Isidis alicuius aut Mithrae...certe ludis Apollinaribus et Eleusiniis tinguuntur idque se in regenerationem et impunitatem periuriorum suorum agere praesumunt.

[2] See Hastings' *Dictionary of the Bible*, s.v. 'Baptism,' III a.

was the effectual sign of the Spirit of God acting by means of the element of water[1].

We see, therefore, that baptism and many of the meanings which Christianity attaches to it already existed before Christ, and may possibly, in great part, have been taken over into the Christian rite of initiation. Nor need this surprise us. Prayer itself is a universal exercise of the human soul, but receives a new meaning through the mediation of Jesus Christ. A similar process of appropriation has taken place in many other instances. Christian institutions are new, not in the sense of being entirely fresh creations, but in the sense that they are transfigured and made new by Him who makes all things new. So it is with baptism : the actual rite of washing, as a religious act, is general among mankind; but it attains fuller meaning and further importance from its relation to Christ's work and the gift of the Holy Spirit.

The actions used in the bestowal of confirmation are two in number: the imposition of the hand and unction, the latter of which is not expressly[2] mentioned in the New Testament in this connexion, but is dealt with here in regard to its origins for the sake of convenience. Both actions are found in the Old Testament and must have been familiar to instructed Jews of the first century of our era.

Imposition of the hand in the Old Testament signifies the bestowal of some spiritual gift; it is used

[1] On this subject see A. Blakiston, *John Baptist and his Relation to Jesus*, chap. III.

[2] But see below, p. 215.

of blessing or of appointment to a particular purpose, as in the laying on of hands upon a sacrifice or upon persons destined for a special function, as Joshua or the Levites. The latter meaning, of dedication or consecration, was prominent in unction in Jewish usage. Thus the significance of both actions is similar; they are a consecration of the individual to his membership in the Church and a dedication to service and ministry in the 'royal priesthood.' But here again the meaning of the acts in an older religion does not exhaust the fulness of meaning of the Christian rite; the association of the gift of the Holy Spirit with confirmation gives it a deeper and richer significance in the use of the Christian Church.

The two centuries following the Apostolic age are marked by great, though almost silent, developement in the rites of the Christian Church, and, in particular, in the rites of baptism and confirmation. At the beginning of the period the performance of the rites was simple, and, even if we make allowance for the paucity and reserve of the documents, consisted of little more than the rudimentary elements. During the post-Apostolic period we meet, here and there, allusions and brief descriptions, which shew that new features had been tacitly added and that the rites were settling into the forms which were later embodied in the liturgical books. At the end of the period, when the Church emerged into the light of publicity and recognition, we find everywhere, in the East and in the West, one general type of rite, containing as

its kernel the simple elements found in the New
Testament, but adding much which experience, reason,
and devotion had suggested, and derived from various
sources.   It is proposed to deal first with the early
descriptions of the rite ; then, in the second chapter,
with the developement and alterations by which the
primitive rite was changed into the full and elaborated
forms of the fourth and fifth centuries.   When the
history has been brought down to that point, we shall
be in a position to consider the character of the rites
of particular areas.

Justin Martyr, in his *First Apology*[1], gives a brief
sketch of baptism, drawn probably from the practice
of the Roman Church.   He writes as follows : ' Those
who believe that our teaching and statements are
true and promise that they can live in accordance
therewith, are taught to pray and entreat, with
fasting, for remission of their former sins from God,
while we pray and fast with them.   Then they are
taken by us to a place where there is water, and are
regenerated with the kind of regeneration with which
we ourselves were regenerated ; for in the name of
the Father of the Universe and the Lord God, and
of our Saviour Jesus Christ, and of the Holy Spirit
they then receive a washing in the water.'   In a later
chapter he carries on the account :—'After thus
washing him who is persuaded and assents, we bring
him to those whom we call brethren, where they are
congregated, to make common prayers for ourselves
and for the enlightened person and for all others

[1] Cap. 61, 65.

everywhere.' A brief description of the Eucharist follows.

Justin's account of set purpose avoids the Christian terminology, partly from a disinclination to use the exact words for sacred things in speaking to heathen, partly to make the meaning clearer by translating Christian language into the terms of common speech. But underneath the periphrastic expressions a good deal of detail appears. The 'catechumenate' is plainly in use, that is, baptism was preceded by a period of preparation and instruction. The catechumens were instructed in right conduct and religious truth; their preparation consisted of fasting, prayer, and confession of sins. Before baptism a profession of belief and a promise to live in accordance with the teaching that had been received, was made; this developed into the 'renunciation' and 'profession' found in later writings. The baptisms were performed in some stream or bathing place, as was convenient; the Threefold Name was used and the rite is called 'regeneration,' and the 'washing' or 'enlightenment[1].' After the baptism all returned to the church or place of religious assembly and the Eucharist followed. It is noticeable that there is no allusion to confirmation.

Another early account is furnished by the *Didache* or *Teaching of the Twelve Apostles*; it is so brief that it can be quoted in full. 'And concerning baptism, baptize ye thus. Having first declared all these things, baptize in the name of the Father, and

[1] λουτρόν, φωτισμός.

of the Son, and of the Holy Ghost in living water. But if thou have not living water, baptize into other water; and, if thou canst not in cold, in warm.   But if thou have neither, pour water thrice upon the head in the name of Father, Son, and Holy Ghost. And before the baptism let the baptizer and him that is baptized fast, and such others as can: and thou shalt enjoin the baptized to fast for one or two days before[1].'   In this account we have a catechumenate like Justin's; the words 'these things' refer to an instruction which occupies the preceding six chapters, and fasting is also enjoined.   The 'living water' signifies water which is fresh and flowing, not from a tank or cistern; such water is also prescribed in Church Orders[2] of the type of the *Ethiopic Church Order*.   The permission to baptize by 'affusion,' that is, by pouring on water, instead of by 'immersion[3]' should be noted, as it is an early instance of a practice which has become general in the West. Here again, as in Justin, confirmation is not mentioned[4].

The baptismal practices of the Gnostics are important and interesting, as they throw a valuable side-light on the usages of a period for which the

[1] Translation from Bigg, *The Doctrine of the Twelve Apostles*, c. VII.

[2] For these Church Orders see below, pp. 39—44.

[3] On these terms and the practice see part II. chapter IV.

[4] Dr J. A. Robinson in *J.Th.St.* XIII. 339 f. ('The Problem of the Didache') discounts the historical value of the *Didache*.   The rite of baptism in *A. C.* VII. 22 is derived from the *Didache*, but has been altered by the compiler to suit his own tastes; see below, pp. 32, 38.

orthodox evidence is scanty. The testimony is, however, to be used with caution, as it often emanates from opponents, and we are never certain how far their use resembled the practice of the Church. It is possible that, as in other matters, so here also the Gnostics may have acted as pioneers and introduced certain features which were afterwards generally adopted.

The baptism of the Gnostic sect called the Valentinians is known to us from the writings of Clement of Alexandria[1]. As a rite it consisted of baptism followed by an imposition of the hand. The closing words of the formula employed at the latter action were 'unto angelic redemption'; the word 'angelic' arises from their doctrine of baptism, according to which St Paul's reference to those 'which are baptized for the dead[2]' is interpreted of the angels who were baptized for mankind dead in sin.

The Marcosians, according to Irenaeus[3], administered baptism with various complicated formulas. The first is: 'Unto the name of the unknown Father of the Universe, unto Truth the Mother of All, unto him who came down upon Jesus, unto union and redemption and communion of the powers.' The second and fourth consist of Syriac words. The third ends with the same phrase as the Valentinian formula, 'unto angelic redemption.' The first form appears to be an adaptation of the orthodox form, altered to suit different theological conceptions; the

---

[1] *Excerpta Theodoti*, 22, 76—86.   [2] 1 Cor. xv. 29.
adv. Haeres. I. xviii. (Grabe).

invocation of the 'name' in some form or other is
common to all.   To the pronunciation of the formula
by the minister of the rite, the candidate responds:
'I am confirmed and redeemed, and redeem my soul
from this world and from all which springs from it,
in the name of Iao, who redeemed his soul unto
redemption in the living Christ.' The congregation
answers: 'Peace to all on whom this name rests.'
Then the neophyte is anointed with balsam[1]. Others
of this sect, according to Irenaeus, thought that the
leading to the water was superfluous, and mixing oil
and water, poured it upon the head of the candidates;
an unction with balsam followed.   It seems possible
to conjecture in this case an early example of two
practices which became very general at a later date
—the use of chrism[2] in the consecration of the
water, and baptism by affusion; the latter is allowed
in the *Didache*, as was noted above.

These Gnostic rites, apart from the bizarre language employed in their formulas, bear a strong
resemblance to the orthodox rites. The double
manner of confirmation is especially noteworthy;
both imposition of the hand and unction are used.
The former action was used in Apostolic times, and
in the West it was general from the second century;
unction is not expressly mentioned in the New
Testament in this connexion, but at a later time was
widely, if not universally, employed in confirmation.

[1] τῷ ὀπῷ τῷ ἀπὸ βαλσάμου v. l. τῷ ὀποβαλσάμῳ.

[2] It is convenient to note here the distinction between oil, that
is, pure olive oil, and chrism, that is, oil mixed with various fragrant
substances; on this subject see part II. chapter I.

Two views may be taken of the above facts: the Gnostic evidence may reflect the general Christian practice, or the Gnostics may have been the originators of confirmation as we know it. In the former case they furnish a link between the use of the imposition of the hand in the New Testament and the later practice, and they might furnish some ground for pushing the use of unction to an early, if not Apostolic, date. In the latter case their practice was rapidly and generally adopted throughout the Church, and the varieties in the manner of confirmation are to be ultimately attributed to the variations of Gnostic rites. The scarcity of orthodox evidence on the subject before the time of Tertullian makes it difficult to decide positively which view is right, and the question must be left open.

In certain Gnostic works of Syrian origin we find the rite of baptism preceded by unction. In the *Acts of Thomas*, which is probably a third century work, a rite of this type is employed; the following passage will serve to illustrate the method of baptizing: 'Mygdonia stood before the Apostle bareheaded; and he took the oil and poured it on her head, saying: "Holy oil, given us for sanctification, hidden mystery wherein the cross was shewn us, thou art the straightener of crooked limbs; thou art the humbler of hard works; thou art he that sheweth the hidden treasures; thou art the offspring of goodness. Let thy power come, and rest on thy servant Mygdonia; and heal her through this unction." When the oil had been poured on her, he bade her nurse

strip her and gird her with a linen cloth; now there
was there a well of water, to which the apostle went
up, and baptized Mygdonia in the name of the Father,
and of the Son, and of the Holy Ghost. When she
had been baptized and had dressed herself, he broke
bread and took a cup of water, and made her communicate in the body of Christ and the cup of the
Son of God, and said: 'Thou hast received the seal,
and won for thyself eternal life'"[1]. A similar rite is
found in the *History of John the Son of Zebedee*[2], and
the practice of an unction before baptism appears
to have been in general use among Syriac-speaking
Christians[3]. Nor is it confined to Syriac works. In
Greek writings an example of it is furnished by the
Gnostic *Clementine Recognitions*[4]. It is also found in
the *Didascalia*[5], which, though extant in Syriac, was
probably of Greek origin, and may have come from
Syria or Palestine. Its date is perhaps 250—300 A.D.
This work deals with baptism incidentally in describing

[1] *Acta Apostolorum Apocrypha*, edd. Lipsius et Bonnet, II. 2.
Acta Thomae 121; cf. 25—27, 49 (46), 131—133, 157. The *Acts
of Thomas* were composed in Syriac (Burkitt in *J. Th. St.* I. (1900)
280 ff., III. (1901) 94). The Syriac text of the *Acts of Thomas* in
Wright's *Apocryphal Acts of the Apostles* has been somewhat con-
ventionalized in its language, and the original text is often better
represented by the Greek translation in Lipsius and Bonnet. See
Preuschen, *Einleitung zu den Thomasakten* in Hennecke, *Neutesta-
mentliche Apokryphen*, pp. 473 f.

[2] Wright, *Apocryphal Acts of the Apostles*, II. 38, 53.

[3] For further evidence of the existence of this rite in East
Syria see the following page and the examples given in Connolly,
Liturgical Homilies of Narsai (*Texts and Studies*, VIII. 1), pp. xlii f.

[4] *Recog. Clement.* III, 67.

[5] M. D. Gibson, *Horae Semiticae*, II. 78. In the later redaction of the work in *A. C.* iii. 16 and the *Ethiopic Didascalia*
(ed. Platt, chap. 16), an unction after baptism is inserted.

the functions of deaconesses, who played an important part in the anointing of the bodies of the women. The account runs as follows: 'The office of a woman Deaconess is required, first, when women go down to the water; it is necessary that they be anointed by a Deaconess, and it is not fitting that the anointing oil should be given to a woman to touch, but rather the Deaconess. For it is necessary for the Priest who baptizeth, to anoint her who is baptized; but when there is a woman, and especially a Deaconess, it is not fitting for the women that they be seen by the men, but that by the laying on of the hand the head alone be anointed, as of old time the Priests and Kings of Israel were anointed. Thou[1] also in like manner, by laying on [thy] hand, anoint the head of those who receive baptism, whether of men or of women, and afterwards, whether thou thyself baptize, or command the Deacon or the Elder to baptize, let it be a Deaconess, as we said before, who anoints the women. Let a man repeat over them the names of the invocation of the Godhead in the water. And when she that is baptized arises from the water let the Deaconess receive her, and teach her and educate her, in order that the unbreakable seal of baptism be with purity and holiness.'

The above rite of baptism long persisted among the Syrian Christians. It is found in Aphraates, Ephraim the Syrian, Narsai and other Syriac writers, and in East Syria it survived till the seventh century,

---

[1] *i.e.* the bishop.

when a post-baptismal unction was added to the Nestorian rite by Isho'yabh III, to whose work we shall return in a later chapter[1].

The recently discovered *Odes of Solomon*[2] deserve notice here among early documents, as they are placed by some authorities in the second century. Dr Harnack and Dr Harris do not allow that they contain any reference to the sacraments, but Dr Bernard[3] contends, on the contrary, that they are really a series of *Hymns of the Baptized*, similar to St Ephraim's *Nativity Hymns*. If we read the *Odes* alone, the contention seems fanciful and far-fetched, as they contain no single definite reference to baptism. But taken in connexion with the Syriac writings on baptism —hymns, homilies, or liturgies, the meaning and purpose of which is indisputable—they assume a different aspect. The allusions to 'water,' the 'seal[4],' 'illumination,' 'vestments' and 'garlands' are seen to be charged with allusions to baptismal practices[5]; the figurative and allusive style of the *Odes* is characteristic of Syriac works, and is found in the parallel examples. The rite used in the *Odes* is uncertain from the indefiniteness of the language, but it was probably of the type which has just been described, that is, unction preceded baptism.

[1] See below, pp. 31, 66—68.

[2] *The Odes and Psalms of Solomon*, J. Rendel Harris; also in *Texte u. Untersuch.* XXXV. 4 (1910), ed. Harnack.

[3] *J.Th. St.* vol. XII. p. 1.

[4] The σφραγίς or 'seal' in liturgical writings properly means the signing with chrism, whereby the Christian was appropriated to Christ, as a sealed article to its owner. In early writers it is sometimes used of baptism as in the *Didascalia* above and Hermas, *Sim.* IX. 16 : ἡ σφραγὶς οὖν τὸ ὕδωρ ἐστίν.

[5] Dr Bernard interprets the 'milk and honey' of Ode IV. 10 as referring to the custom of giving a draught of milk and honey to the newly baptized; but as this custom is confined to Rome, Egypt, and Africa, it is better to take the expression as a metaphor for the felicity of the redeemed.

In this early period our information is very unequally distributed; some districts are fully illuminated, others are left in total darkness. The inequality corresponds, in some degree, to the facts of the case ; all regions did not develope with the same rapidity, nor did all accept new developements at the same rate. The Gnostic and Syriac rites shew early and rapid growth ; and, at a later period, it will be seen that the Syrian Churches were pioneers and leaders in liturgical work. In the West, Africa was similarly a centre of vigorous life and rapid growth. Between the *Didache* and Justin on the one hand, and Tertullian and Cyprian on the other, there is a wide gulf : in the former everything is in a simple and rudimentary state, in the latter the rites have reached the full developement.

In Africa, as early as the time of Tertullian, the catechumenate was well established. The African writers furnish the earliest examples of the use of the word 'catechumen,' though its Greek origin suggests that it was used before in the East. They also employ the Latin word *audientes* or 'hearers,' so called because they 'heard' the lessons and homily at the Eucharist, but were dismissed before the consecration. Tertullian attaches great importance to the maintenance of the discipline of the catechumenate, and strongly censures those heretics who did not observe it[1].

The principal purpose of the catechumenate was instruction; the candidates were taught the rules of

[1] *de Praescript.* c. 41.

Christian conduct, and the fundamental elements of religion. As the time of baptism drew near, the preparation became more strenuous; the candidates devoted themselves to 'prayers, fasts, kneelings, vigils, and confession of sins'; to these we may add the frequent exorcisms which they received[1]. During the catechumenate a preliminary renunciation was made[2]. The length of time which elapsed between the beginning of the preparation and baptism was not fixed; it was, doubtless, prolonged or abbreviated, according to circumstances.

The solemn season for baptism was Easter and the period between Easter and Pentecost[3]. But the sacrament could be administered at other times also[4]. First of all, the candidates before the bishop renounced the 'devil, and his pomp, and his angels[5]'; then the water received a solemn consecration[6]. Baptism was performed with three immersions[7]. At each immersion an interrogation on belief in the Trinity was put to the candidate. The question at the first immersion concerned belief in the Father, at the second, belief in the Son, at the third, belief in the Holy Spirit; the third question was generally expanded, and we know that the African form ended

---

[1] de Bapt. c. 20, Sentent. Episcop. lxxxvii. inter Opera Cypriani, 8, 31, 37 (ed. Hartel, pp. 441, 448, 450).

[2] Tert., de Cor. 3; de Spectac. 13.

[3] id., de Bapt. 19.　　　　　　　　[4] ib. 5.

[5] id., de Cor. 3, de Spectac. 4 and often.

[6] id., de Bapt. 4. Concil. Carthag. A.D. 255=Cypr., Ep. LXX. 1 (ed. Hartel, p. 767).

[7] Tert., de Cor. 3.

with, 'Dost thou believe in eternal life and remission of sins through holy Church[1]'? The whole three questions formed a short creed; to each question the candidate answered in the affirmative. The baptismal formula is unknown, except that the Trinitarian form was employed[2].

Baptism was followed by unction, signing, and imposition of the hand; to the last the gift of the Holy Spirit was attributed[3]. The chrism used in unction had previously been consecrated at the altar[4]. After confirmation followed communion and a draught of milk and honey, as a symbol of the blessings of the Promised Land into which the baptized had entered[5]. During Easter week the newly baptized abstained from the use of the bath[6].

[1] Concil. Carthag. 255 A.D., as above; Cypr., *Ep.* LXIX. 7.

[2] Tert., *adv. Prax.* 26: ...tinguerent in patrem et filium et spiritum sanctum, non in unum. nam nec semel, sed ter, ad singula nomina in personas singulas tinguimur.

[3] id., *de Bapt.* 6—8; *de Resurrect. carnis,* 8; Cypr., *Ep.* LXX. 2; LXXIII. 6; LXXIV. 5.

[4] The unction is said to be made with oil in Tert., *adv. Marc.* I. 14; but chrism is meant as in Cyprian, *Ep.* LXX. 2, where oil and chrism are identified. Quotations from St Cyprian are throughout made from Hartel's edition in the Vienna *Corpus.*

[5] Tert., *de Cor.* 3. Some authorities place the draught of milk and honey between confirmation and communion, or hold that the latter was not associated with baptism. But the above order seems the most probable interpretation of Tertullian's language, in view of general liturgical tradition. Cf. *adv. Marc.* I. 14. See also Lupton's edition of Tert., *de Bapt.* p. xx, and *Encycl. of Rel. and Ethics,* s.v. 'Confirmation.'

[6] *de Cor.* 3.

CHAPTER II

GENERAL SURVEY OF THE DEVELOPEMENT OF THE RITES

THE last chapter began with the rite of baptism in its barest form as recorded in the New Testament, and ended with the rite of Africa, where the developement had been carried to the stage at which the rites in liturgical books were drawn up. Before we discuss the history of the rites in various regions, and the relations of the rites to one another, it will be well to stop for a while and consider the changes that had been made in the rite from the beginning, and the principles which governed the changes. This is the more necessary since many of the more important features of baptism in the first five or six centuries of the Christian era are thoroughly strange and unfamiliar to all who are not versed in Christian antiquities. The discipline of the catechumenate and the incorporation of baptism and its preparation in the Christian year have completely passed out of use, except in the mission field. Yet these two principles condition the developement; and the abandonment of them has brought about equally important changes in the direction of compression and omission. But these principles are again governed by the age of the candidates. For the first four centuries and a little later, the majority of candidates were adults; afterwards, few but infants were presented. It must never be forgotten that all ancient baptismal rites were composed for adults, though now they are used mainly for children.

Easter was the general time for baptism throughout the Church, at least from the time of Tertullian. The rite was administered on the night between Easter Eve and Easter Day and terminated with the solemn mass of Easter morning, at which the neophytes made their first communion. The reason of the association of Easter with baptism is to be sought in that comparison of baptism with Christ's death and resurrection which St Paul[1] expresses. Baptism was likewise administered during the whole of Pentecost, that is, from Easter Day to Whitsunday[2]. The feast of the Epiphany was also a general season for baptism (except at Rome), because the baptism of Christ was then commemorated[3]. An effort was made to confine all baptisms to these seasons, but in case of necessity any day was allowed. Nevertheless, Easter was everywhere the usual time for the solemn performance of the rite. There was a special reason for this. When the candidates for baptism were adults, they were subjected to a long period of preparation, to which Lent was devoted, and which

---

[1] Rom. vi. 4. [2] Tert., *de Bapt.* 19.

[3] Duchesne, *C.W.* pp. 259, 293 f. W. C. Bishop in *J. Th. St.* vol. x. p. 127. Later, baptism was administered on other festivals, but the Roman Church strove to limit it to the days of Easter and Pentecost.

indeed was the cause of the observance of Lent. Those who were baptized at other times would miss these formal instructions, and would require special teaching. There were, therefore, reasons, both practical and symbolical, for confining the rite to Easter. With the spread of infant baptism, the practical reason for the connexion of baptism with Easter disappeared, and the rites of Easter Eve became a mere survival.

At this early period the majority of the candidates were adults and underwent the whole course of instruction. Children and infants were also baptized; they were not treated specially, but went through the same course as the adults, with the natural exception that they did not share in the instructions, and required sponsors to answer for them and to assist them[1]. This is important; for when adults no longer came forward for baptism, infants were treated as at the earliest period, that is, they passed through the successive stages of the rite, except the instructions. Examples of this are furnished by the *Ordo Romanus VII* and the *Gelasian Sacramentary*, in which the full rite is carried out for candidates who were infants. Later, the whole action was curtailed by a process of compression by which the series of initiatory rites with the preparatory catechumenate, lasting from the beginning of Lent to the end of Easter week, was contracted into a single rite, to be performed at any time. Nothing was omitted except a few repetitions. This is the genesis of the baptismal

[1] *Can. Hipp.* 113; cf. Tert., *de Bapt.* 18; *Testament of Our Lord*, II. 8.

rites as set down in the liturgical books, as, for instance, the *Rituale Romanum* and the Greek *Euchologion*. In other cases the compression was accompanied by a remodelling on the lines of the liturgy proper, that is, the Eucharist; this happened in Egypt and Oriental countries. Thus, by a long process of developement, baptism returned to its earliest state, when it was performed with no restrictions of time and season, and as a single action, except that it retained in the structure of the rite traces of its intermediate history, when it was embedded in the cycle of the Christian year.

It might be thought that the instructions given to the catechumens would contain a description and explanation of the sacramental rites in which they were about to participate. But this is not so; instruction on that subject was delivered after the baptism was over, in the week following Easter[1]. Only those who were fully initiated were allowed to learn about the sacred mysteries. From all others the knowledge was withheld. This 'reserve in communicating religious knowledge' is termed the *disciplina arcani*; the name, however, is of no great antiquity, having been invented by a French Calvinist, called Daillé or Dallaeus[2]. The *disciplina arcani* was eagerly seized upon by the Jesuits as a convenient device by which customs and beliefs, for which no early evidence could be alleged, might be thrown

[1] Cf. Cyril Hier., *Cat. myst.* passim, and *Cat.* xviii. 32; Ambros., *de Myst.* i. 2; *de Sacr.* i. 1. 1.

[2] Jean Daillé, 1594—1670 A.D.

back to the earliest period and attributed to Apostolic
authority. It was contended that the Apostles handed
down far more than was written, and that the Church
revealed this deposit, as she thought expedient and
as circumstances allowed ; hence, it was urged, early
writers are silent in regard to many things which at
a later date became universally accepted. The controversy caused no small stir at the time, but its
history is not our present concern. It is certain that
we know all that the *disciplina arcani* ever contained,
and that it consisted of no more than the ordinary
Christian teaching of the time.

Three influences contributed to the formation of
the system of reserve. First, we may set the desire
to withhold sacred truths and practices from the
uninstructed and irreverent, a fear of casting 'pearls
before swine.' Secondly, we may presuppose a pedagogic intention ; by revealing religion to catechumens
gradually and piecemeal they would have their interest quickened and reverence deepened. Some
recent writers have laid great stress on this aspect
of the discipline, and, denying that it existed in early
times, have held it to be merely a pedagogic device
for dealing with the masses of converts who rushed
into the Church in the fourth and fifth centuries.
But this view seems an exaggeration. In the third
place, we may set the influence of the contemporary
mystery-cults, Eleusinian, Orphic, and others, the
language of which was borrowed by Christian writers
from St Paul[1] downwards. This parallel must not be

---

[1] Cf. the words μυστήριον, τέλειος, μυεῖσθαι.

pressed too far. We may suppose a common use of current language, and an independent developement of similar features ; and possibly the Church adapted a useful method of training candidates. But a thoroughgoing adoption of the apparatus of the mysteries is improbable.

The *disciplina arcani* was in vogue from the latter part of the second century until the time when all Christians were baptized in their infancy and heathenism had died out or been abolished ; as there were no longer any catechumens to train or pagans from whom to withhold knowledge, the discipline fell into disuse, though it left deep traces of its previous existence in all liturgical books. The subjects which fell under the reserve were the meaning and rites of the sacraments, and later the creed and Lord's Prayer ; at Rome the Gospels also were withheld, at least in the later forms of that rite. To the *disciplina arcani* are to be attributed several important liturgical features. The terms used to distinguish the two parts of the liturgy—'mass of the catechumens' and 'mass of the faithful'[1]—arose out of this system ; catechumens were admitted to the former, but excluded from the latter. All the unbaptized were dismissed after the sermon, or at Rome after the Epistle ; from this *missa* or 'dismissal' are derived the names of the two parts of the service, and also the word 'mass' itself. Other features due to this discipline are the deliveries of the creed and the Lord's Prayer, and, at Rome,

---

[1] Missa catechumenorum, missa fidelium.

the 'Exposition of the Four Gospels,' which will be
dealt with later. Possibly the silent recital of the
creed and the Lord's Prayer in the Divine Office is
to be assigned to this origin. All these matters were
revealed to the converts gradually, with much precaution and warning that they were a sacred deposit
which must be jealously guarded and never revealed
to outsiders. Of course, this reserve was not everywhere maintained with equal strictness. Justin
Martyr, in his *First Apology*, directed to the
Emperor Antoninus Pius, describes the sacraments,
though not entirely without reserve, still fairly
completely. For this he had special reason in his
purpose of clearing Christians from the foul charges
brought against them; moreover, he wrote at an
early date, though the discipline was not unknown
in his time. We have an example at a much later
date of a difference of attitude with regard to the
disciplina arcani in the treatment of the Nicene
creed by the historians Sozomen[1] and Socrates[2].
The former omits it from his account, the latter
inserts it[3].

The candidates for baptism, from a fairly early
period till the disuse of the catechumenate, were
divided into two classes, the first consisting of those
who had attached themselves to the Church, but
were not considered fit, or had not yet offered

---

[1] *H.E.* i. 20. [2] *H.E.* i. 8.
[3] On the subject of the *disciplina arcani* see Funk, F. X.
Kirchengeschichtliche Abhandlungen und Untersuchungen, vol. iii. 2,
Das Alter der Arkandisziplin.

themselves for baptism; the second consisting of those who were to be baptized at the next public baptism and were being specially prepared for reception among the faithful. The former were called κατηχού-μενοι, ἀκροώμενοι, *catechumeni, audientes*; the second φωτιζόμενοι, *competentes, electi*[1]. The former class was by no means small, especially in the fourth and fifth centuries; the *Confessions* of St Augustine describe the spiritual history of a member of this class. The latter class was the object of the special Lenten preparation, about which something must now be said.

In many, if not all, parts of the Church, services of a special type were used in the period preceding Easter on week-days. It has been mentioned above that the first part of the mass, including the lessons and homily, is called the *missa catechumenorum*; these services also might be called *missae catechumenorum*, for they also consisted of lessons, psalms, and, on occasion, of homilies. Though these special Lenten services may have furnished additional opportunities of devotion for the whole Church, they were designed primarily for the needs of the candidates, and, with the disappearance of the candidates, they gave place to offices of another kind—the day-hours of the monastic type. The system in use at Milan will serve to illustrate the services. On all week-days in Lent, except Saturdays, *missae catechumenorum* were held at the third and ninth hour. Up to Holy Week Genesis and Proverbs furnished the lessons; in Holy Week, Job and Tobit. St Ambrose

---

[1] This is the proper Roman word for the class.

preached to the candidates at these services, and references to the lessons are found in his sermons; the oldest forms of the Milanese books contain complete lists of the lessons read[1]. Vestiges of similar services are found in Spanish books and elsewhere[2].

It was at these services that the candidates were instructed in the rules of Christian conduct and the first elements of religion. Types of the instruction given are found among the works of the Fathers, for example, the *Catecheses* of St Cyril of Jerusalem and many of the sermons and expositions of Scripture of St Ambrose, St Augustine, and St John Chrysostom.

Distinct from these services of instruction were the 'scrutinies' (*scrutinia, scrutamina*), or examinations, which were held, not every day in Lent, but on certain fixed days, varying according to the region. At the scrutinies the candidates were exorcized, and examined whether they were fit for baptism. It was at the scrutinies that the contents of the *disciplina arcani* were unfolded to the candidates. They learnt by heart the creed and the Lord's Prayer[3]; at Rome they were also initiated in the Gospels. Later on in Lent they were required to repeat what they had learnt. The delivery of the Creed, Lord's Prayer, and Gospels was accompanied by explanations; stereotyped forms of these explanations have come down

---

[1] The lessons are given at the foot of the pages containing the offices for Lent in Magistretti's *Manuale Ambrosianum*.

[2] See W. C. Bishop in *C. Q. R.* LXIII. 112 f., LXXII. 34 f. Cf. Ambros., *de Abr.* I. 4. 23, 7. 59.

[3] In some places, *e.g.* Milan, the Lord's Prayer was delivered after Easter.

to us in liturgical books, principally Roman and Gallican.

This system of instruction did not cease with baptism. After Easter it was resumed, but, as the audience was now composed of full members of the Church, the instructor spoke freely and without reserve on the sacraments. Sets of sermons for this purpose have come down to us in the works of the Fathers; St Cyril's *Mystic Catecheses*, St Ambrose *On the Mysteries*, and a nameless author *On the Sacraments* shew us how the newly baptized were dealt with. The last two works are Milanese, and in them the Lord's Prayer is expounded at this time along with baptism, confirmation, and the Eucharist.

We have spoken hitherto of the instruction of the catechumens. But their preparation contained more than instruction. Those who sought admission into the Church were first strictly examined whether they were worthy and sincere. Rigorous enquiry was made into the life and character of the candidates; in particular those who followed certain professions[1] were required to abandon them before being accepted as catechumens. This side of the preparation caused the services for catechumens to be called 'scrutinies' in the West.

Exorcisms play an important part in the preparation for baptism. Exorcizing, or the expulsion of evil spirits, was practised generally in the ancient world,

[1] Cf. *Can. Hipp.* 65—76; Concil. Eliber. can. LXII. (Routh, *Rell. Sacr.* IV. 270 .

and was particularly common in the circles in which the Church grew up. The use of exorcisms among Christians is very ancient[1] and is indicated by references in the earliest writings[2], by the existence of an order of exorcists, and, lastly, by the occurrence of frequent exorcisms in the baptismal rites. The custom is to be traced to the belief in demons and, in particular, to the idea that the activities of heathen gods were due to demonic agency. Those who had been rescued from the heathen world and worship required to be thoroughly purged of all influence of evil spirits. The ceremonies of exorcism were exsufflation or breathing in the face of the candidate that the spirit might be expelled from him—an action which probably arose from the double meaning of πνεῦμα and *spiritus*, which signify both 'breath' and a 'spiritual being,'—imposition of the hand, and signing with the sign of the cross.

Several other practices in the preparation for baptism are mentioned in early writers. Tertullian states that 'those who are to approach baptism ought to pray with frequent prayers, fastings and supplications and vigils, and with confession of all past sins'; the last practice is mentioned also in the *Canons of Hippolytus*[3].

The preparation for baptism was summed up in

[1] Augustine, *de Nupt. et Concup.* II. 29. 51, antiquissimam ecclesiae traditionem.

[2] Acts xvi. 18.

[3] Tert., *de Bapt.* 20; *Can. Hipp.* 103. Cf. Matt. iii. 6; Acts xix. 18.

the renunciation of Satan and the profession of faith
made just before baptism. The renunciation is given
by Tertullian in the form, 'I renounce the devil and
his pomp and his angels[1].' The word 'pomp' had
originally the meaning of 'retinue,' and in the *Canons
of Hippolytus* is applied not only to the retinue of
the devil, but also, in the profession of faith, to the
retinue of God; but at a fairly early date it acquired
the sense of 'pride' and 'display[2].' In the case of infants the renunciation and profession were made by
sponsors. The profession of faith is the culmination
of the dogmatic teaching of Lent, as the renunciation
is of the moral teaching. In form it is parallel to
the renunciation, and as the latter is made towards
the West, the place of darkness, so the profession is
made towards the East, the place of the rising sun
and of light.

Of the actual baptism Tertullian says : 'Thrice
we are plunged, answering somewhat more than the
Lord ordained in the Gospel[3].' These words refer to
the threefold interrogation of the faith which accompanied the threefold immersion. The formularies
given in the Church Orders are doubtless much
expanded; a short and fairly early form is given by
a North Italian writer about the year 400. 'Dost
thou believe in God the Father Almighty ? Dost thou
believe in our Lord Jesus Christ and in his Cross ?
Dost thou believe in the Holy Spirit ?' At each of

---

[1] *de Cor.* 3; *de Spect.* 4; *de Idol.* 6.
[2] Cf. Cyril. Hier., *Cat. myst.* I. 6.
[3] *de Cor.* l.c.

these enquiries the candidate answered 'I believe' and was immersed[1].

It will be seen that we have two professions of faith, (a) that which is parallel to and follows the renunciation, (b) that which, in the form of interrogations, accompanies the immersion. In early rites (b) is generally found, *e.g.* in Tertullian, St Cyprian, the *De Mysteriis*[2] of St Ambrose, and the cognate *De Sacramentis* in the West, St Cyril of Jerusalem in the East and several Church Orders; (a) is found only in the Eastern authorities, not in the earlier Western documents. The Gallican books always lacked (a); in the Roman books the creed was used for it, not a special formula of profession[3]. It would seem that, in the West, (b) was original and (a) added later; for the East our evidence is not quite so early and we cannot say which is there the older.

In confirmation the imposition of the hand continued in use, at least in the West[4]. In Tertullian it is preceded by an unction, to which a sacerdotal significance is attached, and henceforward both formed part of the Western rite; the perplexed history of the double usage in confirmation is further dealt with in the last chapter of this book. In the East imposition of the hand generally died out at an early date, and unction alone remained, except in Egypt which retained both.

In the baptismal rite of Syriac-speaking Churches we find baptism performed without any following

---

[1] *de Sacramentis*, II. 7. 20.   [2] v. 28.

[3] Duchesne, *Christian Worship*, p. 332.

[4] *E.g.* in Spain as in the *Liber Ordinum* and St Ildephonsus. The evidence is given in the chapters on the Roman and Spanish rites.

rite, but preceded by an unction to which great importance was attached. Such is the rite in the *Didascalia Apostolorum*, the *Acts of Thomas*, the Syriac *History of John the son of Zebedee*, and other works of Syriac origin, many of them Gnostic in their teaching[1].

The post-baptismal unction was introduced into the Monophysite rite in the sixth century probably by Severus, Patriarch of Antioch (512—519 A.D.). It was added to the Nestorian rite at the remodelling of the baptismal rite which took place under the Catholicos Isho'yabh III (647—658 A.D.) who had travelled in other countries and borrowed the practice from the rites which he had seen on his journeys.

That this pre-baptismal unction is really the unction of confirmation, seems to be clear from the language of the homilies of Narsai, in which it is connected with the Holy Spirit, and from the word 'seal' applied to it by Ephraim; this view of the unction is supported by the phrase in the Jacobite Order, 'Send thy Holy Spirit upon those who are to be baptized[2].'

Thus we have two distinct uses of unction, one before baptism in Syria, and one after baptism in the rest of the world; both are apparently employed with the same significance and both are made with chrism. But in later rites in the East, in Egypt, and at Rome, there are two unctions, one with oil before baptism, one with chrism afterwards, and the latter is the rite

---

[1] For a complete list of these works see above p. 12, notes 1, 2.
[2] Denzinger, *Rit. Or.* I. 273.

of confirmation, either alone or together with the
imposition of the hand. What is the relation of these
unctions to each other ?

The use of two unctions in one rite first occurs
about the middle of the fourth century in two
different places, in the *Catecheses* of St Cyril of
Jerusalem and in the *Sacramentary of Sarapion of
Thmuis* in Egypt[1]. It is also found in the *Apostolic
Constitutions*, which were composed in Syria in the last
quarter of the fourth century. This last case is very
interesting, as the work shews the process of liturgical
developement in its working. The compiler gives three
accounts of baptism, one his own composition or from
an unknown source, the other two based upon the
Didache and *Didascalia*, which were discussed in
the last chapter. The matter stands thus :

Const. Ap. lib. VII. cap. 22 = *Didache.*
Const. Ap. lib. III. cap. 15—17 = *Didascalia.*
Const. Ap. lib. VII. cap. 39—44 is not from any known
source ; probably the work of the compiler.

Now the third of these accounts shews both
unctions, and to it the other two have been assimilated, that is to say, the *Didache*, which had no
unction, acquired two, and the *Didascalia*, which
had one only, and that before baptism, has now a
second, after baptism. In all cases the former unction
is with oil, the latter with chrism. The latter unction
is twice called 'the imposition of the hand[2]' and such

---

[1] See, below, the chapters on the Syrian and Egyptian rites.
[2] *A. C.* III. 15, VII. 44, χειροθεσία.

importance is attached to it that the whole efficacy
of baptism is made to consist in it, and without it
baptism is declared to be an empty ceremony of
washing. Nevertheless, the gift of the Holy Spirit
is connected with the oil[1]; here we see a trace of the
older Syrian use. The alterations and the confusion
betray the innovator, and we can clearly see that
the older forms were being forced into the newer
mould.

From the *Apostolic Constitutions* alone it might
seem that the two uses of unction, before or after baptism, met in Syria and produced a rite with unctions
before and after baptism. But the other evidence is
against this conclusion; St Cyril and Sarapion are
older, and the confusion of the *Apostolic Constitutions* arises from the action of the newer type of rite,
that of St Cyril and Sarapion, on older and especially
Syrian forms. But the question still remains: Whence
did St Cyril and Sarapion derive the unction with oil
before baptism, and what does it mean? To the former
question our materials do not furnish an answer;
we cannot say whether the practice arose in Syria or
Egypt. As to the latter question, St Cyril of Jerusalem[2] attributes to the 'exorcized oil' of the prior
unction an exorcizing power; and with this the
Egyptian Church Order, the *Canons of Hippolytus*
and the cognate works agree, in so far that they
speak of 'exorcized oil' or 'oil of exorcism.' But
this use of oil for exorcism seems rather strange and

---

[1] *ib.* III. 17, VII. 22.   [2] *Cat. myst.* II. 3.

unusual, and the origin of the unction before baptism is still uncertain[1].

The use of an unction with oil before baptism, in addition to the unction of confirmation, spread over the East fairly rapidly. But in the West the practice extended slowly; in fact, it hardly went beyond the sphere of Roman influence[2]. The common custom in the West, of touching the organs of sense with oil or saliva, appears to have a different origin, and was probably derived from some one centre, possibly North Italy, where the earliest references to it are found.

After the completion of the rite of initiation the newly baptized received the communion; in ancient times when baptism was performed on Easter night, the mass of Easter day closed the rites, and all alike communicated. At Milan, the masses of Easter week were duplicated, one set for the newly baptized and another for the rest of the faithful. Round these great rites a multitude of symbolical ceremonies gathered, which may be mentioned here.

1. *The Kiss of Peace.* The practice of bestowing a kiss on the newly baptized in token of Christian love and fellowship is early and general[3].

2. *The White Garments.* The wearing of white

---

[1] Mr W. C. Bishop suggests that it was originally an unction of the whole body to protect it against the chill of the water in immersion.

[2] It is found in the *de Sacramentis* (I. 2. 4), which claims to follow Roman uses.

[3] Cypr., *Ep.* LXIV. 4; *Apocryphal Acts of the Apostles*, ed. Wright, II. p. 40; *Can. Hipp.* 139; *Test. of our Lord*, II. 9.

garments by the newly baptized was common and must have formed a striking feature of the observance of Easter week in the early ages of the Church. In the eighth century these garments were worn during Easter week and put off on the Saturday after Easter[1]; hence the Sunday was called *in albis depositis*, a name afterwards contracted to *in albis*. The practice of wearing white garments was common to East and West[2] from the fourth century onwards; before then the custom can only have had a limited vogue, as the wearing of distinctive garments at Easter might have exposed the converts to danger.

3. *Crowns of Flowers.* The custom of placing garlands on the heads of the neophytes was common in the East from at least the fourth century and survives in the service books; it is unknown to the West[3].

4. *Milk and Honey.* A draught of milk and honey was given to the neophytes after baptism and communion. This custom is confined to Rome, Africa, and Egypt; in the last region alone it still survives.

[1] [Alcuin], *de Off. eccl.* cap. xxi. de sabbato in albis. Migne, *P. L.* ci. col. 1223.

[2] *Apocryphal Acts*, ed. Wright, ii. 40; Cyril. Hier., *Cat. myst.* iv. 8; Augustine, *Serm.* ccxxiii.

[3] *The Odes and Psalms of Solomon*, ed. Harris, Od. i. 1, v. 10, ix. 8, xvii. 1, xx. 7 (see Dr Bernard's article in *J. Th. St.* xii. 1 f.; the allusions are not certain, as the language is very vague and figurative); Ephraim Syr., *Hymns for the Epiphany*, xiii. 5 and 11 (here the hymns are certainly baptismal and the similarity to the *Odes* confirms Dr Bernard's interpretation of the former); Denzinger, *Rit. Or.* i. pp. 211, 231 (Egyptian), 288, 327 (Syrian); Conybeare, *Rit. Arm.* pp. 99—101 (Armenian).

The practice is symbolical of the spiritual child-hood of the 'regenerate' and of the blessings of the 'promised land' of the Kingdom of Christ[1].

5. *Washing of the Feet.* This custom was very general in the West; it is found at Milan, and in Gaul, Ireland, Africa, and Spain, but not at all at Rome. It was generally performed by a bishop, or at least begun by him, where he was the minister of baptism. The ceremony is an imitation of our Lord's action[2]: as he washed the feet of his disciples, so his repre-sentative washed the feet of the new disciples of Christ. The practice is found in the fourth century in the West, and died out with the spread of Roman influence and customs.

---

[1] *Can. Hipp.* 148; Tert., *de Cor.* 3 (cf. Jerome, *contra Lucifer.* 8); *contra Marc.* I. 14; Clem. Alex., *Paed.* I. vi. 45; Concil. Carthag. III. cap. 24 (Mansi, III. 884); Ioan. Diac., *Ep. ad Senar.* 12; *Leonine Sacramentary* (ed. Feltoe), p. 25; Denzinger, *Rit. Or.* I. p. 232 (Ethiopic) and Proleg. *ib.* p. 37; Jerome, *In Is.* LV. 1, speaks of 'wine and milk' as given to the newly baptized.

[2] John xiii. 4—17.

CHAPTER III

THE LATER CHURCH ORDERS

THE 'Church Orders' are a series of manuals of Christian life embracing moral, legal, and liturgical matter. Their authorship is entirely unknown, and in many cases the date and place of writing are still subjects of much controversy[1]. For the present purpose the Church Orders fall into four sections:

I. The *Didache*, or *Teaching of the Twelve Apostles*.

II. The *Didascalia*.

III. The *Apostolic Constitutions*.

IV. A series of closely related Church Orders.

 (*a*)   The *Egyptian Church Order*.

 (*b*)   The *Ethiopic Church Order*.

 (*c*)   Hauler's *Verona Latin Fragments*.

 (*d*)   The *Canons of Hippolytus*.

 (*e*)   The *Testament of our Lord*.

[1] On the Church Orders see Funk, *Das Testament unseres Herrn u. die verwandten Schriften* (Mainz, 1901), *Didascalia et Constitutiones Apostolorum* (Paderborn, 1905), and Maclean, *The Ancient Church Orders* (Cambridge, 1910).

Of these four classes the first and the second have already been dealt with[1]; the third and fourth still await consideration.

The *Apostolic Constitutions*, as we have seen, contain three accounts of baptism: (*a*) vii. 22; (*b*) iii. 15—17; (*c*) vii. 39—44. Of these three the first is derived from the *Didache*, the second from the *Didascalia*, and the third may be considered the work of the compiler. The first two have been assimilated to the third, as the compiler thought that a baptismal rite should have both an unction with oil before baptism and an unction with chrism afterwards. The third rite of baptism is as follows: A catechumen who wishes to be baptized must be instructed in the renunciation and profession, and in all that concerns Christian conduct. The renunciation runs thus: 'I renounce Satan and his works and his pomps and his worship and his angels and his inventions and all that are under him.' The profession begins: 'I believe and am baptized into,' and proceeds as a creed; it is very similar to the fourth formula of the second council of Antioch (341 A.D.)[2]. After the profession the candidate was anointed with oil, which had previously been blessed by the bishop; the purpose of this unction was remission of sins and preparation for baptism. The water was blessed by the bishop and baptism was performed with the Threefold Formula. After

[1] See above, pp. 7 f., 12 f.

[2] Hahn, *Symbole und Glaubensregeln der alten Kirche*, pp. 139, 187; Funk, *Didasc. et Const. Apost.* I. p. 445, note.

baptism the neophyte was anointed with chrism[1];
a rather obscure prayer and explanation accompany
the unction, the purpose of which appears to be the
ratification and corroboration of the baptism.

The two other forms of baptism contain interesting
explanations of the rite, added by the compiler. In
the third book[2] he says: 'Baptism is given into
the death of Jesus, but the water is instead of burial,
the oil instead of the Holy Spirit, the seal instead
of the cross, the chrism is confirmation of the profession.' Again in the seventh book[3]: 'Thou shalt
first anoint with oil, then baptize with water, and
lastly seal with chrism, that the unguent may be
participation in the Holy Spirit, the water a symbol
of the death, and the chrism a seal of the covenants.'

As we have seen, the *Apostolic Constitutions* are
a Syrian work of the latter part of the fourth century.
The rite, however, hardly appears as developed as
the earlier rite described by St Cyril of Jerusalem.
We see in the first and second rites in the *Apostolic
Constitutions,* possibly also in the third, attempts to
modernize older and simpler traditions of baptism,
particularly in the matter of two unctions. The
curious language which has just been quoted about
the second unction is probably due to the compiler's
acquaintance with rites which had only one unction,
and that before baptism, with the same significance
as the ordinary unction after baptism.

The fourth division of the Church Orders represents a much fuller, more detailed, and more highly

---

[1] μύρον.   [2] III. 17.   [3] VII. 22.

developed rite. Here we are met with the gravest difficulty as to questions of date and locality, both with regard to the separate works and what may lie behind them; to all these questions various answers are given. The rite as shewn in the *Egyptian Church Order* is as follows: A long catechumenate is prescribed; three years is the normal period, but the time may be shortened at the discretion of the catechist. A rigorous examination of the life, character, and pursuits of the catechumen is held; and his conduct during the catechumenate is scrutinized with especial care. During this period the catechumens are diligently instructed and attend the liturgy, but are dismissed after the first part of the mass with laying on of hand and prayer.

As Easter drew near, those of the catechumens who are judged satisfactory are set apart for special instruction; the length of this period is not stated. Henceforth they are allowed to hear the Gospel and are exorcized daily with laying on of the hand; later still they are exorcized by the bishop. On Thursday in Holy Week the candidates bathe, and on Friday they fast. The Easter Vigil begins with a final exorcism by the bishop; after the exorcism he breathes in their faces, and signs the brow, ears, and nose.

The baptismal rite begins with the consecration of the water, which is strictly required to be fresh and flowing, except in case of necessity. Two oils are consecrated by the bishop, an 'oil of thanksgiving' and an 'oil of exorcism.' After a renunciation the candidate is anointed with the 'oil of exorcism';

this unction has an exorcizing power. A profession of faith is made and then the candidates are baptized. Children are baptized first, and sponsors answer for them; then men, and lastly women. Baptism is performed with three immersions, at each of which the candidate professes his belief in a section of the creed; the baptismal formula is not mentioned. After baptism the neophytes are anointed with 'oil of thanksgiving.' Both these unctions are performed by presbyters. Lastly the newly baptized dress and return from the baptistery to the church. Confirmation is administered by the bishop with laying on of the hand, unction of the head with the 'oil of thanksgiving,' and signing of the forehead. The Kiss of Peace concludes the rite and the mass follows immediately. After communion the newly baptized are given a draught of milk and honey.

The above rite is reproduced throughout this series with slight variations. In the *Testament* there is no mention of consecration of the water, and the draught of milk and honey is omitted. In the *Egyptian* and *Ethiopic Church Orders* the profession of faith and the creed are both said in the water, but the profession has ousted the first section of the creed, so that the latter lacks the clauses relating to the Father; in Hauler's *Fragments* the description is mutilated and begins with the second part of the interrogatory creed; in the *Canons of Hippolytus* and *Testament* the creed is completed. In the *Canons of Hippolytus* the baptismal formula is said thrice, once at each immersion;

in the *Testament* the formula is implied[1], in the other documents it is omitted. The creed in the *Canons of Hippolytus*, Hauler's *Fragments* and the *Testament* is of a Roman type; in the *Egyptian* and *Ethiopic Church Orders* it is of the Nicene type.

The *Testament* calls the prayer used at the imposition of the hand by the bishop an invocation of the Holy Ghost. In the *Canons of Hippolytus* the 'oil of thanksgiving' is also termed 'oil of unction' and 'chrism of thanksgiving'; a presbyter anoints with this oil after baptism, but there is no unction by the bishop.

The date and locality of these Church Orders is still a matter of dispute, but it is worth while to note what grounds for settling these points are furnished by the baptismal rite they contain. It must be understood, however, that the following remarks are tentative suggestions rather than definite conclusions, and they must not be pressed too far.

The *Canons of Hippolytus*[2] order that those who wish to join the Church, shall 'learn in church to renounce Satan and all his pomp.' This may mean no more than the prescription in the *Apostolic Constitutions*[3], that the candidate shall learn the renunciation. But it might be an allusion to an earlier renunciation, such as we find in the African and earlier forms of the Roman rite.

Several of these documents have a provision that candidates when accepted shall be allowed to 'hear the Gospel'; such is the case in the *Testament*,

[1] II. 7.   [2] 61.   [3] VII. 40.

and the *Egyptian* and the *Ethiopic Church Orders*.
In the *Testament* it is also provided that the candidates in the earlier stage of their training go out
before the reading of 'the New [Testament] or Gospels.'
These facts seem to indicate that the rite of these
books treated the Gospel as coming under the *disciplina arcani*.   In the *Canons of Hippolytus*[1] there
is a difficult sentence with reference to the approval
and acceptance of candidates: 'then let the Gospel
of that time be read over him.'   It is perhaps
fanciful to connect this in any way with the Roman
'Exposition of the Gospels.'   But in any case the
treatment of the Gospel as part of the *disciplina arcani*
points to Rome, for there alone is that custom found.

In the *Egyptian* and *Ethiopic Church Orders*, the
Testament, and Hauler's *Fragments* there are two
unctions after baptism, one by the priest, another
by the bishop.   This is also a Roman characteristic[2].

The draught of milk and honey is Roman, Egyptian, and African. At Rome it dropped out of use: it
is found in the *Leonine Sacramentary*, which was probably copied in the seventh century but composed in
the sixth[3], but it does not occur in any later work.

In regard to date the works are inconsistent with

---

[1] 104.

[2] There are, however, differences in the manner of these
anointings; at Rome the bishop signed the brow, the presbyter the
head; in the Church Orders there is no distinction, and the bishop
anoints the head. In the *Canons of Hippolytus* the presbyter signs
the brow with chrism in the course of anointing the whole body.
In the *Ethiopic Church Order* (p. 154) the second unction is also
administered by a presbyter; but several MSS. omit the word
'presbyter' (see *ib.* p. 381, ed. Horner).   [3] *C. W.* p. 138.

themselves, since they contain early features, but
have been largely worked over in later revisions. The
sections about 'baptism by blood,' and the general
assumption of a surrounding heathen world, throw
them back before the peace of the Church; on the
other hand, the double unction, before and after
baptism, first appears about the middle of the fourth
century. Again, many of the Roman features mentioned above are only known to us from seventh
and eighth century attestation; it is dangerous to
assign them to a period when they could have influenced Church Orders.

It is difficult to draw any conclusion from the
above indications. Certainly this class of documents
has very puzzling points of contact with the Roman
rite; and the date when the rite was drawn up is
not earlier than the fourth century and may be very
much later. More than this the baptismal rites
do not justify us in saying.

The *Egyptian Church Order* is in Horner, *Statutes of
the Apostles*, pp. 311—320; the *Ethiopic Church Order*,
ib. pp. 147—157[1]; the *Verona Fragments* in Hauler, *Didascaliae Apostolorum Fragmenta Veronensia Latina*, pp.
110 f.; the *Canons of Hippolytus* are printed at the end of
Duchesne's *Christian Worship*, or in the editions of Achelis
and Haneberg; the *Testament of Our Lord* has been
edited by Cooper and Maclean. See also Funk, F. X.,
Didascalia et Constitutiones Apostolorum, and *Das Testament unseres Herrn* (the latter in Ehrard und Kirsch,
*Forschungen zur Christlichen Litteratur- und Dogmen-
geschichte*, Bd. II. Hft. 1, 2).

[1] Pp. 162—178 contain another baptismal rite, which seems to
be based on the later Egyptian and Ethiopic rites.

CHAPTER IV

THE LITURGICAL AREAS

BEFORE discussing the rites of various parts of the Christian world, it is advisable to consider briefly the geographical distribution of liturgical forms, in order that the connexions and relationships between the various sources dealt with in the following pages may not be set before the reader without some word of explanation and introduction.

For the purposes of liturgical history the Church falls into two great divisions, East and West; between these divisions, and looking first to Rome and the West, and later to the East, lies Egypt. These divisions must now be considered in relation to baptismal rites.

For the East, Syria is the starting point. First we have the early Syrian rite, the rite of the native Syriac-speaking peoples, which had an unction before baptism, but none after. It has already been described in connexion with the *Didascalia* and various Gnostic works. In the course of the fourth century another rite was developed in Syria, which had an unction with oil before baptism and with chrism after baptism. This rite, furnished with ceremonial and clothed in appropriate liturgical forms, spread far and wide, and was freely drawn upon by other Churches.

From this source the newly founded city of Constantinople took its rite of baptism ; the Greek or Byzantine prayers are derived from a common stock of Antiochene and Palestinian forms. From the Greek rite are derived the Russian, and all the rites of Churches evangelized by, or under the influence of, Constantinople.

The Armenian Church was founded by missionaries from Caesarea in Cappadocia. But it fell under the influence of Constantinople and has a good deal in common with the Greek rite. The Armenian Church has long been isolated, and to this isolation may be referred many of the peculiarities in its ritual and prayers.

In early days Rome and Alexandria were closely connected, and the original form of the Egyptian rite is related to Western rites. To this relationship we may attribute the use of the first person singular active (e.g. 'I baptize') in formulas, the imposition of the hand in confirmation, and the draught of milk and honey after communion—all features rare or unknown in the East. But after the council of Chalcedon the Egyptian Christians were divided into Melchite[1] (i.e. orthodox) and Monophysite. The former looked to Constantinople, and assimilated their rites more and more to the usages of that

---

[1] From *Malchah*, Syr.=a king, that is βασιλεύς or *imperator* ; in this case the Greek emperor. The title is a sneer at the 'Erastianism' of the orthodox.

see.   On the other hand, the Monophysites identified themselves increasingly with national Egyptian
feeling, and became largely a Coptic-speaking com-
munity.   At the same time, they remodelled their
baptismal rites in close imitation of their brethren,
the Syrian Monophysites; as the later Syrians
assimilated the baptismal rite to the liturgy, so
the Copts also refashioned their rite on the basis
of their own liturgy, but with borrowings which
indicate the originality of the Syrians.   The Coptic
rite was followed by the Church of Abyssinia in the
south, which was dependent on Alexandria in ecclesiastical matters.

In the West the baptismal rites fall into well-
defined local categories, but the relations of these
localities to each other are by no means so simple
as in the East.   Under the denomination of the
West come all the Latin-speaking churches; that
is, Africa (by which is meant the Roman province
of Africa[1]), Rome, Milan, Spain, Gaul, and Britain
with Ireland ; with the cities of Rome and Milan go
the surrounding districts.   It is the custom among
liturgists to divide Western rites of all kinds into two
classes, 'Gallican' and 'Roman,' but in the following
chapter on the various Western baptismal services
and customs no use has been made of that division.   As will be seen in the course of the discussion, the connexions of the various liturgical forms
are too complicated to come under so simple a
classification.

[1] Roughly Tunis and Tripoli.

In one sense, indeed, the rough division is true. There is in Roman rites of all kinds a certain brief simplicity and dry austerity of character which runs through the prayers and the ceremonies; in comparison with the Roman rites, the rites of the rest of the Western world seem florid and emotional. It is not very easy to express this antithesis, but on reading a quantity of Latin liturgical matter the difference is readily felt[1]. From this comparison the African rite must be excluded, on account of our slight knowledge of the literary character of its liturgical forms.

Another strongly marked Roman characteristic is orderliness; the Roman Church loved to have everything carried out in a proper and regular fashion. In this respect Milan must be classed with Rome. The arrangement of scrutinies in these two churches is a good instance. The preparation and instruction of candidates was not left to chance or individual taste, but fixed in rigid forms, performed at stated times; so deeply rooted were these forms that they survived their original purpose for centuries, at Milan even to the end of the Middle Ages.

We will now take a few features which illustrate the relations of the rites in various areas to each other.

The renunciation usually precedes baptism immediately. But at Rome in earlier times, and at Milan

[1] Cf. E. Bishop, *Genius of the Roman Rite*; J. Wickham Legg, *Three Chapters in Recent Liturgical Research*, § 1 (Church Historical Soc. LXXIII.).

after the days of St Ambrose, the renunciation came at the very beginning, when the catechumens became *competentes*; in Africa there were two renunciations. Scrutinies were held at Rome on Sundays in the early period, later on any day but Sunday; at Milan on Saturdays, as also in Africa. The creed was delivered to the candidates on Palm Sunday in Gaul and Spain; at Rome at the third scrutiny[1]; in Africa on the Saturday three weeks before Easter; at Milan on Palm Sunday in early days, later on the Saturday before. The Lord's Prayer was 'delivered' to the candidates in Africa and at Rome[2]; the four Gospels at Rome only and in the sphere of Roman influence, the reason being that at Rome alone were catechumens dismissed before the Gospel.

The consecration of water at Milan is another instance of liturgical interchange. The form *Sanctificare per uerbum Dei* was composed at Milan, whence it spread to Spain; finally it was adopted at Rome, not for its original purpose, but for use in the dedication of a church.

In baptism the formula ends with the words *ut habeas uitam aeternam* in Gaul and Spain. In confirmation the imposition of the hand is very definitely mentioned in Spain and in Africa, and appears to have been common at Rome, but it is scarcely alluded to elsewhere.

The washing of the feet after baptism was never used at Rome; in Spain it was dropped at an early

---

[1] The day for which varied at different periods.
[2] At Milan the Lord's Prayer was delivered after Easter.

date; in Africa it was sporadically employed; at Milan and in Gaul it had a long and vigorous life.

Finally, the draught of milk and honey is common to three regions—Rome, Egypt, and Africa.

Speaking generally, in the West there was a very general interchange of liturgical customs and formularies. The most apparent connexions in this respect are between Milan and Spain, Milan and Rome, and Spain and Gaul. At a later date the Roman rite was freely imitated and borrowed in Gaul, and very curious combinations resulted. The final outcome of the process was that the Roman rite became prevalent everywhere but was strongly influenced and modified by the rites which it ousted.

Of actual liturgical intercourse, in regard to baptism, between East and West, there seems little trace; perhaps the introduction of the Nicene creed into the Roman 'tradition of the creed' is an example.

CHAPTER V

THE EASTERN RITES OF BAPTISM

Sec. 1. *The Syrian Rite*

THERE appear to have been two forms of baptismal rite in Syria and the lands lying to the east of Syria. The one is the native Syriac rite, which has been mentioned in connexion with the *Didascalia* and certain works of Gnostic origin, including the *Apocryphal Acts of the Apostles*; its most marked characteristic is the absence of confirmation or, to put it in another way, the unction before baptism corresponds to confirmation in other rites. This form of rite is the ancestor of the Nestorian rite. The other form belongs to the Greek-speaking Churches of Jerusalem and Antioch; it has a definite rite of confirmation by unction after baptism. This rite is the parent of all existing Eastern rites, except the Nestorian, and even that has been so far influenced as to adopt an unction after baptism.

The history of both these rites is fairly well established, since in the case of both we are fortunate in possessing evidence for their earlier and later forms. The native Syriac rite has already been dealt with[1], and its final fortunes in the case of the Nestorian rite will be considered at the end of this chapter. For the history of the developement of the other rite our earliest information is connected with the Church of Jerusalem, and is contained in the *Catecheses* of St Cyril of Jerusalem. The *Peregrinatio Etheriae*, a description of the sacred places of Jerusalem, written by an abbess from Gaul or Spain who made a pilgrimage to the Holy Land, has commonly been assigned to the time of Theodosius. But more recently a date as late as the fifth or sixth century has been assigned to it[2]. The principal features of the rite as portrayed in these two books will be given, and then it will be possible to consider further developements.

According to Etheria, at Jerusalem Lent lasted eight weeks; all Sundays, and all Saturdays except Easter Eve, were excluded from the fast, so that the total number of days observed as fast days amounted to forty-one[3]. During this period the candidates for baptism at the ensuing Easter, called φωτιζόμενοι or *competentes*, were prepared and instructed by the bishop. The candidates gave in their names the day before Lent began, and on the first day of Lent the bishop, sitting in a chair in the midst of the great

[1] pp. 13—14, 30—34.

[2] See K. Meister, *De itinerario Aetheriae abbatissae perperam nomini S. Silviae addicto* in *Rheinisches Museum für Philologie* (1909), pp. 337 f.

[3] *P. E.* (= *Peregrinatio Etheriae*), IV. The work is conveniently printed at the end of Duchesne's *Christian Worship*.

basilica or *Martyrium*, held an inquiry into the character of the candidates; witnesses were called and a strict examination was held. Those who passed this examination successfully were admitted to the instructions. Each instruction or *catechesis* began with an exorcism[1], performed by the clergy. The bishop then delivered his address; 'beginning from Genesis, through those forty days he will run through all the Scriptures, first expounding carnally, and then explaining them spiritually; also they are taught all about the resurrection, and the faith in those days[2].' Eighteen sermons, together with an introductory discourse, have survived to shew us the character of the preparation given by St Cyril. The preface and the first five are fragments of the series for the first five weeks of Lent; the rest belong to the sixth and seventh weeks. From Palm Sunday to Easter, the commemoration of the Passion, which at Jerusalem was carried out with great elaboration, allowed no time for instruction[3]. On Tuesday[4] after Easter the instructions were resumed, but with this difference, that the Sacraments were now the subject of the discourses; five sermons are provided for the days from Tuesday to Saturday.

[1] *P.E.* VII. 2. St Cyril mentions an insufflation, which was a part of the exorcism; he also alludes to a strange custom of veiling the face: ἐσκέπασταί σου τὸ πρόσωπον ἵνα σχολάσῃ λοιπὸν ἡ διάνοια, *Procat.* 9.

[2] *P.E.* VII. 2.

[3] *ib.* VII. 3.

[4] *Cat.* XVIII. 33. Cf. the pseudo-Ambrosian *de Sacramentis*; why the Monday was omitted in either case is not clear.

After five weeks of Lent had elapsed, the creed[1] was imparted to the catechumens, who learned it by heart and repeated it on Palm Sunday.

Baptism took place in the evening before Easter Day; the hour has already moved back a little from the 'cock-crow' of the *Egyptian Church Order*, probably for reasons of convenience. The rite began in the vestibule, or entrance of the baptistery. The candidates took off all their clothes but the under garment[2]; then they made a renunciation of Satan, turning to the West, and a profession of faith in the Trinity, turning to the East. The scene changed to the baptistery itself, where the candidates undressed completely, and were anointed from head to foot with exorcized oil. This oil had been consecrated, and was believed to possess the power of removing traces of past sins and all malign influences; the position of this anointing, between the profession and the baptism, is noteworthy. The candidates were led to the water, and baptized by trine immersion. The baptism was preceded by a final interrogation, the candidate being asked whether he believed 'in the name of the Father, and of the Son, and of the Holy Ghost'; this interrogation corresponds to the threefold interrogation which accompanies the threefold immersion in early times elsewhere, with the difference that here it precedes the immersions, doubtless by a simplification of the rite.

---

[1] For the creed of St Cyril of Jerusalem see Harnack, *The Apostles' Creed*, pp. 46 ff. (Eng. trans.).

[2] χιτών.

The unction with chrism followed immediately. The manner of its administration must be carefully observed; the neophytes were anointed on the 'brow and the other organs of sense[1],' which expression is further explained as the brow, ears, nose, and breast. Where this unction was performed, in the church or baptistery, and at what point the neophytes resumed their garments, is not stated; but it appears from St Cyril that they wore white robes on the days following their baptism.

The following fragments of liturgical forms are preserved in St Cyril: The renunciation, ἀποτάσσομαί σοι Σατανᾶ....καὶ πᾶσι τοῖς ἔργοις σου....καὶ πάσῃ τῇ πομπῇ [σου]....καὶ πάσῃ τῇ λατρείᾳ σου; the profession, πιστεύω εἰς τὸν πατέρα καὶ εἰς τὸν υἱὸν καὶ εἰς τὸ ἅγιον πνεῦμα καὶ εἰς ἓν βάπτισμα μετανοίας[2]; the profession at the font, ἠρωτᾶτο ἕκαστος εἰ πιστεύει εἰς τὸ ὄνομα τοῦ πατρὸς καὶ τοῦ υἱοῦ καὶ τοῦ ἁγίου πνεύματος[3].

In the writings of St Cyril of Jerusalem we see the baptismal rite in its full developement. The later history is concerned with a double process, a curtailment of the rite in respect of time by contracting it into a single service, and an elaboration of the service so produced. The latter stage is represented by the extant liturgical books; for the former we have the writings of the pseudo-Dionysius and James of Edessa.

[1] τῶν ἄλλων σου αἰσθητηρίων, Cyril Hier., *Cat. myst.* III. 3.
[2] *ib.* I.
[3] *ib.* II. 4. Cf. for the renunciation Jerome, *Comment. in Euang. Matth.* I. c. v. 25, and for Antioch Chrys., *Cat. II. ad illuminandos*, 4, 5.

The works which pass under the name of Dionysius the Areopagite were composed by an unknown writer, possibly Syrian, about the year 500. The rite of baptism is contained in the second section of the second chapter of the *Ecclesiastical Hierarchy* and, divested of the turgid and bombastic language in which it is described, is as follows:

The person desiring to be baptized is brought to the bishop by some Christian who is willing to act as sponsor. The bishop inquires what he wishes; the candidate in reply states his need and desire of baptism. The bishop then delivers an instruction on the Christian life, and when the candidate has promised to live in accordance therewith, he lays his hand on him, signs him, and instructs the priests to enter the names of the candidate and sponsor. This portion of the rite is all that remains of the catechumenate, already reduced to a mere survival and soon to vanish entirely. The deacons now divest the candidate of all his garments save one, and he is made to stand facing West and to renounce Satan thrice; the renunciations are preceded by a threefold exsufflation of Satan, presumably symbolizing the rejection of all malign spiritual influences. After this he turns to the East, and, with hands uplifted to heaven, professes his adherence to Christ and his teachings; a threefold confession of faith follows. He is now completely undressed, and the unction with oil takes place, begun by the bishop with three signings and completed by the priests over all the body. While the priests are thus engaged, the bishop

consecrates the water; the consecration is performed
with the ceremonies usual in the liturgical books,
with prayers and the pouring in of chrism crosswise,
together with three *Alleluias*[1]. The candidate and
sponsor are summoned by name, and the bishop
baptizes with threefold immersion and enunciation
of the formula. The neophyte is clothed by his
sponsor in white garments; the bishop signs him
with chrism, and finally makes him a participator in
the Eucharist.

The importance of this description lies not so
much in the information it furnishes about the
Syrian rite as in the insight it gives into the process
of transition from the long series of instructions and
ceremonies found in earlier writers to the single rite
of the extant books. We are able in the pseudo-
Dionysius to surprise the process while it is still
going on. We see the long preparation dwindling
to a mere preface to baptism; there is but one
catechesis, and that is a mere form. Baptism appears
to be performed at any time, not at Easter only.
The description of the rite contemplates an adult
as the recipient, but it appears from a later passage
that infants were commonly baptized, confirmed, and
communicated just as at the present day in the
East[2]. The renunciation and profession have taken

---

[1] Maximus Confessor, in his Scholia *ad loc.* interprets the
words of Dionysius τὸ ἱερὸν τῆς τῶν θεολήπτων προφητῶν
ἐπιπνοίας μελῴδημα as referring to Ps. xxviii. (xxix. in P. B.
version) and the *Alleluia*; the psalm is not, however, found in the
liturgical books at this point (Migne, *P. G.* iv. 125).

[2] *Eccl. Hier.* vii. 3, § 11.

the threefold form. The consecration of the water, though possibly less elaborate, is substantially the same as in the books. The unction is divided between the bishop and priests, just as in the Maronite books it is divided between the priest and deacon.

A still further stage is marked in the description of baptism by James of Edessa[1]. He divides the rite into two parts, and notes that in olden days a long period of time elapsed between the two parts, and that meanwhile the candidates were called Christians; the period to which he alludes is the catechumenate, but the division of the rite is not accurate, as he places in the first part the renunciation and profession of faith, which in earlier days immediately preceded baptism. In the second part he places the creed, the first unction, the consecration of the water with insufflation and pouring in of chrism, the baptism, and chrismation. It appears from the various liturgical books that the chrismation of confirmation was applied to the whole body. We saw that in St Cyril it was applied to the organs of sense; it was extended to the whole body at a later date, by analogy with the unction before baptism. In this the confirmation of the Syrian rite differs from the Greek and Western rites. At the end of baptism communion was given to the newly baptized, as is still the custom in the East.

This order of baptism of James of Edessa is of considerable importance, since his translation of a baptismal service written in Greek appears to be the

[1] Denzinger, *Rit. Or.* i. p. 279.

foundation of all the Monophysite Syrian forms of
baptism. The author of the Greek form was probably
Severus of Antioch[1]; if so, the Monophysite rite is
derived from Severus through James of Edessa. The
rite which bears the name of James[2], together with
three others[3], the last of which bears the name of
Severus, is divided into two parts, according to the
description of James. Two later rites have altered
this and placed the creed in the first part, that is,
in the office of the catechumens[4]. In all these rites
the office of baptism is simplified, as in James of
Edessa. The manner of dealing with the rite of the
catechumenate is especially noteworthy; in these
liturgical redactions it is reduced to a signing, exorcism, renunciation, and profession of faith. The
unction before baptism is divided in the Monophysite
rite by the consecration of the water; before the
consecration the priest anoints the brow and signs
it; after it he anoints the whole body, in either
case with oil. The genesis of this peculiarity is not
difficult to see. In the rite of the pseudo-Dionysius
the bishop began this anointing with signings, and
the priests finished it over all the body, while he consecrated the water; in the remodelling by Severus
the priest alone played both parts, so that he began
the anointing, then consecrated the water, and finally
completed the anointing. It might have been simpler
for him to complete the anointing when he began it,

---

[1] Monophysite Patriarch, 512—519 A.D.
[2] *Rit. Or.* i. p. 280.   [3] *ib.* pp. 288, 295, 302.
[4] *ib.* pp. 273 and 312; the latter also bears the name of Severus.

but the compiler wished to retain the old custom and the ancient procedure. The candidates are undressed before the exorcism, and after the final chrismation they are clothed in white, crowns are set on their heads, and they are girded with girdles; an office was composed for the removal of these crowns and girdles after seven days[1]. The oil and chrism were not consecrated at the service, but on Maundy Thursday by the bishop[2]. The chrism of confirmation was applied to the whole body, beginning at the brow. The infants (who alone are contemplated in these rites) are communicated at the end of the service.

The above is the general form of the Monophysite, or Jacobite Syrian baptismal rite. But the service at which it is performed is of an entirely different character. Anyone who should attempt to read the forms of service as they are set out in Denzinger's *Ritus Orientalium* would have some difficulty in detecting the ceremonies and rites of baptism amid the mass of enveloping liturgical forms. It remains now to speak of the framework of the rite.

When infant baptism became common, nothing remained of the catechumenate, as we have seen, but a few ceremonies introductory to baptism. The rite, at this stage, is exhibited in the pseudo-Dionysius and James of Edessa. The next stage was the elaboration of this simplified rite. When this took place is not clear. The silence of James of Edessa is not conclusive that he was unfamiliar with the later

[1] Denzinger, *Rit. Or.* I. p. 327.   [2] *ib.* p. 361.

elaboration; the fact that his name is associated
with one of the rites suggests that he himself may
have added some of the liturgical framework; in any
case we must set the remodelling of the rite at a
date before the divisions of the East became fixed,
in order to explain the resemblances of the Maronite
and Jacobite rites. The liturgical composer, whoever
he was, was struck by the presence in the baptismal
rite of the creed (which, by this time, had been
inserted after the profession of faith), and of a consecration of the element of water. These features
suggested the Liturgy[1] proper, or Eucharist, as a
model on which to base the baptismal service. This
idea was not peculiar to this region, but appears to
have been very general in the East at the period;
it is carried out, even more thoroughly, in the
Maronite, the Nestorian, and also in the Egyptian
rites; in fact, it was evidently at one time the pre-
vailing liturgical fashion. The method of execution
in the Monophysite rite is as follows.

The rite opens with a number of liturgical compositions, including a respond, a *cyclion*, a *prooemium*
with its prayer, and a *quqaya* (corresponding to the
Greek κανών). These are borrowed from various
sources, some from St Ephraim; particularly interesting is that in which an apocryphal account of
our Lord's baptism is given[2]. The psalm and lessons

---

[1] The creed was introduced into the Eucharistic Liturgy at
Antioch by Peter the Fuller soon after 470 A.D.

[2] *Rit. Or.* I. p. 310. For an explanation of the technical terms see
ib. p. 268; the respond and *cyclion* are psalms 'farced' or interspersed

follow; the latter are two in number, except in the second rite of Severus, where the number is increased to three by the addition of a lesson from the Acts[1]. At this point the exorcism, renunciation, and profession of faith are inserted, and the office of the catechumens, corresponding to the 'mass of the catechumens,' ends. The second office, corresponding to the 'mass of the faithful,' begins with the creed. The priest then pours water into the font and covers it with a veil; this answers to the Offertory. At this point the unction of the brow with oil takes place. A *prooemium* with a prayer and another *quqaya*, followed by a prayer, leads up to the consecration of the water, itself a complicated formula. After the consecration, the rite proceeds with the rest of the unction, baptism, confirmation, and vesting in white, concluding with the Lord's Prayer and the communion; here also metrical compositions and prayers are freely inserted. It only remains to mention the formulas of baptism and confirmation. The former is: 'N. is baptized in the name of the Father. Amen. And of the Son. Amen. And of the Holy Ghost unto life eternal. Amen.' This formula is slightly elaborated in some cases; for instance: 'N. is baptized that he may be a lamb in the flock of Christ,' or 'unto holiness and salvation and blamelessness and to a blessed resurrection from the dead.' The formula of confirmation

---

with matter suitable to the occasion; a *prooemium* is an introduction to prayer; and a *quqaya* is a metrical composition.

[1] Denzinger, *Rit. Or.* I. p. 311.

is: 'With holy chrism, the sweetness of the odour of Christ, the seal of true faith, the fulness of the gift of the Holy Spirit, N. is sealed in the name of the Father. Amen. And of the Son. Amen. And of the living and Holy Spirit, unto life eternal. Amen.'

The above rites of baptism are of considerable length and are suited for performance in a church. In case of necessity, such as imminent death, something shorter was needed. For this purpose two short rites are supplied. The first, which bears the name of Severus[1], is simply the rite of James of Edessa without any liturgical framework. The second, which bears the name of Philoxenus of Mabug[2], is still briefer; the rite is reduced to a signing of the brow with oil, a very short consecration of the water, baptism, and signing with chrism. In both cases communion concludes the rite.

The Melchites, or orthodox Syrians, translated the Greek rite for their use into Syriac. Two versions[3] of this are extant, the first a mere translation of the Greek, the second a mixture of Greek and Syrian usages. The latter is also used by the Monophysites. Both versions bear the name of St Basil; they are not of sufficient importance to require a full description.

The Maronites, or Monothelite Syrians, separated from the orthodox Church after the condemnation of the Monothelite heresy by the sixth Ecumenical Council[4]. In 1182 A.D. they were admitted to communion with the Roman Church, and they have since

[1] *Rit. Or.* i. p. 316.   [2] *ib.* p. 318.
[3] *ib.* p. 318.   [4] 680—681 A.D.

then retained a more or less close connexion with
that portion of the Church. From these two facts—
the separation of the Maronites from the Greeks and
their connexion with the Latins—two results have
followed. (*a*) Their rite has not shared the fortunes
of the Jacobite rite and has remained untouched
by the alterations which the latter has undergone
since the seventh century. The Maronite rite is,
therefore, an older form of the Syrian rite than
the Jacobite; their common features indicate that
they had a common history before the separation.
(*b*) The Maronite rite has been Romanized in several
features. The discussion of the baptismal rite and
its liturgical framework will bring out both these
points.

There are two Maronite rites[1], the former of which
bears the name of Jacob of Serug. The rite of Jacob
of Serug begins with a service for the entry of mother
and child into church, in the course of which the
child is signed twice, the second time with oil consecrated in the service. The consecration of the
oil during the service is an ancient feature preserved
in this rite both at this point and later in the service
when the oil is consecrated for the unction before
baptism. The baptismal rite itself is the same as
the Monophysite[2], except for the consecration of oil
during the service; chrism, however, is consecrated

---

[1] The Maronite rites are in Denzinger, *Rit. Or.* I. pp. 329, 351.

[2] A small point of difference is that the deacon, not the priest,
anoints the body of the candidate after the consecration of the
water.

on Maundy Thursday, as elsewhere. One feature is missing in the Maronite rite, that is, the change of place during the service; in the Monophysite rite, the first service, that is, the service of the catechumens, is performed in the church, the second service in the baptistery; after confirmation the neophytes are brought to the altar. On all this the Maronite rite is silent. A Roman feature is the use of the active voice in the formula of baptism, 'I baptize thee'; the formula of confirmation remained unaltered. Stephanus Aldoensis, the Maronite patriarch, who died at the beginning of the eighteenth century, introduced many more Roman details into the rite. The neophytes were presented at the end with a lighted candle[1]; infant communion was abolished, and priests were not allowed to confirm, or, at least, they were only permitted to anoint the top of the head, unction of the brow being reserved to bishops.

The liturgical framework of the rite is more closely assimilated to the Eucharist than in the case of the Jacobites; the liturgy to which it bears most resemblance is naturally that of St James. The following are the main features which the baptismal rite has borrowed from the liturgy: the *Trisagion*, Psalm, Epistle, *Alleluia*, Gospel, Dismissal of the unbaptized, Creed (which is, of course, common to both), Salutation, *Sursum corda*, *Sanctus*, Invocation of the Holy Spirit, Lord's Prayer, Final dismissal. Besides these, the baptismal service contains a number of prayers, litanies, and metrical compositions, which

[1] From the Roman rite of baptism.

can be paralleled from the eucharistic liturgy. The dismissal of the unbaptized is particularly worthy of note, as it is a once universal feature which survives only in a few places. The total result is that we have an ancient Syrian rite, slightly Romanized, and enclosed in a liturgical setting borrowed from the liturgy of St James.

The Maronites have also a shorter rite, which bears the name of St Basil of Caesarea. The rite consists of an unction of the brow, a consecration of the water, a further unction, baptism, signing with chrism, and communion. The use of the first person active in the baptismal formula proves that the rite is Maronite. Two short forms, for loosing the girdle and cutting the hair, follow the Maronite rite in Denzinger's collection. They are made up of prayers which were later adopted by the Greeks. The same remark applies to the Jacobite forms for removing the crown and girdle from the newly baptized after seven days. The identity of the prayers with the Greek shews that these ceremonies came into use at an early date.

The native Syriac rite, with its unction before baptism instead of after it, held its ground longest in East Syria[1] among the Nestorians, where a post-baptismal unction is not met with till the patri-archate of Isho'yabh III in the middle of the seventh century. That patriarch[2] subjected the baptismal

---

[1] It is found even in the Antiochene Theodoret, Bishop of Cyrrhus, *in Cant.* I. 2 (Migne, *P. G.* LXXXI. 60).

[2] The Nestorian rite has been translated and furnished with

rite to a revision much more drastic than any other rite experienced. The preparation for baptism is reduced to an imposition of the hand and a signing; the exorcism, renunciation, and profession of faith[1] also disappear. At the back of these changes stands the Pelagianism of the Nestorians, which denied original sin; the infants could not be treated as requiring liberation from alien spiritual influences, as they had no inherited taint of sin from which they needed to be delivered. Accordingly the prayers contain a curious mixture of Pelagian and older expressions, now denying, now implying original sin. After the consecration of the water an unction of the whole body of the candidate takes place. He is then baptized, and confirmed by an imposition of the hand and a signing of the brow with oil; the rite closes with communion. Chrism is not used, but oil alone, both for the consecration of the water and for confirmation; the oil is consecrated in the service. The baptismal formula is: 'N. is baptized in the Name of the Father, in the Name of the Son, in the Name of the Holy Ghost, for ever and ever. Amen'; the people respond 'Amen' at the words 'Father,' 'Son,' and at the end of the formula. We have spoken of a confirmation in this rite; but it is doubtful whether it really possesses it. The prayer at the imposition of the hand presupposes that the

valuable introduction and notes by Diettrich (*Die nestorianische Taufliturgie*); cf. also Denzinger, *Rit. Or.* I. pp. 364—383.

[1] The creed is retained, but is as purely liturgical a feature as the lections.

Holy Spirit is already received, and is, indeed, rather a thanksgiving than a prayer. At the signing with oil on the brow, the formula is : ' N. was' [or 'has been'] 'baptized and perfected in the Name of the Father, and of the Son, and of the Holy Ghost.' The word 'perfected' is equivalent to 'confirmed'; but here again the action is regarded as past. Further, the use of oil is generally omitted in the signing, so that it is difficult to see, in the Nestorian post-baptismal ceremonies, whether in their present or earlier form, any rite really corresponding to confirmation.

Isho'yabh's remodelling of the service furnished the above rite with a very formal framework, parallel to the Liturgy, and divided into eight parts, each beginning with a prayer and ending with a hymn or metrical composition. The whole service is divided into two parts by the dismissal of the unbaptized and the penitents at the end of the fourth part. The other liturgical features are introduced as in the rest of the Syrian rites ; a peculiarity of this rite is that the consecration of the oil as well as the water is placed in the *Anaphora* after the *Sursum corda*.

In conclusion, the Syrian rites (apart from the Nestorian) possess a common character which may be summed up as follows. The rite is curtailed by shortening the preparatory portion, and this abbreviated rite is set in a framework borrowed from the liturgy. The features in the rite which require notice are the dividing of the unction before baptism into two parts, and the application of the unction of confirmation to the whole body. The features common to Syrian and other Oriental rites are that the priest is the ordinary minister of confirmation and that communion follows immediately upon confirmation; the formulas are all in the passive, except in the Maronite rite, where Roman influence has introduced the active voice.

Sec. 2. *The Greek Rite.*

The rite of the Church of Constantinople and the Churches dependent on it was ultimately derived from the rite current in the Churches of Western Syria and Palestine, and is in all essential points identical with the rite found in Cyril of Jerusalem and Dionysius the Areopagite. The principal source of information is the rite in its final form as embodied in the *Euchologion*[1]; our information, apart from this source, is scanty.

We glean a little knowledge of the early history of the Greek rite from the canons of the Trullan Council (692 A.D.). Sponsors are mentioned in a canon which forbids their marriage with the widowed parents of the children baptized[2]; we have here evidence for infant baptism, though the practice was so well established by the seventh century that it is hardly needed. The catechumenate was, however, still in use; it is enjoined that catechumens

[1] The best edition is that in pp. 389—412 of Conybeare and Maclean's *Rituale Armenorum.*
[2] Can. 53.

shall learn the creed and repeat it on the Thursday before Easter[1]. The ninety-fifth canon of this Council contains a statement of the practice of the Church of Constantinople in receiving heretics, which dates from the middle of the fifth century[2], and furnishes early evidence of the manner of confirmation among the Greeks; it is administered by signing with chrism the brow, eyes, nose, mouth, and ears, with the words, 'The seal of the gift of the Holy Spirit.' From the same source we learn the order of the ceremonies of the catechumenate in the case of reconciled heretics. The first day they were made Christians, the second day catechumens[3], the third they were exorcized with insufflation of the face and ears; before they were baptized a period of instruction elapsed.

The eighth century Barberini manuscript[4] preserves an ancient form for the renunciation and profession. The antiquity of the service is proved by its primitive character; the archbishop presides, the archdeacon assists, and the congregation consists of adult catechumens. This service is held, not on Easter Eve, as we should expect, but on Good Friday; baptism still takes place in the night of the Easter Vigil. The interesting feature is the instructions which precede and follow the renunciation and profession; we are favoured with examples of early

---

[1] Can. 78.   [2] Cf. *infra*, p. 193, note 5.

[3] Possibly the 'making of a Christian' = originally 'the making of a catechumen,' and the 'making of a catechumen' = the 'making of a "competent."' Already the rites are beginning to lose their earlier meaning.

[4] *Rit. Arm.* p. 438.

catecheses on the subject of the moral obligation of the covenant made by the catechumens in renouncing Satan and professing Christ. In this document we have a glimpse into the manner of performing one part of the baptismal rite, before the final developement took place, and the ceremonies of the catechumenate became merely a prefatory part of the baptismal service.

Let us now turn to the consideration of the baptismal rite in its developed form[1]. Before it are placed two prayers, the first 'for sealing the child when it receives a name on the eighth day after its birth'; the second 'when it enters the church on the fortieth day after its birth.' Both prayers are suited only for infants; they are both, however, found in the Syriac, the former in the Jacobite, the latter in the Maronite.

The rite which follows may be divided into four parts[2]:

I. The entry into the catechumenate. II. The exorcisms. III. The renunciation and profession. IV. Baptism and confirmation.

I. The first part is entitled 'Prayer for making a catechumen.' The candidate is divested of his shoes, and his clothing except the under garment; the priest sets him to the East, breathes on him thrice, and signs his brow, mouth, and breast,

---

[1] The rite is given in the Greek *Euchologia*; a critical edition is furnished in *Rit. Arm.* pp. 389—406.

[2] Dom Puniet in the *D.A.C.L.* II. col. 287. In this chapter the texts in the *Rit. Arm.* are mainly used.

accompanying the actions with a prayer. The section, of course, represents the beginning of the catechumenate.

II. The second part contains as much of the system of instruction and preparation as survived the disuse of adult baptism. It consists of a triple exorcism, followed by a fourth exorcism to be used immediately before baptism. The ceremonies of the exorcizing are insufflation and signing of brow, mouth, and breast.

III. For the third part our evidence is rather fuller, as we possess, in addition to the *Euchologion*, the ancient form of service described above. It is best to begin with the form in the Barberini manu-script[1], as it is our oldest complete description.

The archbishop enters at the sixth hour and ascends the *ambo*. The archdeacon salutes the congregation and the archbishop bids the catechumens sign themselves and take off their shoes and clothes, except, presumably, the under garment or *chiton*[2], and proceeds to deliver an address. The renunciation follows. The catechumens turn to the West; thrice the archbishop says the formula, ' I renounce Satan, and all his works, and all his service, and all his angels, and all his pomp,' and thrice they repeat it. Thrice he asks them, ' Have you renounced Satan?'; and thrice they reply, ' We have renounced.' They now turn to the East, and with similar repetitions

---

[1] *Rit. Arm.* p. 438.
[2] Cf. what has been said on the Syrian rite above, p. 54.

make the profession; the formula is, 'I profess[1] Christ, and I believe in one God,' *i.e.* the 'Nicene' creed; the archbishop asks, 'Have you professed Christ?'; and the candidates reply, 'We have professed.' The candidates are bidden to worship Christ, and, while they kneel, a prayer or ascription of praise to God[2] is said over them; this prayer is not in the ancient manuscripts but appears in the printed texts. Another address is given, followed by a litany of a general character. The archbishop then makes the sign of the cross over the people, and prays. After the prayer he bids the catechumens dress, and proceeding to the altar prays, while the deacon recites a litany; the prayer still remains in the rite[3]. Finally the catechumens are blessed and dismissed.

This service is incorporated in the later rite with very few alterations. The command to undress and take off the shoes still appears in the books, although the candidates are already undressed. The litanies have disappeared, and all the prayers but one; the addresses are also omitted. In the modern printed text the command to worship Christ which succeeds the profession of faith is followed by the response, 'I worship Father, Son, and Holy Spirit, consubstantial and undivided Trinity,' and the ascription of praise to God. Neither of these forms appears in the oldest complete text of the rite, but the former appears first in a slightly different form in the tenth

---

[1] συντάσσομαι τῷ Χριστῷ.

[2] εὐλογητὸς ὁ Θεὸς κ.τ.λ.

[3] Δέσποτα Κύριε ὁ Θεὸς προσκάλεσαι κ.τ.λ. *Rit. Arm.* p. 396.

century Grotta Ferrata manuscript, and the ascription of praise is already found in the Good Friday service quoted in the last paragraph. The renunciation of Satan is, in all texts, early or late, followed by an exsufflation; to this, since the late mediaeval period, has been added the spitting at him, as a sign of contempt, which now appears in the printed texts[1].

IV. In the modern Greek *Euchologia*, the first three parts into which the service is divided appear as one service, under the title ' Prayer for making a catechumen.' The fourth part is entitled ' Service[2] of Holy Baptism.' The modern service is headed by a rubric for the vesting and entry of the priest. In the eleventh century Grotta Ferrata manuscript[3] this rubric is given in an older form, in which the ministry of the patriarch on Easter Eve is contemplated. At the beginning of the second lesson[4] at Vespers, the patriarch descended from the throne and entered the baptistery through the vestry ; here he puts on a white vestment and white shoes and, going to the font, censed it on all sides ; then, giving back the censer, he made the sign of the cross thrice with candles, while the deacon said the litany. In the modern service, while the litany still goes on the priest (in earlier days, the bishop or patriarch) says silently an *apologia*, or prayer for himself as minister. On the completion of the litany the consecration of the water is performed in a loud voice. In this consecration oil, not chrism, is used. The oil is hallowed after

---

[1] *D.A.C.L.* II. col. 290.
[2] ἀκολουθία.
[3] *Rit. Arm.* p. 396.
[4] φωτίζου=Is, lx. 1—16.

the blessing of the water, and the priest makes three crosses on the water with it. The candidate is also signed with the oil on brow, breast, and back; the formula is: 'N. is anointed with the oil of gladness, in the name of the Father, and of the Son, and of the Holy Ghost'; the deacon then completes the unction of the whole body. Baptism follows, with the formula: 'N. is baptized in the name of the Father, and of the Son, and of the Holy Ghost.' The manuscript quoted above[1] on the baptism states that the patriarch puts on cuffs and takes a towel and baptizes as above, making an immersion at the name of each person of the Trinity; afterwards he washes his hands and lays aside the towel and cuffs. The formulas used at the unction and at baptism go back to the Syrian originals. They have, however, received some slight additions in the course of time; the words, 'the servant of God' have been prefixed to the name of the candidate since the tenth century or earlier; in the modern books 'Amen' is said after the name of each person of the Trinity, after the manner of the Syrians.

Baptism is connected with confirmation by a prayer referring to both rites. The confirmation is very simple, and consists merely of a signing of the brow, eyes, nostrils, mouth, and ears with the chrism which has been consecrated on Maundy Thursday; the formula is: 'The Seal of the Gift of the Holy Spirit.' The liturgy, at which the newly baptized communicated, followed the confirmation in older days.

[1] Grotta Ferrata MSS. *Rit. Arm.* p. 404, note *a*.

After seven days the newly baptized are brought to
church, and the parts which received the chrism are
washed. The prayers which accompany this ceremony
are derived from Syrian sources, and, as in both
cases they are used for the same purpose, it appears
that this washing goes back to a considerable antiquity.

The variants given in the *Rituale Armenorum* for this
last part of the rite are interesting[1]. In the first, which
is from a twelfth century manuscript, the rite of confirmation is Egyptian in character; the brow, nostrils,
ears, hands, and heart are signed with chrism with the
same formulas as in the Alexandrian rite[2], but the other
unctions and the imposition of the hand which appear
in the Egyptian rite are not reproduced. A second brings
before us the ancient ritual of baptism very vividly;
it is from a manuscript which we have twice quoted
above. 'The patriarch takes off the baptismal vestments and puts on those for the liturgy. And as the
singer chants "As many of you as were baptized into
Christ," he confirms. And after this, singing with the
choir boys "Blessed is he whose unrighteousness is forgiven," he enters the church and celebrates the divine
liturgy. And on other feasts [than Easter] when baptisms take place in the little baptistery, the patriarch
descends and does all according to the above-written
type.' In this description we have a note of the extension
of baptism to other festivals; the rite was still a great
ceremony, not yet to be performed at any time, but by a
concession permitted to be administered on certain other
festivals with the Easter ceremonial, but still by the
patriarch as minister. A further note in the same manuscript states that after confirming the patriarch sits
awaiting the Emperor; but the choir boys and singers,

[1] p. 405, note *a*.   [2] *Rit. Or.* I. p. 209.

chanting 'Blessed is he whose unrighteousness is forgiven,'
lead the newly enlightened into the church. Here we are
brought into the church of St Sophia and see the great
personages of the court, along with the Emperor, attending
the liturgy of Easter.

A third variant prefaces the Greek rite of confirmation
with a Greek translation of the Roman prayer for the
sevenfold Spirit.

In the printed edition of the rite, the chant 'As many
of you as were baptized into Christ, have put on Christ'
follows confirmation. Then two lessons are read, an
Epistle (Rom. vi. 3—11) and a Gospel (Matt. xxviii.
16—20), and after a litany the congregation is dismissed.
The connecting link between these additions and the
ancient rite is to be found in the liturgy of Easter Eve.
There the above chant is used as a substitute for the
Trisagion and the above Epistle and Gospel are read;
afterwards the liturgy of St Basil is said. The liturgical
matter at the end of the baptismal rite as now performed
is really a 'mass of the catechumens,' and is a survival
of the time when baptism was part of the Easter Vigil and
was followed by the Liturgy.

The Greek (Byzantine) rite is very similar to the
Syrian rites of the Monophysites and Maronites.
This fact will be clear from a comparison of the rites
in the tables at the end of the book. The resemblance is natural, as they are all ultimately derived
from the fourth century rite of Western Syria and
Palestine. The similarity, however, extends to the
language of the prayers and formulas; indeed, the
Greek originals, from which the later Syrian rites
were translated, were practically identical with the
Byzantine form. We have, in fact, an instance of
the general tendency to assimilation of rites which

had by this time taken place in the East. Whether this assimilation was due to the original dependence of the Greek Byzantine rite on the Churches of Western Syria and Palestine, or to later borrowing on the part of these Churches from the rite of the Imperial City, must be left undetermined ; but both influences were probably at work. The Greek rite, however, has preserved the old forms more faithfully, since it has not undergone the liturgical transformation of the later Syrian rites.   Not only does it lack the framework of chants and lessons, but it has maintained the division into parts—preparation, renunciation and profession, baptism—which in the later Syrian rites have been effaced by subsequent changes.   Three exorcisms remain in the Greek service, whereas in the Syrian rites this part of the preparation has been more extensively curtailed, so that no trace remains of the numerous *catecheses.* Further, the 'sealing' with chrism of the Greeks is administered by unction of the organs of sense only, not of the whole body ; in this respect the Greeks stand nearer to St Cyril of Jerusalem than the Monophysites and Maronites.

The following table gives a list of the corresponding prayers.

Denzinger, *Rit. Or.*		Conybeare, *Rit. Arm.*	
p. 267.		p. 389.	
p. 329.		p. 390.	
p. 312.		p. 398.	
p. 275. } p. 276. }		p. 401.	
p. 278.		p. 404.	
p. 361.	Te deprecamur.	p. 408.	Σὲ ἱκετεύομεν.
p. 360.	Domine Deus noster.	p. 410.	Δέσποτα Κύριε.

In addition to this the whole blessing of the water is the same as in the Syrian rite, save the first prayer Μέγας εἶ Κύριε, which is derived from the Greek rite for blessing the waters on the feast of the Epiphany.

SEC. 3. *The Armenian Rite*[1]

The Armenian Church has been subject to three separate influences, Syrian—from its first missionaries; Cappadocian—from St Gregory the Illuminator, who in the fourth century came from the Cappadocian Caesarea and became the national apostle of the Armenians; and Greek—when the Church of Constantinople became dominant in Asia Minor. During the fifth century the Armenian alphabet was invented and the liturgical books were translated into the Armenian language. It is to this period that tradition ascribes the arrangement of several offices, among them the baptismal rite, by John Mandakuni[2], catholicos of the Armenians. At the end of the ninth century St Mashtotz revised the offices, and it is for this reason that the Armenian service book is called a Mashtotz to this day. Finally, the Armenian Church in 491 A.D. denounced the council of Chalcedon and henceforward was separated from the rest of the Church. It is evident from the above that the Armenian rite of baptism has passed under a variety of influences; but as we know scarcely

[1] See Conybeare and Maclean, *Rit. Arm.* pp. 86—108, and Denzinger, *Rit. Or.* I. pp. 383—401; the second rite in Denzinger is very modern, and has borrowed much from the Roman rite.

[2] *Rit. Arm.* p. xxxiii.

anything of the Cappadocian rites, we are unable to
say definitely what parts of the baptismal rite must
be attributed to that source.   But it is clear that,
whereas the Greek and Syrian rites stand in most
intimate connexion, the Armenian rite stands apart
from either of those sources, both in ceremonial and
prayers ; whether the differences are to be attributed
to the Cappadocian sources or to the various revisions
is not clear, but no doubt the isolation of the Armenian
Church is responsible for a good deal of peculiarity
in the rite.

The service begins with the bringing of the child
to church on the eighth day after birth, for which is
appointed a single prayer.   On the fortieth day the
child and its mother come to church, several prayers
are said over them, and they are blessed.   At the
present time children are baptized a few days after
birth; accordingly the first office is prefixed to baptism,
and the second is said *after*[1] baptism—inconsistently,
for its language presupposes that baptism is yet to
come.   In Armenia adult baptism lasted longer than
elsewhere, though by the eighth century, as we learn
from John of Odsun, children were baptized when
eight days old.   But the rubric which precedes the
next part of the rite represents the older custom.
It runs as follows : ' The Canon of Baptism, when
they make a Christian.   Before which it is not right
to admit him into church.   But he shall have hands
laid on him beforehand, three weeks or more before

[1] *Rit. Or.* I. p. 400.   The following account of the rite is derived
principally from the *Rituale Armenorum.*

the baptism, in time sufficient for him to learn from
the Wardapet [that is, Doctor] both the faith and
the baptism of the Church.   First of all the Godhead
of the Holy Trinity, and about the creation and
coming to be of all creatures ; and next about the
election of just men.   After that the birth of Christ,
and in its order all the economy, and the great
mystery of the cross, and the burial and the resurrection and ascension unto the Father, and the
second coming, and the resurrection of all flesh, and
the rewarding of each according to his works.   In
teaching this the Wardapet shall instruct him to be
untiring in prayer[1].'   This rubric belongs to a time
when adult baptism was the rule, and is inconsistent
with the prescriptions for bringing a child to church
on the eighth and fortieth days, since it forbids those
who are not yet catechumens to be admitted to the
Church.   The description of the instruction to be
given to the catechumens is exactly in accordance
with the ancient discipline ; in fact we have here
surviving the antique ritual of the catechumenate, as
is shewn by the rest of the rubric : 'This is the order
for those of ripe age.   First the catechumen shall have
hands laid on him, whether of full age or a child.'
The office, although used for children, was felt to be
designed for adults.   Two prayers are said over the
candidate, then an exorcism, at the end of which,
according to a marginal note in one text[2], the priest

---

[1] *Rit. Arm*. p. 89.

[2] *ib*. p. 91, note *g*.   This is confirmed by a quotation from the
catholicus John the Philosopher ; *Rit. Or*. i. p. 386, note.

lays his hand on the catechumen. The renunciation is made three times; at each renunciation, according to the Barberini manuscript, the candidate spits on Satan, a detail which also appears in the mediaeval Greek rite. The profession of faith is couched in a peculiar form. The priest asks, 'Dost thou believe in the all-holy Trinity, in Father and Son and Holy Spirit? Dost thou believe in the Father? Dost thou believe in the Son? Dost thou believe in the Holy Spirit?' To each question answer is made 'I believe.' According to two ancient manuscripts the Nicene creed is said; the rest omit it. It appears that up to the sixth century the Armenians used the Nicene creed; about the sixth century they adopted a new form of symbol, based upon an 'Interpretation of the creed' attributed to St Athanasius, but borrowed from Syrian sources, and this they employ in place of the Nicene creed[1].

The prayer of consecration of the oil follows. Here we must consider briefly the use of oil and chrism among the Armenians. The unction of a catechumen before baptism has entirely vanished from the Armenian rite, in both modern texts and manuscripts. But in ancient days there was an unction of catechumens with oil consecrated by this prayer (which is now said over already consecrated chrism), and the consecration of the water and confirmation were, as now, performed with chrism consecrated

---

[1] *D.A.C.L.* II. col. 296; *Rit. Or.* I. p. 392, note; cf. also Hahn, *Bibliothek der Symbole*, pp. 151—156.

by the catholicos at Etchmiadzin on Maundy Thursday[1]. The text of the *Rituale Armenorum* mentions holy oil only for the consecration of the water and confirmation; nevertheless chrism, or μύρον, is now used and has always been used, according to the testimony of Armenian writers[2].

The consecration of oil is followed by the pouring of water into the font and by a section of liturgical matter, consisting of psalm, Old Testament lesson, epistle, gospel, and litany, all with special reference to baptism. This liturgical matter recalls the Syrian rites which we have already dealt with; but the manner of inserting it is altogether different. In the Syrian rites the creed follows the lections, and the whole rite is assimilated to the Liturgy; here the creed precedes the lections, and no attempt is made to remodel the rite on the lines of the liturgy. The section was inserted at this point probably because it is the division between the preparation and the baptism proper. The reason of its insertion was a natural desire to illustrate the rite by suitable passages from Scripture.

The form of consecration of the water is very short and contains no exorcism. It begins with the praise of God for his work in creation, proceeds with a commemoration of the institution of baptism, and then prays for the descent of the Holy Spirit on the water and for bestowal of the gifts of baptism on the

[1] *Rit. Or.* i. pp. 35, 55.
[2] Cf. *ib.* and *Rit. Arm.* p. 107, where an ancient Armenian tract on baptism is given.

candidate, among which is mentioned[1] the reception of the Holy Spirit. At the end of this prayer chrism is poured crosswise into the font.

The catechumen now undresses, an action which is accompanied by a prayer from the Greek rite[2], selected for its verbal appropriateness by reason of an allusion to stripping 'him naked of the oldness of sin.' Baptism then takes place. The ordinary formula in manuscripts is: 'N. is baptized in the name of Father and Son and Holy Spirit, redeemed by the blood of Christ from the slavery of sin, receiving the freedom of adoption as son of the heavenly Father, having become a co-heir with Christ, and a temple of the Holy Spirit, now and ever and for eternity.' The first section of this formula agrees with the usual Eastern form. Mr Conybeare in the *Rituale Armenorum* translates, 'N. *shall be* baptized,' on the authority of certain old manuscripts; but this strange and unexampled reading is not supported by tradition or by ancient Armenian writers. The mode of administration is a threefold affusion or pouring of water over the head, followed by threefold immersion, accompanied by threefold repetition of the formula. Complete submersion is ordered by the synod of Tvin (A.D. 527) under Nerses the Graceful. After baptism the account of our Lord's baptism is read from the Gospel according to St Matthew.

---

[1] According to *Rit. Arm.* p. 95; in Denzinger's text there is no mention of 'the reception of the Holy Spirit.'

[2] It is the last prayer in the office 'for making a catechumen' in the printed Greek rite; the reading in *Rit. Arm.* p. 396, is different.

Confirmation among the Armenians takes a peculiar form. The neophyte is anointed with chrism on brow, eyes, ears, nostrils, mouth, palms of the hands, heart, back, and feet. No mention is made of the Holy Spirit in the formulas which accompany these acts, but the word 'seal' is frequently used. The gift of the Holy Spirit is definitely associated with baptism both in the consecration of the water and in the baptismal formula. But in the prayer before the unctions occur the words, 'replenish him with the grace of the Holy Spirit,' which may refer to the following rite[1]. The priest is the minister of confirmation; there is no trace in the Armenian rite of the original ministry of the bishop in the rites of initiation.

Finally the newly baptized is clothed in white raiment and crowned, and receives communion at the altar. On the eighth day the crown is removed by the priest.

The following prayers in the Armenian rite correspond to the Greek; the references in both cases are to the *Rituale Armenorum*.

Armenian	Greek
p. 86.	p. 389.
p. 88.	p. 390.
p. 94, the litany is similar to that on p. 397.	

The following prayers correspond with the Greek *Euchologion*: The prayer 'O Lord our God' on p. 87 is found in the office εἰς γυναῖκα λεχώ, and the prayer 'Lord,

---

[1] The prayer is derived from a Syrian source (*Rit. Or.* I. p. 315), where it is used at the end after communion.

who hast called' on p. 96 corresponds most closely to the last prayer of the Greek office 'for making a catechumen.'

The prayer on p. 97, 'O God, that art,' is from the Syrian rite; cf. *Rit. Or.* I. p. 315.   Several manuscripts of the Armenian insert in the consecration of the water a prayer which is mainly Syrian in origin and is taken from that part of the Syrian form of consecration which the Greeks did not take over; cf. *Rit. Arm.* p. 101 with *Rit. Or.* I. pp. 275, 276.

CHAPTER VI

THE EGYPTIAN RITE

THE *Egyptian Church Order*, the *Canons of Hippolytus*, and the cognate works, which are often attributed to an Egyptian source, and certainly bear several Egyptian characteristics, have already been considered in the chapter on Church Orders. We now proceed to discuss the documents of a distinctively Egyptian origin, of which the first in order is the so-called *Sacramentary of Sarapion of Thmuis*[1]. This recently discovered work is attributed in its title to Sarapion, bishop of Thmuis, a friend of St Athanasius, whose diocese was in the Delta. The book is a collection of thirty prayers, each with a title indicating its function; those numbered 7—11, 15, 16, 28, concern us here. Their titles are as follows:

7. Consecration of waters.
8. Prayer for those who are being baptized.
9. Prayer after the renunciation.
10. Prayer after the † assumption †.
11. Prayer after baptism and ascent [from the font].
15. Prayer for the oil of those who are being baptized.

[1] So termed by Brightman; the late bishop of Salisbury gave it the name of *Bishop Sarapion's Prayer Book*.

16.   Prayer for the chrism wherewith the baptized are anointed.

28.   Imposition of the hand upon catechumens.

There is not at first sight much information to be gleaned from these titles; and indeed there is not very much that is specifically Egyptian apart from the doxologies of the prayers.

No. 28.   This prayer was used when the catechumens were dismissed at the end of the first part of the Liturgy.   This is the only piece of information the book furnishes on the catechumenate, but the silence is not surprising, since it is a collection of prayers to be said in the formal services of the Church by the officiating bishop or priest; the catechumenate enters into their range only at this point.

No. 7.   In the manuscript the consecration of the water stands first in the prayers for baptism, and this may be its right position, as in the *Egyptian Church Order*.   In all developed rites the consecration is placed later, in immediate proximity to baptism, and such is the case in the Egyptian rites. This prayer is, of all the baptismal prayers, most akin to the forms in liturgical books.   The order of subjects is:

1.   God's work in creation.
2.   God's work in redemption.
3.   Prayer that God will look upon the waters and fill them with the Holy Spirit.
4.   'Let thine ineffable Word come to be in them and transform their energy, etc.
5.   Prayer for the candidates.

6. 'As thy only-begotten Word coming down upon the waters of the Jordan rendered them holy, so now also may he descend, etc.'

7. Another prayer for the candidates.

The invocation of the Word in 4 and 6 is characteristic of Alexandria, and occurs also in Sarapion's Liturgy. The emphatic word 'change[1]' in 4 may just possibly be connected with the emphasis laid on a change in the water in later Egyptian theology[2], an emphasis which led to the introduction of a prayer for the re-changing of the water to its former nature. The other subjects mentioned are usual in consecration prayers, but the treatment is not very similar to anything in later rites[3].

No. 8 is an introductory prayer to the rite. No. 9 is, in title, connected with the renunciation, but in substance refers also to the profession of faith. No. 15, according to its title, is a prayer over the oil of the unction before baptism, but in substance is a prayer for the administration of the unction. No. 10 is entitled a 'prayer after the assumption[4],' a phrase which, if right, is difficult to explain. Various meanings are suggested: the

---

[1] μεταποιησάτω; the references are to the text of the *Sacramentary of Sarapion* in *J.Th.St.* I. (1900), 88—113, 247—277.

[2] See below, p. 167.

[3] But cf. ὡς κατελθὼν ὁ μονογενής σου Λόγος ἐπὶ τὰ ὕδατα τοῦ Ἰορδάνου ἅγια ἀπέδειξεν, οὕτω καὶ νῦν ἐν τούτοις κατερχέσθω καὶ ἅγια καὶ πνευματικὰ ποιησάτω with *Rit. Or.* I. p. 204, quoniam unigenitus Filius tuus D. N. J. C. qui in Iordanem descendens eius aquas mundauit.

[4] μετὰ τὴν ἀνάληψιν.

'assumption' of the catechumen into the baptistery
(*i.e.* the prayer follows the passage from the vestibule
to the font); the 'taking up' of the neophyte from
the font by the sponsors (Brightman); the 'acceptance
of the candidate by God, or the bishop' (Wordsworth).
Brightman emends the text to 'unction[1],' a course
which furnishes an easier meaning. In any case, it
appears from the language that it ought immediately
to precede baptism.

The baptism is not described, as would be
expected from the character of the collection; but
No. 11 is a prayer which follows baptism immediately. Confirmation is referred to in No. 16; but
the prayer itself must belong to the beginning of the
rite, as it is a prayer of consecration of chrism, not
of its administration. Of the latter no account is
given, but there is a reference to the 'printing of
the sign of the life-giving cross,' to the 'gift of the
Holy Spirit,' and to the 'seal'; perhaps in the words
'thy mighty hand' we may see an allusion to the
imposition of the hand, which, as far as we know,
was always used in Egypt, and has survived to
the present day.

The above rite does not seem to have had any
influence on later developements. None of its
prayers are reproduced in the fully-developed rite,
and there are but few points of contact in language.
The consecration of the water has most resemblance
to other forms, but even here the similarity is not
strongly marked.

[1] μετὰ τὴν ἄλειψιν.

Apart from this work we have but little information about the baptismal rites in Egypt in ancient times. The two series of *Canonical Responses* attributed to Timothy of Alexandria[1] throw some light on the changes which were taking place. The catechumenate was still in existence as a working system for adults[2], but infants were baptized on the seventh day after birth[3]. In the latter case the old terms 'to be catechized and baptized' still adhered to the rite, though the former word had now lost its real meaning. St Cyril of Alexandria mentions the sponsors and their duty to say the *Amen* at the unctions before and after baptism[4]. In the fifth century, as we learn from the spurious *Responses* of Timothy, the rite was in a fluid state. Baptism was frequently performed by a presbyter and at any time in the year; but the necessary rearrangements of the rite and the ministers were still under consideration. The question was asked, 'May a deacon prepare the catechumens to renounce[5]?' The reference is to the work of the deacon in directing the catechumen to the proper attitude and in leading the renunciation. An affirmative answer is given, and, in accordance with it, the deacon still performs

---

[1] Timothy was Bishop of Alexandria 381—385 A.D. The first series of *Responses* is genuine; the second cannot be genuine, owing to the mention of Christmas (*Resp.* [xviii.]; Duchesne, *C. W.* p. 259), but it may be attributed to the fifth century (Brightman, *J. Th. St.* I. 248[1]). The latter series I have quoted in brackets. For text see Pitra, *Iuris Eccles. Graec. Hist. et Mon.* I. 630—645.

[2] I. II. VI. [II.].　　　　[3] [IV.].

[4] *In Ioan.* XI. 26 (Migne, *P. G.* LXXIV. 49).　　　[5] [X.].

those duties in the Coptic rite. The subject of the renunciation is further dealt with[1] in an answer which directs that 'if a deacon is present, he shall make the renunciation; but if there are two presbyters, one shall be appointed for the renunciation, the other shall baptize.' The order of the rite also comes in question[2]: 'If a presbyter is left alone, and has to perform baptism, how shall he deal with the order [of the rite]? Shall he perform the renunciation of the catechumens and the unction with oil after the consecration of the water of the laver of regeneration? Or shall he consecrate the Jordan, that is, the water of the font, after the renunciation? Or shall he baptize immediately after the consecration, without leaving the font to go out to the renunciation?' The answer is: 'Let him first perform the renunciation; then let him go into [the baptistery] and perform the consecration of the water, and thus baptize.' Here also the Coptic rite is framed in accordance with this answer. In regard to the baptism itself, a question is asked: 'May a reader or subdeacon present a catechumen for baptism, and call out the names of the catechumens[3]?' The reply is that 'if a deacon is not present, a subdeacon may present; and if a subdeacon also be not found, even a reader presents on account of the necessity.' In the rubrics of the rite, a deacon is mentioned for

[1] [IX.].
[2] [VIII.]. Note the use of the word 'Jordan,' which is a characteristic word in the Egyptian rites.
[3] [XI.].

this office, as it properly appertains to him; the exceptional cases are naturally not provided for.

In these *Canonical Responses* we see the method of treating the various questions arising from the alteration in manner and age of baptism. In every part of the Church the same problem was demanding a solution at this time, namely, how baptism should be performed in the case of infants throughout the year, and how the rite, and, in particular, the ceremonies of the catechumenate, should be suited to altered circumstances. We have just considered the process: let us turn to the finished result[1], taking first the rite and then the liturgical framework.

The baptismal service opens with a prayer over the mother of the infant. This takes place on the fortieth or eightieth day after birth, according as the child is a boy or a girl; on this day the child is brought to church to be baptized, accompanied by the mother. The office of the catechumens follows. This office still bears a trace that it represents a series of *catecheses* in the repetition of the rubric, 'The priest asks the names of the candidates.' In the first *catechesis* the candidates are anointed with oil on various parts of the body; this oil[2] is consecrated in the service and is supposed to possess an exorcizing power. The second *catechesis* consists of

[1] Denzinger, *Rit. Or.* i. pp. 191—235; Evetts, B. T. A., *The Rites of the Coptic Church*, pp. 17—43. In *Rit. Or.* the Ethiopic rite is given along with two Coptic redactions.

[2] It is called the 'oil of catechesis.' For the exorcizing power compare the language of St Cyril of Jerusalem (p. 54) and the *Egyptian Church Order* (p. 40).

various prayers. The last of them is a prayer for the delivery of the catechumen from malign spiritual influences and is accompanied by an imposition of the hand; this must be considered as the representative of the exorcisms of older days. After this catechesis, or as a part of it, stand the renunciation and profession. The formula of renunciation opens with the words, 'I renounce thee, Satan,' to which St Cyril of Alexandria bears witness[1]. The profession of faith is made in the ordinary terms: 'I confess thee, Christ our God, and all thy saving laws, and all thy life-giving religion and thy works which bestow life.' We should expect the creed to be recited here as in other rites. But in this rite the creed is said at a later point, without any relevancy, as a part of the liturgical framework. But at this point occurs a most interesting survival, an old profession of faith, much shorter and simpler than the creeds. It runs as follows: 'I believe in one God, the Father Almighty, and his only-begotten Son Jesus Christ our Lord, and the Holy Spirit, the giver of life; the resurrection of the flesh, and his one, only, catholic, apostolic, holy Church.' To this the Ethiopic adds, 'one baptism for the remission of sins.' This short creed is a very ancient feature, which everywhere else has been superseded by one of the fuller creeds, the Nicene or the Apostles'[2]. A parallel is furnished by the profession in St Cyril of

[1] *In Ps.* XLV. 11 (*P.G.* LXIX. 1044).

[2] Some, however, think that this form is merely an abbreviation of a longer creed; see Hahn, *Bibliothek der Symbole*, p. 158.

Jerusalem[1]; the interrogations at the water in the early Roman and Milanese rites are similar. In early days the profession of faith was made in formularies such as these; from them the creeds were formed, with additions for dogmatic and controversial purposes; later the fuller creed displaced the shorter form very generally, but in the Egyptian rite the latter still remains.

An unction now takes place; the formula which accompanies it begins: 'I anoint thee,' that is, the active voice is used, as in the Western rites[2]. The ceremonies of the preparation conclude with an imposition of the hand and an exorcism.

At this point the baptistery is entered, and baptism begins. The water is consecrated, and the candidate baptized. The baptismal formula is Egyptian, and agrees with Western, not Eastern, use. In the Ethiopic rite it is: 'I baptize thee in the name of the Father, and of the Son, and of the Holy Spirit the Paraclete. Amen.' In the other Egyptian rites this is amplified, by the addition of an *Amen* after the name of the Father and the Son; or, still further, by making a triple formula, thus: 'I baptize thee, N., in the name of the Father, Amen. I baptize thee, N., in the name of the Son, Amen. I baptize thee, N., in the name of the Holy

---

[1] See p. 55.

[2] This formula is borrowed from the Syrian rite, but the words 'N is signed' are altered into the active voice, which alone is found in Egypt in such forms. This unction is the unction before baptism, to be distinguished from the unction of the catechumenate at the beginning of the rite.

Spirit, Amen'; each phrase is accompanied by an immersion. The Ethiopic is the earliest form; it is already attested in the fourth century by Timothy of Alexandria, who orders that in a case where it is doubtful whether a child has already been baptized, he shall be baptized with the formula, 'If thou hast not been baptized, I baptize thee in the name of the Father, and of the Son, and of the Holy Ghost[1].' After baptism the water is de-consecrated by a prayer that it may be changed into its former nature.

Confirmation is performed by unction of various parts of the body with chrism, beginning with the brow. It is to this unction that the gift of the Holy Spirit is ascribed in the prayer which precedes this rite[2]. The unctions are accompanied by a number of formulas such as, 'The unction of the grace of the Holy Spirit,' 'The unction of the earnest of the kingdom of heaven,' etc.; the last is, 'I anoint thee with holy oil,' in which we have again the first person active, characteristic of the Egyptian rite. An imposition of the hand follows, by way of blessing, as appears from the accompanying formula, 'Mayest thou be blessed with the blessing of heaven and the blessing of the angels : may the Lord Jesus Christ bless thee in his name.' In the Ethiopic there is, in addition to this blessing, an imposition of the

---

[1] *Resp.* xxxviii.

[2] The oil of the unction before baptism and the chrism of confirmation are both consecrated by the patriarch on Maundy Thursday; therefore the prayers at this point are not consecratory. See *Rit. Or.* i. p. 194, note 1; p. 230, note 2.

hand before the unction, which appears to be a confirmation; the action of laying on of the hand is accompanied by a prayer, 'We thank thee, Lord, that thou hast made thy servants worthy of the second birth and the stainless robe, Amen. Send also upon them the riches of thy mercy, and the Holy Spirit, which thou didst send upon thy Apostles; say to them, Receive the Holy Spirit, the Comforter; and in the same way give him to thy servants and handmaids.' In this rite the prayer over the chrism does not speak as definitely as in the other Egyptian rites of the gift of the Holy Spirit as mediated by the unction with chrism. In the Coptic rite, after the imposition of the hand, the priest breathes in the face of the neophyte, saying, 'Receive the Holy Spirit, and be a pure vessel'; this action is, of course, imitated from our Lord's action[1], but it leaves it a little uncertain what the 'matter' of confirmation is supposed to be in Egyptian rites, whether unction, imposition of the hand, or insufflation. As, however, the last action is only present in one of the printed versions, it must be considered as an illustrative ceremony, rather than of the essence of the rite[2].

At the end of the rite, the neophytes are clothed in white, girded, and crowned. They receive communion and finally a draught of milk and honey. This last ceremony survives completely only in the

[1] John xx. 22.
[2] It is found in *Rit. Or.* i. p. 209, but not in the other version on p. 220 nor in the Ethiopic, p. 231, nor in Evetts' edition.

Ethiopic rite[1]. On the eighth day the infants are brought to church and the girdles are removed; an office for this purpose is furnished[2].

A short order of baptism is found in Denzinger[3] and may be noted here. Though it is stated that it is not in use, nevertheless it is interesting as shewing the ideas current about the essentials of the rite. The composer, in a preface, states that certain distinguished ecclesiastics had desired to shorten the office, on account of its inordinate length, and the slight Scriptural or other authority which much of the rite possessed; he, accordingly, proceeds to frame a rite on Scriptural grounds. The following is the outline of the rite: Renunciation, Profession (based on the Nicene creed), the Lessons (from the longer rite), Consecration of the water, Baptism, Confirmation *by imposition of the hand alone*. The rite is of no liturgical importance, but the eagerness to retain nothing that is not justified by Scripture and the rejection of ceremonial adjuncts[4] recall the liturgical work of the Reformation period.

The Egyptian rite, as we have described it, has a definitely marked character. It is neither Eastern nor Western, but has points of agreement with both. In its use of the active voice in formulas, its retention of the imposition of the hand at confirmation, its employment of a draught of milk and honey after the baptismal communion, it resembles the West, and particularly Rome. This may be attributed to

[1] In Egypt honey only was given; Vansleb in *Rit. Or.* I. p. 37. But one manuscript (quoted *ib.* p. 221, note) refers to milk only.

[2] *Rit. Or.* I. p. 213.   [3] *ib.* p. 233.

[4] *E.g.* the last rubric is, 'Then the priest shall clothe them in their own garments'; thus the use of white garments is discarded.

the intercourse and connexion between Rome and Alexandria in early days. But there the resemblance stops. The prayers are quite different from Roman prayers; and in the liturgical framework and redaction of the rite the Egyptian service is entirely Eastern. After the troubles which arose out of the Council of Chalcedon and the Monophysite schism, Egypt was divided into two sections, the orthodox or Melchites, who looked to Constantinople, and the Monophysites, who looked, not to Constantinople, least of all to Rome, but to their brethren in Syria and the East. It remains to consider this latter stage, and to discuss the liturgical framework of the rite and the sources of the various parts.

The liturgical framework of the Coptic rites is derived from the Liturgy, like that of Syria. But this process is here carried out less skilfully; an enormous amount of material is laid upon the baptismal rite, without regard to space, time, or relevancy, and to this material the enclosed rite is adapted and assimilated.

Let us begin with the consecration of the water. For this purpose there are three formularies; all three appear in the Ethiopic rite, and the first and third only in the various recensions of the Coptic rite[1]. Each of the three forms is a complete form of consecration and their multiplication is an

[1] These are the references for the three forms: (1) *Rit. Or.* p. 204, Deus coelorum and Aquarum auctor=p. 218=p. 226=Evetts, p. 31. (2) *Rit. Or.* p. 227 (Ethiopic rite), Domine, O Domine pater bone. (3) *ib.* p. 205, Ad te Domine oculos nostros=p. 219 =p. 228=Evetts, p. 33.

instance of the clumsiness of the redaction. The first form appears to be the genuine Egyptian consecration of the water. The second, which occurs only in the Ethiopic, is a translation of the Syrian form. The third is probably also Syrian, but is not arranged quite as in the Syrian rite[1]. The third form (in the Ethiopic the second) is furnished with a *Sursum corda*, and thus the appearance of an *Anaphora* is given to the consecration of the water.

From the consecration of the water let us turn to the general structure of the rite, which is modelled on the Egyptian Liturgy, just as the Syrian baptismal rite was modelled on the Syrian Liturgy.

The ceremonies of the catechumenate are placed at the beginning. After the entry into the baptistery the lessons are read; they are four in number as in the Liturgy—Catholic Epistle, Pauline Epistle, Acts of the Apostles, Gospel. Then eight long prayers are said; these appear[2] to be the same as are said in the Great Thanksgiving in the *Anaphora*[3] of the Egyptian Liturgy and constitute the Intercession of the Liturgy. According to the compiler's procedure they ought to appear in that part of the

---

[1] *D.A.C.L.* II. col. 696. Observe that oil is mixed with the water before consecration, and that the second, or purely Syrian form, ignores this, while the first and third speak of a blessing of 'oil and water.'

[2] They are not given in full in the editions of the rite, which contain only the titles.

[3] The *Anaphora* of an Eastern liturgy includes the Great Thanksgiving (='Preface'), the *Sanctus*, the Consecration, and an Intercession. In the Egyptian *Anaphora* an Intercession is placed within the Great Thanksgiving before the *Sanctus*.

baptismal rite which corresponds to the *Anaphora,*
that is, the consecration of the water. But of the
three forms of consecration of the water provided
in the Egyptian baptismal rite, the first has not the
structure of an *Anaphora,* and the other two are
Syrian, and do not admit of an Intercession within
the Great Thanksgiving of the *Anaphora.* It is
quite true that there is not the slightest reason
why they should appear anywhere in a baptismal
rite, but as they occur in the Liturgy, the compiler
felt bound to work them in without regard to their
irrelevancy. The prayer that follows, 'over the
Jordan or baptistery,' is the 'prayer of the veil,'
and is succeeded by the three prayers which occupy
this position in the Liturgy, namely, the prayers 'for
peace, for the fathers, and for the congregation.'
After these prayers the creed is said. The consecration of the water follows, concluding with the
Lord's Prayer, and a 'Commixture' of chrism and
water takes place. All is now ready and baptism is
performed. After baptism the water is de-consecrated
and the font washed out with fresh water; this is
parallel to the ablutions which take place at the
end of the Liturgy.

From the above account it will be seen that we
have a baptismal rite interpolated with materials
from an Egyptian Liturgy. The place of the *Anaphora* is supplied by forms for consecration of the
water borrowed from Syrian baptismal rites, these
latter being themselves in the form of an *Anaphora.*
The analysis given below shews that two of the

prayers in the above rite were taken from the Byzantine baptismal rite. There were, therefore, three stages in the developement. First, there was a genuine Egyptian rite. Secondly, it was remodelled in imitation of the later Syrian rites. Thirdly, one or two prayers were taken over from the Greek rite employed by the Melchites.

The following analysis of the formularies of the rite will enable the reader to check the above statements. Except when otherwise stated, the rite analysed is the first rite in Denzinger's *Ritus Orientalium*[1].

Pages 197—199 do not present obvious affinities.

200. Ungo te = D. 273, except that the Egyptian alters the passive to the active; in Evetts' version the passive is used and the second person for the first.

200. Ens, Dominator Domine = C. 394, ὁ ὤν, and 395 ἐξέλασον.

201. Voca = C. 396, but the text of this prayer in the *Euchologion* is nearer the Egyptian.

201. The four lessons, Pauline Epistle, *Catholicon*, Acts of the Apostles, and Gospel = B. 152—155.

201. The prayers at this point are from the Liturgy.

> Oratio gratiarum actionis = B. 147.
> Censing = B. 150.
> Thuribulus aureus est uirgo = B. 150.
> Domine scientiae = B. 153.
> Domine Deus noster, qui per sanctos Apostolos tuos = B. 154.
> Absolutio ad Patrem = B. 183.
> Oratio Actuum Apostolorum = B. 154.
> Euangelii oratio = B. 155.

---

[1] The following symbols are used: R. = Renaudot's *Liturgiarum Orientalium Collectio*, vol. I.; D. = Denzinger's *Ritus Orientalium*; C. = the *Rituale Armenorum*; B. = Brightman's *Liturgies Eastern and Western*.

202. Longanimis, multae misericordiae = B. 157.

202. Eight prayers = B. 166—171.

202. Oratio super Iordanem = The Prayer of the Veil, B. 158.

203. Clemens, misericors = D. 271, 312 and C. 398; in position it corresponds to the last.

203. Three prayers and creed = B. 160—161.

205. Orate pro perfecta pace = B. 227.

205. Accedite pro more = R. 12.

205. Misericordiam pacis, baptisma laudis = ἔλεος εἰρήνης, θυσία αἰνέσεως, B. 164.

205. Charitas Dei = B. 49 ; it is the Syrian form.

[227. Domine, O Domine, pater bone *to* 228 in saecula saeculorum = D. 275, 276, C. 400, 401. The Egyptian form agrees with the Greek in omitting the Invocation of the Holy Spirit (D. 276, Miserere), but agrees with the Syrian against the Greek in retaining the section of the praise of the works of God (D. 275 Domine Deus = D. 227 Domine, O Domine), which the Greek replaces by another form borrowed from the Epiphany blessing of the waters. The *Sanctus* concludes this prayer[1].]

205. Ad te, Domine *to* 206 puritate plena, is another form on the Syrian model[2], but arranged in an order different from that of the Syrian rite. The *Sanctus*[3] is Syrian in form = B. 86.

206. The Consignation = B. 180.

207. Pater noster; borrowed from the Liturgy, B. 182.

207. Ita Domine. Tu Domine inclinasti = R. 35.

207. Oratio absolutionis ad Filium = B. 148.

207. Unus Pater sanctus = B. 184.

207. Pouring in of chrism = Commixture, B. 184.

208. Ps. 150 = B. 185.

---

[1] This form is only found in the Ethiopic rite, and is the second of the three sets of consecration prayers.

[2] *D.A.C.L.* 'Bénédict. de l'eau,' col. 696—698.

[3] In the Ethiopic it is placed earlier.

208. Ego te baptizo = D. 277; the formula is assimilated to the Syrian by the insertions of *Amens* in it, according to this redaction.

211. Benedictus = The Dismissal, B. 187.

The above examination of the sources displays the method adopted in the remodelling of the Egyptian baptismal rite. The work was probably done after the Syrian remodelling and on the same plan. The composer had the Syrian rite in front of him, and took from it forms of consecration of water and inserted them in the Egyptian rite. He has also adopted the prayers of an Egyptian Liturgy, and inserted them piecemeal at various points in the baptismal rite. Both the Egyptian rite of baptism and the Egyptian Liturgy received Syrian touches in the process. By subtracting the prayers which are paralleled in the Liturgy and Syrian rite, we obtain a residuum which represents the original Coptic rite and which has a marked local character in its language; particularly noticeable is the repeated epithet of God, 'lover of men.' The original Egyptian rite is readily obtained by removing the liturgical framework and cutting out the Syrian and Greek forms (p. 200, *Ungo te* and *Ens, Dominator*; p. 201, *Voca*; and p. 203, *Clemens, misericors*; also the Syrian consecrations of the water). The resultant rite is the original Egyptian form. Cf. the table on pp. 236-8.

CHAPTER VII

THE WESTERN RITES

Sec. 1. *Africa*

The complete ruin which befel African Christianity has involved the destruction of all African liturgical books. We are, therefore, reduced to the quotations in the African Fathers for information on the subject of the rites of that Church. Fortunately the writings of the African Christians are both numerous and full, so that a fairly complete account of baptism can be pieced together. A portion of the evidence has been dealt with in the first chapter on account of its early date. It remains now to deal with the later writers and authorities, among whom St Augustine is pre-eminent in bulk and value.

The entry into the catechumenate was marked by a signing with the sign of the cross, accompanied by a 'prayer of imposition of the hand'; this was followed by the 'sacrament' of the giving of salt[1]. The catechumen was now called a 'Christian'; although he was not baptized, he had passed out of the heathen

---

[1] Aug., *Conf.* I. 11. 17; *de Bapt. c. Donat.* IV. 21. 28; *de Pecc. Mer. et Remiss.* II. 26. 42. The word 'sacrament' is here used for a symbolical act, not in its later, strictly technical, sense.

world[1].   The above rites were performed at any time in the year and were administered to children without any idea of immediate baptism[2].

When the catechumen wished to be baptized, he gave in his name[3] and entered on a period of special preparation, marked by prayers, exorcisms[4], and, above all, by instructions, of which we have examples among the works of St Augustine[5].   During this period the candidates were called *competentes*[6]; they had previously been called *audientes*[7].   In Africa, as at Rome and in Gaul, the special examinations of the *competentes* were called ' scrutinies[8].'

On the Saturday before Mid-Lent Sunday (as we term it) the creed was delivered to the catechumens; this delivery was preceded by the first renunciation[9]. On the following Saturday the creed was repeated and the Lord's Prayer delivered.   On the succeeding Saturday the Lord's Prayer was repeated by the candidates.   The lapse of another week brought Easter Eve and a final repetition of the creed[10].   It appears,

---

[1] *In Ioan. Evang. Tract.* XLIV. 2.

[2] Aug., *Conf. l.c.* Concil. Hippon. can. 3 (Mansi, *Concil. ampl. coll.* III. col. 850, 919).   [3] Aug., *Serm.* CCXXIX.

[4] id. *de Fide et Opp.* VI. 9.

[5] Cf. *Serm.* LVI.—LIX. and CCXII.—CCXVI. and the *de Catechizandis Rudibus.*

[6] *de Fide et Opp.* VI. 9.   [7] *Serm.* CXXXII.

[8] *de Fide et Opp.* VI. 9, Catechizantur, exorcizantur, scrutantur.

[9] Ferrand., *Ep.* XI. (*ad Fulgent.*), 2 (Migne, *P.L.* LXV. 378). Aug., *Ep.* CXCIV. 43; *Serm.* CCXV. 1. Cf. the spurious *Serm. de Symbolo*, 2 (*P.L.* XL. 637).

[10] *Serm.* LVIII. 1, 13, LIX. 1, CCXIII. 1, 8.   Cf. the sermon *de Symbolo* quoted in the last note and the two following sermons, all three of unknown authorship.

therefore, that Saturday was, in St Augustine's time, the fixed day for scrutinies in Africa; this fact is of importance in comparing rites.

Easter was, as we should expect, the normal time for baptisms[1]. Before the Easter Vigil the creed was repeated, and the baptisms took place after the Vigil service[2].

Before baptism a second and final renunciation was probably made, as in the earlier period[3], and the three questions on the faith were still united to the three immersions in the water[4]. In some parts of Africa the baptismal formula ended with the words 'unto remission of sins'; the addition is found in a Gallican rite[5] and a similar phrase was added in Spain.

The chrism for use at confirmation was consecrated at the altar by the bishop; presbyters were frequently forbidden to usurp this function[6]. After the unction of the candidate came the imposition of the hand[7]. A draught of milk and honey was

---

[1] Ferrand., *ut supra*. Aug., *Serm.* ccx. 2. For baptism at the Epiphany in Africa, cf. Victor Vitensis, *Hist. Persec. Vandal.* II. 17 (Migne, *P.L.* LVIII. 216).

[2] Aug., *Serm.* LVIII. 13.

[3] Optat. Milev., *de Schism. Donat.* v. 7.

[4] Concil. Carthag., can. 1, A.D. 348 (Mansi, III. 145, 153).

[5] *Codex Canonum Ecclesiae Africanae*, cx. Cf. *Missale Gothicum*, xxxv. (Migne, *P.L.* LXXII. 275).

[6] Aug., *de Bapt. c. Donat.* v. 28. Concil. Carthag. II. can. 3; Concil. Carthag. III. can. 36; Concil. Hippon. can. 34 (Mansi, III. 869, 885, 923). Ioannes Diaconus, *Ep. ad Senarium*, 8. Cypr., *Ep.* LXX. 2.

[7] Optat. Milev., *op. cit.* IV. 7. Aug., *Serm.* cccxxiv.

blessed at the altar and given to the neophyte after confirmation and communion[1].

The ceremony of washing the feet of the newly baptized—a widely spread custom in all Latin countries but Rome—had also some currency in Africa, though its position was less secure than in Gaul and North Italy. St Augustine was consulted about the custom by a certain Januarius, and replied : 'Concerning the washing of the feet, since the Lord commanded it as a type of that humility which he came to teach, as he himself afterwards explained, the question was raised at what time so great a truth could best be taught by example, and that time [viz. baptism] occurred as one to which the injunction might be assigned with greater solemnity. But lest it might be thought to belong to the sacrament of baptism, many were unwilling to adopt it as a custom ; some did not hesitate even to abandon the practice ; some again to honour it by a more sacred season and yet distinguish it from the sacrament of baptism, chose the third day of the octave [of Easter]...or even the octave day itself for the purpose[2].'

It appears from this that the custom of washing the feet of the newly baptized was practised in Africa with considerable varieties of usage. The fear expressed by St Augustine that the ceremony might come to be held essential to baptism and itself sacramental, is justified by the teaching of St Ambrose,

---

[1] Concil. Carthag. III. can. 24 = *Cod. Can. Eccl. Afric.* XXXVII. (Mansi, III. 884).   [2] Aug., *Ep.* LV. (*ad Ianuar.*), 33.

that St Peter's hereditary sins were removed by the washing of his feet[1]. Such excesses naturally brought the practice into suspicion.

The later African rite described above shews some signs of advance on the earlier type represented by Tertullian and Cyprian. The preparation for baptism is much more definite; the Saturday scrutinies with their deliveries and repetitions of the creed and Lord's Prayer obviously belong to a later age and more fixed organization. One or two new ceremonies appear—the giving of salt at the beginning of the catechumenate and the washing of the feet after baptism. But the whole is, as far as we can judge, similar to the earlier form but a little more organized.

The evidence for the African rite shews its affinities with various other rites. The washing of the feet is found all over the West except at Rome; the draught of milk and honey is found in Egypt, and at Rome, but nowhere else in the West. The addition to the baptismal formula has parallels in Gaul and Spain. In the absence of liturgical books it is dangerous to go further, and it is possible that the facts we possess represent the actual situation, and that the African rite was not of one definite type, Roman, Spanish, or Gallican, but agreed now with one, now with another. Such a conclusion would be entirely in harmony with the complicated interrelations which other Western rites display.

[1] *de Myst.* VI. 32; cf. *de Sacr.* III. i. 4—7.

Sec. 2. *Rome*

There is some difficulty in determining the order to be adopted in dealing with the other Western rites. For some reasons it would seem better to conclude with the Roman rite, as it finally ousted all other rites (except the Milanese) and, in great part, rests on later evidence. On the other hand, the rites of the Roman Church, occupying, as they did, an ever higher and higher position in the eyes of men, profoundly affected all developements in other Western rites and form a canvas on which the changes which took place at Milan, in Spain, Gaul, or Ireland, may be depicted. For the latter reason the Roman rite is dealt with in this place.

Our earliest evidence from Rome is the *First Apology* of Justin Martyr, which has already[1] been considered; as it possesses no local colour, it may be ignored at this point and we will begin with John the Deacon[2] and the earliest forms in the *Sacramentaries*[3], and then trace the later developements.

Senarius, a distinguished official of the time of Theodoric, had asked a question about the scrutinies and their meaning and purpose ; in answer John the

---

[1] pp. 6—8.

[2] Mabillon, *Museum Italicum*, tom. I. pt II. p. 69 (Migne, *P.L.* LIX. col. 402).

[3] For the *Sacramentaries* see Duchesne, *C.W.* pp. 120—144. Of the three types the *Leonian* contains little or nothing to our purpose; the *Gelasian* and *Gregorian* are later, and display an admixture of other elements. A Sacramentary is a book containing the officiant's prayers at Mass, Baptism, Ordination, etc. The names ' Leonian,' ' Gelasian,' ' Gregorian,' are purely conventional, and the books cannot be ascribed to any of these Popes.

Deacon gives an account of the scrutinies in an early
form. This account, combined with certain other
references, furnishes the earliest description of the
Roman discipline of the catechumenate.

Those of the catechumens who proposed to be
baptized at Easter gave in their names in the early
part of Lent[1]. They were then called *electi* or
'selected candidates.' Their reception as 'elect' was
performed as follows according to the *Gelasian
Sacramentary*[2]. The priest breathes in the face of
the candidate, signs his brow, and lays his hand on
his head with an accompanying address. After a
prayer, the candidate receives salt, and, after signing
himself, is blessed. John the Deacon is a little
fuller; he speaks of an exsufflation, exorcism, and
giving of salt, and refers to a renunciation and
'tradition of the creed.' The reference to a renunciation at this early stage is interesting and agrees
with the African rite[3]. During Lent the 'elect' were
present daily at the prayers of the Church, and
received frequent impositions of the hand.

The candidates had now learnt the text of the
creed; explanation of it and examination in it was
the function of the scrutinies which followed. These
were three in number and took place on the third,
fourth, and fifth Sundays in Lent; the masses for the
scrutinies are preserved in the *Gelasian Sacramentary*[4]. The third scrutiny was followed by a special

---

[1] Siricius, *Ep. ad Himer. Tarr.* 2 (*P.L.* XIII. 1134).
[2] *Sacramentarium Gelasianum*, ed. Wilson, I. lxxi.
[3] Cf. also Leo, *Serm.* XL. 2; *Can. Hipp.* 61.
[4] I. xxvi. xxvii. xxviii.

rite : the ears and nose were touched with oil[1] and the breast was anointed. The position of this last rite is not quite clear; the *Canones ad Gallos*[2] order an unction at the third scrutiny, and John the Deacon appears to connect the above rite with the scrutinies rather than with baptism ; but according to the later rite Easter Eve would seem the right time for the anointing of the ears and nose (called the *Effeta*) and of the breast. At some later time in Lent the creed was repeated publicly before the congregation[3].

The above preparation for baptism underwent a considerable amount of modification between the fifth and eighth centuries, partly by way of elaboration and amplification, but also by way of misunderstanding, as the disuse of adult baptism took away the significance of the preparation.

The first step was the introduction of the ceremonies of the Exposition of the four Gospels and the ' tradition ' of the Lord's Prayer. It is probable that these, together with the ' tradition ' of the creed, were attached to the three scrutinies—the Exposition of the Gospels to the third Sunday, the ' tradition ' of the creed to the fourth, and the ' tradition ' of the Lord's Prayer to the fifth Sunday in Lent. At a later date the Exposition and the two ' traditions ' came together at the third scrutiny. The Exposition of the four Gospels had by this time assumed the

---

[1] John the Deacon is not quite clear about the meaning of this ceremony.

[2] Can. 8 in Mansi, *Concil. ampl. coll.* III. 1137.

[3] Cf. Rufin., *Comm. in symb. Apost.* 3. Aug., *Conf.* VIII. 2. 5.

name of the 'opening of the ears[1],' a title which originally belonged to the *Effeta*[2]; at the same period the *Effeta* changed its character and was performed with saliva, not with oil. The creed used was from Byzantine times the 'Nicene' creed, not the 'Apostles'' creed, and it was said in Greek and Latin.

The history of the *Effeta* and the *aurium apertio* is by no means clear. At the beginning of the fifth century we find both terms applied in North Italy to a rite performed on Easter Eve, as is shewn by the citations in the note on the above paragraph. In the later form of the Roman rite in the *Gelasian Sacramentary* (to be considered in the next paragraph), the term *aurium apertio* is annexed to the Exposition of the four Gospels, and the *Effeta* still attaches to the rite of touching the ears and nose on Easter Eve. Between these stands John the Deacon; does the 'touching of the ears and nose with oil,' which he describes, belong to the third scrutiny, as in the *Canones ad Gallos*, or to Easter Eve, as in St Ambrose? If the former alternative is right, then the Roman *Effeta* or *apertio aurium* originally belonged to the third scrutiny, and the 'traditions' were placed after it, so that it served as a preparation for them; later, the *Effeta* was removed to Easter Eve as in North Italy, and the name *apertio aurium* remained alone at the third scrutiny[3]. On the

---

[1] *apertio aurium.*

[2] Ambros., *de Myst.* I. 3; *de Sacr.* I. i. 2; Petrus Chrysologus, *Serm.* LII; Maxim. Turin., *Tract.* I. *de Bapt.* For the placing of the 'traditions' on successive Sundays compare the *Capitula Euangeliorum Neapolitana* (*Anecdota Maredsolana*, tom. 1, *Liber Comicus*, append. iv. p. 432); also the African custom of 'traditions' on successive Saturdays.

[3] This would be analogous to the Spanish rite; Ildephonsus, *de Cognit. Bapt.* 29; *Liber Ordinum* (*Mon. Eccl. Lit* vol. v.), col. 73,

second alternative the *Effeta* or *aurium apertio* took place originally at Rome, as in North Italy, on Easter Eve, but, for some unexplained reason, the Exposition of the Gospels robbed the *Effeta* of the name *aurium apertio* and henceforth appropriated it to itself, until the name and the ceremony of the Exposition fell into disuse and became extinct.

In the *Ordo Romanus Septimus*[1] a different arrangement of the preparation for baptism is found. The scrutinies are now seven in number, and they no longer take place on Sundays, but on weekdays. Of these seven the third is the greatest. With this arrangement of scrutinies, the Sunday masses *pro scrutinio* cease to have a meaning and accordingly they are replaced in the *Gregorian Sacramentary* by proper masses for the Sundays. In the *Gelasian Sacramentary* the older system of three scrutinies and the newer of seven are mixed together incongruously; the three Sunday masses *pro scrutinio* still remain[2], but later on[3] the services for weekdays are inserted according to the system of the *Ordo Romanus Septimus*. The newer system, while more elaborate than the older, is also a degeneration; the

---

where the *Effeta* is performed on Palm Sunday, and would be in exact accord with Amalarius, *de Eccl. Off.* i. viii, and with certain other authorities; see *D.A.C.L.* 'Apertio aurium,' col. 2532.

[1] Mabillon, *Museum Italicum*, tom. ii. pp. 77—84. The *Ordines Romani* are a series of descriptions of Roman rites, to assist those who had to perform them, and, particularly, those who, in distant countries, wished to follow Roman usage. They represent the mediaeval *Ordinale* and *Consuetudinarium*, and are analogous to rubrics, but have a wider purpose.

[2] i. xxvi., xxvii., xxviii.

[3] *ib.* xxix.—xxxvi.

purposes of the various parts are no longer understood. Whereas originally at Rome a distinction
was made between the wider class of catechumens,
and the smaller class of 'elect,' who were the catechumens accepted for baptism at the following
Easter, the *Gelasian Sacramentary* uses the title
*Orationes super electos, Ad catechumenum facien-
dum*[1], thus confusing the two classes. Moreover,
the scrutinies are no longer examinations and instructions in a creed which had been already learnt ;
the 'tradition' of the creed does not come till the
third scrutiny. Why these changes were made, and
where they originated—at Rome or in Gaul—is still
obscure.

The following is the description of the system of
seven scrutinies according to the *Ordo* and the
Gelasian Sacramentary. The first scrutiny takes
place in the third week in Lent[2]. At the third hour
the office *ad catechumenum faciendum* is performed.
The names of the candidates and of their sponsors
are taken down by an acolyte, and they are ranged
in rows, males on the right, females on the left. A
presbyter signs their brows, and, laying his hand on
them, recites certain prayers ; then he exorcizes salt
and puts a fragment in the mouth of each. The
office concluded with a benediction[3].

The candidates are now sent out of church and

---

[1] *Sacr. Gelas.* I. xxx.
[2] Monday, Tuesday, or Wednesday according to various versions. *ib.* I. xxix. ; *Ordo Rom. VII.* 1.
[3] *Sacr. Gelas.* I. xxx.—xxxii. ; *Ordo Rom. VII.* 1.

mass begins; the mass appointed to be said in the
Ordo is that which in the *Gelasian*[1] *Sacramentary* is
assigned to the third Sunday in Lent *pro scrutinio*,
but it is here said on a weekday.   After the collect
the candidates are recalled for the first scrutiny;
this consists of exorcisms, of which there are three
sets, belonging originally to the three scrutinies of
earlier times, but now combined into one.   The
exorcism is all that remains of the scrutiny; the
examination has naturally vanished, as all the candidates are infants in the arms of their sponsors.
The scrutiny proceeds as follows : The candidates
are arranged in rows as before ; the deacon proclaims,
'Pray, ye elect, kneel' and, after a space for private
prayer, he says, 'Rise, finish your prayer together
and say, Amen.'   After the 'Amen,' the deacon
again makes a proclamation 'Sign them, approach
for a blessing' ; thereupon the godfathers and god-
mothers sign them.   Then an acolyte[2] signs the male
candidates, and, laying his hand on their heads,
recites a prayer *Deus Abraham* and an exorcism
Ergo maledicte.   The female candidates are exorcized
in the same way, except that the prayer in their
case is *Deus caeli*, in place of *Deus Abraham* in the
case of the males.   The first exorcism is succeeded by
a second, performed with the same proclamations
and ceremonial ; the acolyte recites over the men
the exorcism *Audi maledicte*, over the females the
prayer *Deus Abraham...qui tribus* and the exorcism
Ergo maledicte as above.   Then a third acolyte

---

[1] I. xxvi.   [2] Originally an exorcist; Duchesne, *C.W.* p. 299, n. 1.

performs a third exorcism; this time two exorcisms, *Exorcizo te* and *Ergo maledicte*, are said over the males, and two also, *Exorcizo te* and *Ergo maledicte*, over the females. The exorcism *Ergo maledicte* is the same on each of the five occasions that it is used; the other forms of prayer and exorcism vary in each case. Finally a priest recites a prayer of blessing over the candidates, accompanying it with a signing and an imposition of the hand. The mass proceeds to the gradual, after which the candidates are dismissed, the deacon proclaiming, 'Catechumens, retire; if any be a catechumen, let him retire; catechumens, go forth[1].'

On the Saturday in the same week the second scrutiny was held; the days on which the next four took place are to some extent left to the discretion of the presbyter who conducts them, but the third fell in the fourth week, the fourth and fifth in the fifth week, and the sixth in the week before Easter; according to the *Ordo* the seventh was that at the third hour on Easter Eve, but according to the Gellona[2] manuscript the seventh scrutiny was on Wednesday in Holy Week, and the Easter Eve service belonged to baptism. The sacred number of seven is ascribed to a correspondence with the seven-fold gifts of the Spirit.

The first six scrutinies were all performed in the manner described above. On the third scrutiny, which was of special importance, after the exorcisms

---

[1] *Sacr. Gelas.* I. xxxiii.; *Ordo Rom. VII.* 2.
[2] See *D.A.C.L.* s.v. 'Catéchuménat,' col. 2609.

the Exposition of the Gospels began. Four deacons came from the sacristy, bearing the four Gospels and preceded by two candles and incense. The Gospel-books were placed on the four corners of the altar and the Exposition began. The priest gave an address on the Gospels, then the beginnings of the four Gospels were read. The order of the Evangelists is that of the Vulgate, Matthew, Mark, Luke, John, from which fact it is clear that the ceremony dates from a period when the Vulgate was the text generally in use; each reading was prefaced by the deacon's salutation, 'Stand in silence, listen attentively,' and a short address on each Gospel followed the reading. The five addresses, which were quite short and formal, are preserved in the *Gelasian Sacramentary.*

The 'Exposition of the Gospels at the Opening of the Ears to the Elect'—such is the title of the ceremony—is succeeded by the 'tradition' of the creed, which is headed, 'Here beginneth the Preface of the Creed to the Elect.' The priest gives a short address on the creed; then an acolyte brings a male child, and the priest asks, 'In what language do they confess our Lord Jesus Christ?' On receiving the answer, 'In Greek,' he bids the acolyte recite the creed; the acolyte accordingly recites the 'Nicene' creed in Greek. This is done again with a female child, then the whole is repeated with the 'Nicene' creed in Latin, and the priest gives a closing address on the creed.

This ceremony of the tradition of the creed has

come down to us in a formal and stereotyped condition ; the recital of the creed first in Greek then in Latin, over two male and two female infants, is an almost meaningless survival. The custom goes back to days when Rome was a bilingual city, that is, before the final extinction of the Byzantine power. But why the 'Nicene' creed[1]? It is certain that earlier at Rome the 'Apostles'' creed was used, as also in later times ; nor did the Roman missionaries who spread the Roman rite over northern Europe ever take with them any other baptismal creed than the 'Apostles'.' A possible explanation is that the use of the Greek 'Nicene' creed in Rome drew along with it the Latin 'Nicene' creed ; where Latin only was used, the 'Apostles'' creed re-asserted itself.

The next ceremony is headed, 'Also the Preface of the Lord's Prayer.' The deacon's bidding is heard as before, 'Stand in silence, hear attentively,' and the priest begins an address on the Lord's Prayer in the course of which he expounds it clause by clause. At the end the deacon again makes his proclamation. The catechumens are then dismissed and mass proceeds[2]. The fourth, fifth, and sixth

---

[1] 'Nicene' creed here means the Constantinopolitan creed without the *filioque* sanctioned by the third Council of Toledo (589 A.D.). 'Apostles'' creed is used in this volume to denote the various forms of the old Roman creed current in different parts of the West.

[2] *Sacr. Gelas.* I. xxxiv.—xxxvi. ; *Ord. Rom. VII.* 4—8. The *Gregorian Sacramentary* retains three fragments of the above system, a blessing of salt, the first prayer in the making of a catechumen, and the blessing of the priest that closes each scrutiny, together with a rubric referring to the Exposition of the Gospels.

scrutinies are performed as the first two. On Maundy Thursday the chrism and oil are consecrated at the *missa chrismalis* between the communion of the Pope and of the rest of the people[1].

On Easter Eve the last scrutiny took place after the third hour; as no mass was said on that day, the scrutiny stood by itself. In the *Gregorian Sacramentary* the candidates repeat the creed, and the Pope exorcizes them with the form *Nec te lateat satanas*; it is to be observed that the office is not now assigned to an acolyte or exorcist. The *Effeta* follows; then an unction of the back and breast with oil, and the renunciation in threefold form, 'Dost thou renounce Satan, And all his works, And all his pomps?' the candidate after each phrase answering 'I renounce.' In the *Gelasian Sacramentary*, as also in the *Ordines Romani I.* and *VII.*, the repetition of the creed is placed after the renunciation. The creed used in the first *Ordo* is the 'Apostles',' in the seventh it is the 'Nicene'; in the *Gregorian Sacramentary* it is called *pisteugis*[2], which is indefinite but points to a bi-lingual repetition. The *Effeta* in all these documents, except the *Gregorian Sacramentary* which is silent about it, is performed with saliva; the use of saliva instead of oil is posterior to John the Deacon and is due to an assimilation to our Lord's miracle[3]. Even in the time of Leidrad of Lyons[4] there was

[1] Einsiedeln MS. 326 in Duchesne, *C.W.*, Eng. trans. p. 482. *Sacr. Gelas.* I. xl.

[2] I.e. τὸ πιστεύεις, or the creed in Greek.

[3] Mark vii. 31—37.

[4] Migne, *P.L.* XCIX. 857; circa 800 A.D.

variety of practice; 'some,' he says, 'touch the ears and nose of catechumens with holy oil, others again with saliva; others without saliva and oil; others also touch the mouth with oil after the Lord's example.' Here we have a variety of customs: the first is that of John the Deacon, the second of the later Roman books, the third is that of the *Gregorian Sacramentary*, the *de Sacramentis*, and the *de Mysteriis*. The formula of the *Effeta* is as follows: *Effeta, quod est adaperire, in odorem suauitatis. Tu autem effugare, diabole, appropinquauit enim iudicium Dei.* The creed in the documents, apart from the *Gregorian Sacramentary*, which represents an earlier tradition, is repeated by the priest holding his hand on the candidates' heads; but this is merely an alteration to suit infant baptism. After the repetition of the creed, the candidates are dismissed, to return later for baptism.

Baptism at Rome followed the Easter Vigil, and therefore originally took place in the night; but with the lapse of time the hour of the Vigil was moved further and further back until it joined the last scrutiny[1]. After the lessons of the Vigil service the Pope and the choir went to the font, singing a litany. On arriving at the font the Pope proceeded to consecrate the water. The form of consecration consists of a series of prayers, of a similar character

[1] The Vigil begins at the eighth hour in the *Ordo* of St Amand (Duchesne, *C.W.* p. 469) and the *Gelasian Sacramentary*; at the ninth in the first Roman *Ordo*; at the seventh in the Einsiedeln *Ordo* (*ib.* p. 483); in the seventh Roman *Ordo* it appears to follow the scrutiny.

and arrangement to the Eastern forms. In the older books, the *Ordines* and the *Gelasian Sacramentary*, we have simply a number of prayers; from the *Gregorian Sacramentary* onwards the prayers are thrown into the shape of a Eucharistic prayer, by the addition of the *Sursum corda* and *Vere dignum*. This change must not be confused with the Syrian and Egyptian assimilation of the baptismal rite to the Liturgy; it is of an entirely different character. The consecration of the water, by reason of its importance, was arranged in the most solemn and stately manner of prayer; but the fanciful and elaborate remodellings of the East are foreign to all Western rites[1].

The baptism now began. The candidate was led to the water and thrice immersed; the immersions were accompanied by a threefold question: 'Dost thou believe in God, the Father Almighty?' R. 'I believe.' 'Dost thou believe in Jesus Christ, his only Son, our Lord, who was born and suffered?' R. 'I believe.' 'Dost thou believe in the Holy Ghost, the Holy Church, remission of sins, the resurrection of the flesh?' R. 'I believe[2].' Later these interrogations were placed before the immersions, for the sake of convenience, and the questions were slightly amplified. The formula, as in the West generally and in Egypt, was: 'I baptize thee in the name of the Father, and of the Son, and of the

[1] An analysis of the prayer and its developement will be found at the end of the book.

[2] *Sacr. Gelas.* I. lxxv.

Holy Ghost'; after the interrogations had been placed before baptism, the formula of baptism was divided among the three immersions; we do not know how it was combined with the interrogations in the earlier period. The Pope baptized one or two, but the bulk of the baptizing was left to the inferior clergy. After baptism, a presbyter signed the top of the heads of the neophytes with his thumb dipped in chrism; the prayer is: 'God Almighty, the Father of our Lord Jesus Christ, who hath regenerated thee from water and the Holy Ghost, and hath given unto thee remission of all thy sins, He anoints thee with the chrism of salvation in Christ Jesus our Lord to life eternal.' They are then clothed in white[1] and brought to the Pope, who lays his hand on them, reciting meanwhile the prayer for the sevenfold Spirit[2], and finally signs them saying, 'In the name of the Father and of the Son and of the Holy Ghost, peace to thee,' or, 'The sign of Christ to life eternal[3].'

There are various slight differences in the manner of performing confirmation in the ancient books. The *Gregorian Sacramentary* entitles the prayer for the seven-fold Spirit, 'A prayer for signing infants,' and says nothing of an imposition of the hand. The *Gelasian Sacramentary* attaches to the signing with chrism the words, 'The sign of Christ to life eternal,' omitting the invocation of the Trinity. The first and seventh *Ordo Romanus* say nothing of an imposition of the hand; they state that the Pope

[1] Ioan. Diac., *Ep. ad Senar.* 6.
[2] Familiar to us from its use for Confirmation in the Prayer Book of the English Church.
[3] *Ordo Rom. VII.* 12; *Sacr. Gelas.* I. xlv.

before confirmation gives each of the neophytes a stole, a chasuble, a chrisom (or cloth to cover the head after the unction of confirmation), and ten coins. The Einsiedeln *Ordo* mentions signing and unction; the *Ordo* of St Amand conjoins a touching of the head with the prayer[1]. The oldest authority, John the Deacon, speaks of unction only. From this it is clear that the imposition of the hand was not regarded as very important; the unction was the main thing. But it would be rash to deduce from silence that there was no imposition of the hand; nevertheless, that which is considered unimportant has an insecure position and may easily be omitted.

In the *Ordo* of St Amand the priest, after baptism, signs the head with exorcized oil, not chrism as elsewhere.

While the Pope confirmed, the choir in the church were singing the litany, repeating the invocations, first seven times, then five times, then thrice. At the end the Pope entered, and began the *Gloria in excelsis*, thus commencing the Easter mass. At the end of the Canon he blessed the draught of milk and honey which was given to the newly baptized after their communion. This draught is found in John the Deacon and the *Leonian Sacramentary*, but later it vanished entirely[2].

The modern Roman rites of baptism and confirmation mainly follow the Gelasian rite, that is, the rite which is placed in Lent in the *Gelasian Sacramentary*; but there is a considerable admixture of

---

[1] Duchesne, *C.W.*, pp. 470, 483.

[2] *Sacr. Leon.* (ed. Feltoe), p. 25. Ioan. Diac., *op. cit.* 12...in sacratissimum calicem lac mittatur et mel, et Paschae sabbato cum sacrificiis offeratur...baptizatis ergo hoc sacramenti genus offertur...

other elements, from the rite in the *Gelasian Sacramentary* at Pentecost, from Gallican books, and from other sources. The rites of baptism are in the *Rituale*; separate and different forms are furnished for infants and adults. The rite for infants begins with the entry into the catechumenate, performed with exsufflation and signing of brow and breast; the giving of salt follows. The scrutinies are represented by the third of the Gelasian set of exorcisms. Then the creed and the Lord's Prayer are said. After a final exorcism, the *Effeta* and renunciations are performed, and the children are anointed with oil. The interrogations on the faith are made, and baptism takes place. After baptism the head is anointed with chrism. A white linen cloth is placed on the head with a Gallican formulary[1], and a lighted candle is placed in the child's hand. The order for adults is longer. Various psalms are said first. The rite has a double renunciation, at the beginning and just before baptism. An exsufflation of the unclean spirit and an insufflation of the good Spirit follow; the formulary used with the latter is similar to that used in the *Bobbio Missal* at the same point[2]. A number of signings of various parts of the body are made, and here again Gallican formularies are used[3]. After the giving of salt, the three sets of exorcisms from the *Gelasian Sacramentary* are said, with all the accompanying biddings and signings. After the creed and Lord's Prayer, the final exorcism *Nec te*

---

[1] As in the *Missale Gothicum* and *Bobbio Missal*.
[2] See p. 156. [3] Cf. the *Missale Gothicum*.

lateat satana is recited, and the *Effeta*, second renunciation, and unction with oil are performed. The rest of the rite proceeds as in the case of infants.

The rite of confirmation is given in the *Pontificale*. The prayer for the sevenfold Spirit is said with extended hands. Signings of the brow with chrism follow ; the formula is, ' I sign thee with the sign of the cross, and I confirm thee with the chrism of salvation, in the name of the Father, and of the Son, and of the Holy Ghost. Amen.' A curious ceremony follows ; the bishop strikes the confirmed person lightly on the cheek, saying, 'Peace be with thee.' Possibly this ceremony descends from the *alapa* of Roman manumission[1]; as the liberated slave received a blow in the course of his manumission, so those who receive the freedom of the Gospel and spiritual emancipation similarly receive the *alapa*, or blow on the cheek.

Sec. 3. *Milan*

The Church of St Ambrose is profoundly interesting to all students of ecclesiastical history and antiquities, not only for the great part it has played in the past, but also because it alone[2], in the Latin West, has

---

[1] Cf. *Schol. on Persius*, 5, 75 : quia quotiens manumittebant, eos alapa percussos circumagebant et liberos confirmabant. *Novell. Iust.* 81. praef.: si emancipationis actio...facta cum iniuriis et alapis liberabat eos huiusmodi uinculis. These references are from the new *Thesaurus Linguae Latinae*, s.v. 'alapa.'

[2] The Mozarabic rite, revived by Cardinal Ximenes, survives in so feeble and artificial a form that it cannot be taken as an exception.

succeeded in maintaining its own peculiar rites and service books right down to the present. Spanish, Gallican, British rites—all sank beneath the advancing tide of the Roman rite; at Milan alone a different rite holds its ground. A further point of interest is the exceptionally good and early information which we possess about this rite. St Ambrose's work *de Mysteriis* and the cognate but anonymous *de Sacramentis* (probably composed about the year 400 A.D.) furnish full and detailed descriptions of baptism as it was carried out at that time; the former work is Milanese; the latter emanated from some North Italian town within the sphere of Roman influence. In either case the work consists of sermons addressed to the newly baptized in Easter week, to explain the sacraments that they had just received. It follows that we have very little about the catechumenate, since all the explanation that it needed had already been given before baptism; but from them and other sources we gain a certain amount of knowledge about the preparation for baptism.

The catechumens who wished to be baptized at Easter gave in their names and were signed with the sign of the cross; henceforth they were called *competentes*[1]. On the Sunday before Easter the creed was delivered to the candidates[2]; as they were not dismissed before the Gospel, the tradition of the Gospels had no place; the Lord's Prayer was explained after baptism[3]. During Lent the candidates

[1] *de Sacram.* III. 2. 12; *de Myst.* IV. 20; Ambros., *Ep.* xx. 4.
[2] Ambros., *Ep.* xx. 4.   [3] *de Sacram.* v. 4; VI. 5. 24.

were instructed daily in Christian morals and the
elementary principles of religion. The instruction,
at this early period, was given at the *missae catechumenorum* or special Lenten services, consisting of
Old Testament lessons and psalms ; the sermons of
St Ambrose to candidates refer to the passages
of Scripture which were read[1]. These services were
held at the third and ninth hours on weekdays in
Lent, except Saturday ; Genesis and Proverbs were
read during the first five weeks of Lent, and Job and
Tobit in Holy Week[2].

The *Effeta*[3] and renunciations formed the immediate prelude to baptism ; this is in agreement
with Gallican use, and different from the earlier and
later Roman use. The *Effeta* was performed by
touching the ears and nose ; the action is brought
into close relation to the Gospel narrative, but neither
saliva nor oil is mentioned. To this ceremony the
name of 'the mystery of opening' was given ; the
minister was, in the case of the *de Sacramentis*,
the bishop.

The scene now changed to the baptistery.
According to the author of the *de Sacramentis*
the candidates were anointed on the whole body.
Both writers speak of the renunciation, which was
apparently twofold ; this is different from the single

[1] *de Myst.* I. 1. Cf. *de Abraham* generally, and, in particular,
I. 4. 25, 7. 59, 9. 89.

[2] See the sections from earlier books at the foot of the pages in
the *Manuale Ambrosianum* (ed. Magistretti).

[3] The following description is drawn almost entirely from the
de Myst. and *de Sacram.*

Gallican and the triple Roman form[1]. The *de Sacramentis* places after the renunciation a sentence which has always maintained its place in the Milanese rite: *memor esto sermonis tui et nunquam tibi excidat tuae series cautionis.*

The following is a comparison of the various forms of the Milanese tradition of renunciation. The *de Mysteriis*: renuntiasti diabolo et operibus eius, mundo et luxuriae eius ac uoluptatibus? the *de Sacramentis*: abrenuntias diabolo et operibus eius? abrenuntio . abrenuntias saeculo et uoluptatibus eius? abrenuntio . memor esto *ut supra*; the *Liber Manualis*[2]: abrenuntiat diabolo et operibus eius? abrenuntiat . saeculo et pompis eius? abrenuntiat . memor esto sermonum tuorum, ut a te nunquam abscedant . memor ero; the *Ordo* of Beroldus[3] and the modern books have practically identical forms.

The unction and the renunciation were assigned to priests and deacons, and while they were thus engaged the bishop consecrated the water[4]. The

[1] In *de Myst.* II. 7, for 'cui renuntiandum in os putaris' Dom Morin reads, by conjecture, 'cui renuntiando in os sputares'; if this reading is right, the spitting is parallel to that in the Greek rite. *Revue bénédictine*, t. XVI (1899), pp. 414—418.

[2] *Manuale Ambrosianum*, ed. Magistretti, II. 467.

[3] Ed. Magistretti, p. 92. The *Ordo* of Beroldus is a mediaeval description of the rites of the cathedral of Milan, to guide those who had to perform them both in the cathedral and in other churches. See *D.A.C.L.* s.v. 'Bérold.'

[4] The following are the references: *de Myst.* III. 8...uidisti... summum sacerdotem...consecrantem; *ib.* 14, aqua...cum...salutaris fuerit crucis mysterio consecrata, tunc ad usum spiritalis lauacri et salutaris poculi temperatur; *de Sacram.* I. 5. 18, ubi primum ingreditur sacerdos, exorcismum facit secundum creaturam aquae, inuocationem postea et precem defert, ut sanctificetur fons et adsit praesentia Trinitatis aeternae; *ib.* II. 5. 14, uenit sacerdos, precem dicit ad fontem, inuocat Patris nomen, praesentiam Filii et Spiritus sancti.

language of St Ambrose is too slight to determine
the form of prayer used, and the phrases used by
the writer of the *de Sacramentis* are puzzling ; he
speaks of 'an exorcism over the creature of water,
afterwards...an invocation and prayer, that the font
may be hallowed, and the presence of the eternal
Trinity may come upon it '; again, 'the priest comes,
he says a prayer at the font, he invokes the Father's
name, and the presence of the Son and Holy Spirit.'
The allusion to an exorcism agrees with the later
Milanese and Gallican forms, where very distinct
exorcisms are found ; but the emphatic references to
an 'invocation' and 'the presence' do not agree
with anything in later forms. The references to Old
Testament types of baptism in both writers agree
with the extant Ambrosian prayers, but they also
agree with the mass lections of the day, so that here
again the matter remains in uncertainty. St Ambrose
appears to refer to a signing of the water[1].

The font consecrated, the clergy descended into it,
and the bishop stood by it. The method of baptism
is minutely described in the *de Sacramentis*[2]: 'Thou
wast asked : Dost thou believe in God the Father
Almighty? Thou saidst, "I believe," and wast immersed, that is, thou wast buried. Again thou wast
asked : Dost thou believe in our Lord Jesus Christ
and in his cross ? Thou saidst, "I believe," and wast
immersed ; therefore thou wast also buried with Christ :
for he who is buried with Christ, rises with him.
A third time thou wast asked : Dost thou believe also

---

[1] *de Myst.* III. 14, IV. 20.　　　　[2] *de Sacram.* II. 7. 20.

in the Holy Spirit? Thou saidst, "I believe," thou
wast immersed the third time, that the threefold
confession might remove the manifold fall of the
previous life.' With this St Ambrose, as far as he
goes, agrees[1]; neither writer mentions the baptismal
formula, nor gives any hint when it was said. The
form of the second of the above interrogations, 'Dost
thou believe in our Lord Jesus Christ and *in his
cross*?' is supported by St Ambrose[2], but is otherwise
unknown; it is not found in any other author or book,
and was replaced in the later Milanese rite by the
Roman form, 'Dost thou believe in Jesus Christ, his
only Son, our Lord, who was born and suffered?'
The alternation of interrogations and immersions is
a feature common to many early rites, but everywhere
abandoned later, for reasons of convenience and
economy of time.

After the baptism came an unction of the head
with chrism by the bishop[3]; to this action the *de
Sacramentis* assigns the prayer which the Roman rite
employed at the signing of the head by a presbyter,
with a few verbal differences[4]. The unction was
followed by the 'washing of the feet' of the newly
baptized in imitation of our Lord's action. When
the bishop had washed the feet of one or two, the

---

[1] *de Myst.* v. 28.   [2] *ib.* v. 28.

[3] sacerdos.

[4] This is the text from the S. Gall. MS. 188: deus pater
omnipotens qui te regenerauit ex aqua et spiritu concessitque tibi
peccata tua ipse te unguet in uitam aeternam (the Roman form is
in *Sacr. Gelas.* ed. Wilson, I. xliv.). μύρον was used; see *de Sacram.*
III. 1. 1.

presbyters completed the ceremony.   About the time
when the *de Sacramentis* was written the 'washing
of the feet' was the subject of some controversy in
North Italy.   Many disapproved of it because the
custom was not in use at Rome; and their dis-
approval was intensified by the unguarded language
of St Ambrose, who said that St Peter's 'foot is
washed, that his hereditary sins may be removed;
for our own sins are loosed through baptism.'   The
writer of the *de Sacramentis* defends the custom of
his Church, but very carefully guards against any
idea of attaching a quasi-sacramental notion to the
ceremony; '*every* fault,' he says, 'is washed away
in baptism[1].'   The newly baptized were then clothed
in white garments.

The rite closed with the 'spiritual seal,' the
spiritale signaculum, as both writers term it; this
consisted of a signing of the neophyte by the bishop.
Nothing is said about the use of chrism or the part
of the body which was signed; from the silence of
our authorities it would appear that this signing was
equivalent to an imposition of the hand.   The action
is definitely associated with the sevenfold gifts of the
Spirit; a prayer equivalent to the Roman form may
have been used, but the readings are so very different
that it is not safe to speak with certainty[2].

---

[1] *de Myst.* VI. 32; *de Sacram.* III. 1. 4—7.

[2] *de Myst.* VII. 42; *de Sacram.* III. 2. 8, spiritus sapientiae
et intellectus, spiritus consilii atque uirtutis, spiritus cognitionis
atque pietatis, spiritus sancti timoris.   *Sacr. Gelas.* I. xliv. p. 87,
spiritum sapientiae et intellectus, spiritum consilii et fortitudinis,
spiritum scientiae et pietatis; adimple eos spiritum timoris Dei.

After baptism the whole assembly proceeded to church and the Easter mass began, at which the newly baptized communicated.

At a later date the Milanese rite was completely altered in its arrangement[1]. A good deal of the older matter, both of words and ceremonies, survived, but the order of the parts of the system was entirely revolutionized. When the change took place we do not know; the resultant form bears a rough resemblance to the Roman rite as described by John the Deacon, but whether there is a connexion, and whether the Milanese rite is prior or posterior is not clear. The main features of the change are that the renunciation is placed at the beginning, when the catechumens become *competentes* or candidates for baptism at Easter, the *Effeta* disappears, and there are three scrutinies, held on Saturdays.

On the Sunday called 'Of the Samaritan woman[2],' after the Gospel at mass the deacon gives notice that candidates must give in their names. On the 'second Saturday' after mass the celebrant blesses ashes[3]

[1] This rite is described in the *Ordo* of Beroldus (ed. Magistretti), pp. 92—95, the *Manuale Ambrosianum* (ed. Magistretti), II. pp. 123—125, and is referred to in the text and notes of the services for Saturdays and Sundays in Lent; cf. also the *Codex Sacramentorum Bergomensis*, p. 42 (Solesmis, 1900).

[2] The Sundays and Saturdays in Lent were thus named at Milan: Dominica in capite quadragesimae, sabbatum I de quadrag., dominica I de Samaritana, sabb. II, dom. II de Abraham, sabb. III, dom. III de Caeco, sabb. IV [de Lazaro], dom. de Lazaro, sabb. in traditione symboli, dom. in ramis oliuarum [*or* palmarum]; thus the Saturday and its following Sunday go together.

[3] The ashes are spread in the shape of a figure called *chrismon* ; see *DACL*. 'Catéchuménat,' col. 2615.

spread on sackcloth in the middle of the church. Meanwhile the children stand at the doors of the church. The deacon approaches them and puts to them the twofold questions of the renunciation; the subdeacons reply for the children. After the renunciation the deacon says : ' Be mindful of your words, that they never depart from you'; the subdeacons reply, 'We will be mindful.' The candidates then entered the church and stood round the ashes ; certain of the clergy made an 'exsufflation' of the ashes, saying : *Exsufflo te, cinis cilicio aspersus, in nomine Patris et Filii et Spiritus sancti.* After this strange ceremony exorcisms are said over the candidates and they are signed ; the exorcism used is that called the 'Exorcism of St Ambrose[1].' Finally the candidates are dismissed with a blessing. All these ceremonies constituted the scrutiny[2], which was repeated after the Gospel at mass on the following two Saturdays ; on Sundays they were blessed after the Gospel as on the 'second Saturday.' On the Saturday 'of Lazarus' the scrutiny was preceded by an unction of the breast at the door of the church with the words, 'I anoint thee with the oil of salvation in Christ Jesus our Lord unto eternal life.' The scrutiny followed ; on this Saturday the signings were repeated eight times, on the 'third Saturday' six, and on the 'second Saturday' thrice.

On the Saturday before Palm Sunday the creed was delivered to the candidates; its delivery is

---

[1] To be found in the *Man. Ambros.* II. 469.
[2] *ib.* p. 169, line 21.

introduced and followed by an address[1]. It is not
clear when the creed was repeated. There is no
'Exposition' of the four Gospels or of the Lord's
Prayer; in this respect also it resembles the earlier
form of the Roman rite. On Maundy Thursday the
chrism and oil were consecrated at the mass; the
forms are peculiar to the Milanese rite, and the consecration takes place between the prayer *super oblata*
and the beginning of the Canon, not at the end of the
Canon, as at Rome[2].

On Easter Eve the baptismal service began with
the consecration of the water. First, the collect[3] is
said which precedes the Roman form of consecration;
then the consecration prayer itself, which falls into
three parts: (*a*) a preface or invitation of the people
to prayer, (*b*) an exorcism of the water, and (*c*) a
blessing of the water. For (*a*) two forms are furnished as alternatives; (*b*) is a longer form of the
section of the Roman blessing of the water beginning
Unde benedico te, turned into an exorcism by altering
benedico to *adiuro*[4]. The blessing (*c*) is exceedingly
interesting. It begins *Sanctificare per uerbum Dei*,
and is based on a passage in St Ambrose's *Exposition
of St Luke*[5]. From it is derived the Spanish blessing
of the font[6] and the blessing of water in the Roman

---

[1] The *Ordo* of Beroldus and the *Man. Ambros.* contain detailed
and complicated descriptions of the above scrutinies and ceremonies;
a full account would occupy more space than can be afforded here.

[2] *Cod. sacram. Bergom.* p. 62. *Pontificale* in *Monumenta
ueteris liturgiae ambrosianae*, vol. I. pp. 97—103.

[3] *Gelas. Sacr.* I. xliv. adesto magnae pietatis tuae mysteriis.

[4] *ib.* I. xliv. and lxxiii.   [5] x. 48.   [6] *Liber ordinum*, 29, 30.

Pontifical; in the latter case the last part of the prayer is different, in accordance with its different purpose[1]. At the beginning of (b) an insufflation is performed; at the end of (c) chrism is thrice poured into the water in the form of a cross with the words, 'This font be holy, hallowed, and anointed in the name of the Father and of the Son and of the Holy Ghost.'

This consecration of the font is a valuable instance of the growth and diffusion of liturgical forms. The phrases are seen taking shape in the writings of one of the great doctors of the Church, at a time when the exalted style of speaking and liturgical language touched each other. In the elaborate rhythms, the crisp, epigrammatic phrases, and, in particular, in the formal doxologies which end many sermons, we see the diction of the sacramentaries, not as a specially sacred manner of speaking, but as the natural style of elevated discourse, taught in the schools, and practised both in the world and in the Church. In such an environment the masterpieces of the Latin service-books grew; and the forms thus composed circulated freely from Church to Church, each borrowing from the other what it needed or admired. The result is that no sacramentary or service-book stands in isolation, but each is connected with others by relations of mutual borrowing.

The actual baptism begins by a dialogue between

---

[1] *Pontif. Rom.* 'De ecclesiae dedicatione seu consecratione.' *Sacr. Greg.* 'Ordo ad ecclesiam dedicandam' (Greg. Magni, *Opera*, ed. Benedictin. III. col. 146), *D.A.C.L.* 'Bénéd. de l'eau,' col. 693—5.

the principal minister (bishop[1] or priest) and the
deacons, who are to baptize. The latter are asked
'what they have come to do'; they reply, 'to
baptize'; and the bishop, after satisfying himself of
the belief of the candidates by the three questions,
grants them permission to baptize. The three
questions are the Roman form of interrogations at
the font; the older form which we mentioned as
occurring in the *de Sacramentis* has disappeared.
Later a transformation took place; the dialogue
between the bishop and the deacons became a
dialogue between the priest and the candidates (or
their sponsors); the priest asked, 'What have you
come to do?' or 'What dost thou seek?' and they
answered, 'To be baptized[2].' During the baptism a
litany was sung.

After baptism came confirmation, the history of
which at Milan is not quite clear. In the *de
Mysteriis* and *de Sacramentis* there is an unction of
the head with a prayer, and also a signing to which
the gift of the sevenfold Spirit is attributed. In the
Ordo of Beroldus[3] the archbishop rises after the litany,
and signs the baptized on the brow in the form of a
cross, reciting the same prayer in its Roman form:

[1] At Milan the books presuppose the presence and ministry of
the archbishop; but in his absence another bishop would act, and
in later times the service was naturally adapted to the use of
presbyters.

[2] In the same way at the beginning of the Roman and Milanese
rites, the minister asks, 'What do they seek?' the answer is,
'Faith.' In fact, there has been an assimilation of the one form
to the other.

[3] p. 112.

' Almighty God, the Father of our Lord Jesus Christ, who hath regenerated you with water and the Holy Ghost, and hath given you remission of all your sins, he anoints you with the chrism of salvation, in Christ Jesus our Lord, unto life eternal.' This appears to be the rite of confirmation; if so, it corresponds to the early form. But we cannot infer from the allusions to the sevenfold Spirit in the *de Mysteriis* that the Roman prayer of confirmation was then used, for no allusion is found to it in Beroldus or the *Manuale*. In other books the presbyter signs with chrism on the head, and confirmation must be supposed to follow later. Indeed, the Roman rite of confirmation has long been used in Milanese regions[1]. The situation then is this. In early times there was an unction of the head with the prayer *Deus qui te regenerauit* followed by a signing; this survived when the archbishop was minister until the Middle Ages, the unction and signing being combined. But when presbyters baptized, the unction of the head was performed as in the Roman rite, and the Roman confirmation followed. Finally the Roman confirmation entirely ousted the Milanese form and was alone used.

When a bishop baptized, the washing of the feet was still practised; it is found in the *Manuale* and Beroldus. The rite closes with a thanksgiving, *Celebratis atque perfectis diuini baptismatis sacramentis*[2].

---

[1] *Pontificale* in *Mon. uet. lit. ambros.* ed. Magistretti, p. xxii.
[2] *Sacr. Bergom.* p. 67; *Manual. Ambros.* II. 209.

In all parts of the Church baptism and its preparation were organic parts of the Lenten and Easter services; and in all parts, when, with the growth of infant baptism, the rite was shortened and consolidated, something of the preparation for baptism remained in the final form. But at Milan the connexion of the preparation for baptism with the Lenten services and the solemn baptism at Easter survived to the end of the Middle Ages; there is no other parallel to this tenacious retention of the ancient discipline of the *competentes*. The system, however, belonged properly to a cathedral church, and particularly to the cathedral church of Milan. For the use of parish priests another order was in use, from which the present Milanese baptismal rite is descended. This latter rite is found in books which also contain the former, the one being incorporated in the Christian year, the other appearing as an appendix. The shortened form[1] still retains many specially Milanese features, such as the placing of the renunciation at the beginning of the order 'for making a Catechumen,' and the use of the 'exorcism of St Ambrose'; but a good deal of borrowing from the Roman rite has also taken place, in particular, the re-introduction of an *Effeta*, now performed with saliva. After baptism the child is communicated by intinction[2]. The first part of the rite, that which

---

[1] *Cod. Sacr. Berg.* cclxxii—cclxxiv; *Man. Ambros.* i. 143—147, ii. 466—473.

[2] The words of administration are: 'Corpus Domini nostri Iesu Christi, *sanguine suo tinctum*, conseruet animam tuam in uitam

corresponds to the preparation, is entitled 'An Order for making a Catechumen'; the second part, 'for baptizing a sick child' or 'for sick baptism,' from which it appears that it was at first intended to be used only in urgent cases; but later both were conjoined into one service.

The Milanese mass-book provides masses through Easter week for the newly baptized. The institution of these masses is of great antiquity and the lections read at them are alluded to in the *de Mysteriis* and the *de Sacramentis*.

SEC. 4. *Spain*

In the baptismal rites of the regions which now remain to be dealt with, there is scarcely any trace of the scrutinies which occupied so much space in the treatment of Rome and Milan. It does not follow from this that no preparation was given to the candidates for baptism in Spain and Gaul, but merely that, when the baptism of adults ceased, the preparation for baptism died away without trace; whereas at Rome and Milan the skeleton of the system of instruction survived for many centuries after the life and purpose had vanished. But the ceremonies of the entry into the state of catechumens or of *competentes* and of the delivery of the creed remained in the rites of Spain and Gaul as long as the rites lasted, that is, until they were superseded by the Roman rite.

aeternam.' In the modern Milanese books, of course, this has disappeared through Roman influence, and the rite has been generally altered in a Roman direction.

For the baptismal rite of Spain we have three principal sources, the second book of the *De ecclesiasticis officiis* of St Isidore of Seville[1], the work *De cognitione baptismi* of St Ildephonsus of Toledo[2], and the *Liber ordinum* recently edited by Dom Férotin[3]. St Isidore and St Ildephonsus both belong to the seventh century; the *Liber ordinum* is found in manuscripts not earlier than the eleventh century, but the matter is drawn from ancient sources, as is shewn by its close agreement with St Ildephonsus[4]. All the works deal with infant baptism, but it is not difficult to reconstruct the earlier stage.

At the Council of Elvira, a catechumenate of two years is prescribed; pagans are received into the catechumenate by an imposition of the hand, and are then called Christians[5]. The Council of Valencia ordered that the Gospels should be read before the dismissal (*missa*) of the catechumens. The name *competentes* is found in the *Pilgrimage of Etheria*[6];

---

[1] Migne, *P.L.* LXXXIII. 814 foll. This work is to be used with caution, since the writer freely drew on various sources, not necessarily Spanish; cf. *Ep. Missoria, ib.* 738.

[2] *ib.* XCVI. 111 foll.

[3] *Monumenta ecclesiae liturgica*, vol. v. The lateness of the book accounts for the absence of a system of 'scrutinies.' But Isidore and Ildephonsus are also very sparing of information on the subject of 'scrutinies.'

[4] The *De cognitione baptismi* is a version of an earlier work; it is connected or identified with the *Liber responsionum ad quendam Rusticum de interrogatis quaestionibus* of Justinian, bishop of Valencia (died after 546).

[5] Can. XXXIX. XLII.

[6] VII. 1. Duchesne, *C.W.* p. 519. Though the work relates to Eastern rites, the authoress was Gallican or Spanish; cf. p. 52.

the first canon of the Council of Braga ordered that the exorcisms shall take place at least twenty days before baptism, and that within the twenty days the catechumens shall be taught the creed. In Isidore and Ildephonsus a clear distinction is made between catechumens and *competentes,* that is, between unbaptized Christians in general and those who had given in their names for baptism.

The rite began with exorcisms according to the two writers mentioned above. The *Liber ordinum* has not preserved the full exorcisms in the baptismal service, but they have survived in the ' Order for one who is vexed by an unclean spirit[1],' which agrees with the details preserved by Ildephonsus. The deacon pronounces an exorcism, *Recordare Satanas,* which is thrice repeated. The bishop then reads three portions of Scripture called *capitula*[2]. Lastly the deacon recites an exorcism *Deprehensae sunt insidiae tuae,* which is quoted by the Spanish bishops in the Adoptianist controversy[3]. The exorcisms are assigned to deacons in the *Liber ordinum*; this sounds strange, but on referring to Ildephonsus[4], we find, as we should have expected, that exorcists were the original ministers of these exorcisms.

According to Isidore salt was given at this point. Ildephonsus alludes to the custom with some contempt; apparently it was not received at Toledo. The *Liber ordinum* makes no reference to salt.

---

[1] xxvi. col. 73.　　　　[2] Zech. iii. 2, Mark viii. 33, Rev. v. 5.
[3] Ildeph., xxv; *Liber ord.* xxvi; *Epistola ad episcopos Franciae* in Migne, *P.L.* ci. 1329.　　　　[4] xxii.

The 'Order of baptism to be celebrated at any time' in the *Liber ordinum* has the above ceremonies in a shortened and somewhat altered form. The priest exorcizes the child with insufflation ; then he signs and names the child. The accompanying prayers have their parallels in the Milanese rite[1]. The adjuration of Satan, *Recordare Satanas*, mentioned above, is said at this point, and the first stage in the preparation closes. Isidore speaks of an unction in connexion with the exorcizing ; either it is the unction of the *Effeta* which will next be mentioned, or it is a preparatory unction which has disappeared.

The *Effeta* took place in Spain on Palm Sunday at the early morning service. The lections at this service are mentioned by Ildephonsus as preceding the exorcisms[2] ; it would appear, therefore, that the exorcisms were repeated at the other services for candidates or 'scrutinies.' The ears and mouth of the candidate were touched with hallowed oil, and the following words were said : ' *Effeta, effeta*, with the Holy Spirit for a sweetsmelling savour. He hath done all things well : he maketh both the deaf to hear, and the dumb to speak.' In spite of the difference of method the ceremony is closely connected by the Spanish writers with the passage in the Gospel. The *Effeta* is considered as a preparation

---

[1] *Lib. ord.* 25, 26 ; *Manuale Ambros.* II. 467, 468.

[2] Ildeph., XXVIII ; *Liber comicus*, ed. Morin, pp. 132—134. The lections are Is. xlix. 22—26, I Pet. i. 25—ii. 40, Mark vii. 31—37. The ceremony was called in Spain *Effetatio*.

for the reception of the creed. The varieties in the position of the *Effeta* in the Western rites are noteworthy. At Milan in early days it was placed just before baptism, as in Gaul and in later times at Rome; at Rome in earlier days, according to John the Deacon, it was performed at some time during Lent, perhaps before the delivery of the creed, as in Spain; lastly, at Milan, in the shorter rite, it was shifted to the very beginning of the preparation. To resume: on the same day, after the sermon at mass, the creed was delivered to the candidates[1]. The creed used is the Spanish form[2] of the 'Apostles'' creed, and it is preceded and followed by short discourses of a formal character. The candidates signed themselves at the recitation of the creed[3]. The creed thus received was repeated on the following Thursday, as in the East[4]. It appears that the chrism was consecrated on this day as in Gaul.

On Easter Eve the service of the Easter Vigil was held. During the third lesson, which was from the fifty-fifth chapter of Isaiah, beginning, ' Ho, every one that thirsteth,' the bishop and his clergy went to the font, which had been locked and sealed throughout Lent; the bishop now opened it with a prayer. The

---

[1] *Lib. ord.* col. 184; *ib.* col. 28. In the latter passage a blessing (a cento of texts from the first three chapters of St. Luke), with an imposition of the hand, intervenes between the *Effeta* and the tradition of the creed. The blessing may represent a dismissal in older days.

[2] Hahn, *Bibliothek der Symbole*, pp. 64—69.

[3] *Lib. ord.* col. 184; Ildeph., xxx.

[4] Ildeph., xxxiv.; Concil. Laod. can. 46; Concil. Trull. can. 78.

water for the font was ordered to be taken, not from cisterns, but from running streams—a rule reminiscent of the Church Orders ; on the altar in the baptistery stood the chrism. The blessing of the water begins with a preface for which two forms are supplied[1] ; the actual consecration[2] falls into three parts : (*a*) an exorcism, (*b*) the consecration of the water, and (*c*) a prayer for the candidates. The exorcism (*a*) is accompanied by three 'exsufflations,' or breathings on the water as a symbol of the removal of alien spiritual influences. The second prayer (*b*) is the same substantially as the Ambrosian form *Sanctificare* which was discussed in the last section. At the end of it a cross is made on the water with oil[3]. This blessing of the water is similar to the Milanese ; the definite exorcism puts it in the same class as the Gallican and Milanese, and separates it from the Roman forms.

Before baptism the renunciations and professions are made. The threefold form of each is attested by all authorities. The renunciation in the *Liber ordinum* is as follows : 'Dost thou, servant of God, N., renounce the devil and his angels ?' 'I renounce.' 'His works ?' 'I renounce.' 'His commands (*imperiis*) ?' 'I renounce.' The same form is found in Ildephonsus ; the word *imperiis* is a Spanish characteristic[4]. The profession of faith is made in three

---

[1] *Lib. ord.* pp. 218, 219. [2] *ib.* col. 29—31.

[3] *ib.* col. 31; Ildeph., cix.

[4] Ildeph., cxi. has *abrenuntio tibi diabole et angelis tuis, operibus tuis et imperiis tuis*; the same words occur in Ambros.,

clauses, 'Dost thou, N., believe in God[1] the Father Almighty?' 'And in Jesus Christ, his only Son, our God and Lord?' 'And in the Holy Spirit?' To each the candidate replies, 'I believe.' The form of the second clause, 'his only Son, our God and Lord,' is distinctively Spanish, and is supported by many authors[2].

Baptism is performed by single immersion as a protest against Arianism[3]. The baptismal formula ends with the words 'that thou mayest have life eternal'; this clause is characteristic of the Gallican rites and we shall meet it again in the next section.

After baptism the neophyte is signed with chrism on the brow; the formula is, 'The sign (or seal, *signum*) of life eternal, which (*quod*) God the Father Almighty hath given through Jesus Christ his Son to those who believe unto salvation.' This formula is similar to the Gelasian, 'The sign of Christ to life eternal.' The chrismation is followed by an imposition of the hand joined to a prayer for the seven-fold Spirit. The imposition of the hand is rather important in the Spanish rite; the signing with chrism is interpreted by Isidore and Ildephonsus as appointment to the 'chosen generation, the royal priesthood.' In the *Liber ordinum* both the signing and the imposition of the hand are performed by the

Hexaem. i. iv. 14; the address in the second person has an Eastern sound. There appears to have been a good deal of borrowing from Milan in Spain, and the formula with *imperiis* may be added to the account.

[1] *Dominum* (*Lib. ord.* 32, line 7) should surely be *Deum*.

[2] Cf. Hahn, *l c.*   [3] Ildeph., cxvii.

priest. Isidore and Ildephonsus, however, speak of the imposition of the hand as limited to bishops, and support the limitation by the rule laid down by Pope Innocent[1] with regard to the unction of the brow ; they consider the Spanish imposition of the hand as equal to the Roman unction of the brow. But in practice the presbyter both laid on the hand and signed the brow.

The washing of the feet of the newly baptized is mentioned in the canons of the Council of Elvira, where it is ordered that clerks, not priests, shall perform it[2]. But afterwards the custom was entirely dropped, and nothing further is heard of it in Spain.

Communion follows immediately upon baptism. The third day after baptism, according to the *Liber ordinum*, the children were brought to church, to lay aside the white garments which they had received after confirmation. In earlier times they doubtless wore them through Easter week.

In the time of the author of the treatise *De cognitione baptismi* (which has been cited as the work of Ildephonsus) there were two seasons for baptism, Easter and Pentecost, and, except in the case of large dioceses, the rite was confined to cathedral churches[3]. But at a later date the rule was relaxed and baptism was administered at any

---

[1] Cf. *infra*, pp. 196—7.

[2] Can. XLVIII. neque pedes eorum lauandi sunt a sacerdotibus, sed clericis. But some texts read *uel* for *sed*; if this is right, then the practice was forbidden and the silence of all later authorities is explained. Routh, *Rell. Sacr.* IV. p. 268.

[3] Ildeph., *op. cit.* CVIII.

time in the year[1], and by a priest, who confirmed after baptizing. At the same time the rite was compressed into a single service, containing everything from the first exorcism to confirmation; this stage is represented in the *Liber ordinum* in the 'Order of baptism to be celebrated at any time[2].' Still later, the Roman rite so completely superseded the Spanish that, even at Toledo where the Mozarabic use was revived by Cardinal Ximenes and still exists, it is completely forgotten that there once existed in Spain a rite of baptism different from the Roman[3].

For the traces of the *missae catechumenorum* or special Lenten services for the instruction of candidates see Mr W. C. Bishop in *C.Q.R.* LXXII (1911), 34 f. The original arrangement provided for a three weeks' course only, but later alterations extended the course to six weeks. The lessons read consisted of selected portions from the Sapiential books, formed into a cento, a regular course of sections from the Books of the Kings, and selections from the prophets. These services were held at the third, sixth, and ninth hours, and vestiges of them remain in the Mozarabic Missal and Breviary.

SEC. 5. *Gaul and Ireland*

In Gaul the preparation for baptism was of a less fixed and formal character than at Rome or Milan. The word 'scrutiny' is almost unknown[4], nor has

---

[1] For baptism at the Epiphany and a three weeks' preparation, see Mr W. C. Bishop in *J.Th.St.* vol. x. (1908), 127.

[2] *Lib. ord.* col. 24—36.

[3] See the remarks of Dom Férotin in *Lib. ord.* p. xvi.

[4] In the *Missale Gallicanum Vetus*, sec. XIII. bears the title *Praemissiones ad scrutamen*; but in sec. IX. of the same book the

the practice of holding scrutinies left traces in the
books.   And again, the distinction between catechumens and *competentes*, between those who had
abandoned heathenism and those who wished to be
baptized, seems to have been blurred and indistinctly
conceived.

Persons who deserted heathenism were received
with the sign of the cross[1]; if they wished to be
baptized, they were prepared in the Lent preceding
their baptism by the imposition of the hand and
unction[2], by exorcism and exsufflation[3], and on the
Sunday before Easter, they received the creed.   The
absence of scrutinies does not mean that candidates
for baptism in Gaul were not adequately prepared;
but it does mean that the services of exorcism and
examination were so far informal and undeveloped,
that when the need for them ceased, the services
silently disappeared, whereas at Rome and Milan the
framework of these services was so complete and
their articulation into the Christian Year so strong,
that they could stand alone for centuries after their
original meaning and purpose had died away.

The authorities for the baptismal rites of Gaul
and Ireland consist of four service books and St
Germanus of Paris.   The books[4] are all more or

title *Ad faciendum scrutinium* is merely a guess of the editor ; see
D.A.C.L. II. 2600.

[1] Paulinus, *de uita S. Martini*, l. i. in *P.L.* LXI. 1011.

[2] Second Council of Mâcon (585 A.D.), can. 3.

[3] *Auctoritates de gratia Dei*, c. IX. (printed among the works of
Prosper of Aquitaine in *P.L.* LI. 210).

[4] For the description of these books see Duchesne, *C.W.*,
Eng. trans. pp. 151—160.   The books will be found as follows :

less affected by Roman influence. The least Roman is the *Missale Gothicum*, which emanated from the Church of Autun and is probably to be assigned to the beginning of the eighth century. Of about the same date is the *Missale Gallicanum Vetus*, which contains more Roman elements. The *Sacramentarium Gallicanum* or *Bobbio Missal*, and the *Stowe Missal* are connected with each other in baptismal rite; they are both almost completely remodelled on Roman lines, and the non-Roman elements emerge but fitfully. All these books are in considerable confusion; the parts are disarranged, and the combination of Roman and non-Roman elements in the last three is clumsily effected, so that there is much reduplication of material. The second letter of St Germanus of Paris furnishes a few details about the ceremonies of Palm Sunday.

As there are no Gallican scrutinies to deal with, the discussion of the baptismal ceremonies falls into three sections, the entry into the catechumenate or 'making of a Christian[1],' as it was called, the 'tradition of the creed' with other attached matter on Palm Sunday, and finally baptism itself. It is proposed to give a description of what appear to be common features and then to discuss the four books separately.

Missale Gothicum and *Missale Gallicanum Vetus* in Mabillon, *De Liturgia Gallicana*, Lib. III.; *Sacramentarium Gallicanum* in Mabillon's *Museum Italicum*, tom. I, pt. ii.; these three are also in Migne, *P.L.* vol. LXXII. and Muratori's *Liturgia Romana Vetus*; the *Stowe Missal* in Warren's edition; St Germanus in *P.L.* LXXII.

[1] Sulp. Sev., *Dial.* II. 4.

The entry into the catechumenate was performed by a signing of the brow and other parts of the body. The creed was delivered to the candidates on Palm Sunday; this is clear from the liturgical books[1]. The form used was always the 'Apostles'' creed; St Hilary says that he had been a bishop for some time before he heard the Nicene creed[2], and the books shew the 'Apostles'' creed only. On this day also, as appears from St Germanus[3], the oil and chrism were consecrated, and the candidates were anointed; but this may have been a local custom and the liturgical books do not furnish any precise information on the point. The *Missale Gallicanum Vetus* seems to refer to the consecration of the chrism in the *Immolatio* or preface for the mass of Maundy Thursday[4]. The same book (as also the *Sacramentarium Gallicanum*) contains an 'Exposition of the Gospels,' and St Germanus appears to allude to it; but as in Gaul the catechumens were not dismissed before the Gospel[5], the ceremony would be a meaningless and unintelligent borrowing from Roman customs.

The solemn season for baptism was Easter[6], but other seasons were grudgingly allowed. During Lent

---

[1] Cf. also St Germanus; in this sense is probably to be taken can. 13 of the Council of Agde (Concil. Agathense, 506 A.D.).

[2] *de Synodis*, 91.

[3] *Ep.* II. In this passage *catechumenus* and *competens* are used interchangeably. Palm Sunday was called *dies unctionis* in Spain (Ildeph., *De cognit. bapt.* XXXIV.) on account of the reading on that day of the story of our Lord's anointing at Bethany.

[4] *Missal. Gallic. Vet.* XVII.   [5] German., *Ep.* I.

[6] Second Council of Mâcon (585 A.D.), can. 3; Council of Auxerre (578 A.D.), can. 18.

the baptisteries were closed as in Spain[1]. The baptismal service on Easter Eve began with the consecration of the font. The form for this purpose consisted of an exorcism and a blessing; the exorcism is exceedingly prominent in these rites, and separates them, along with the Spanish and Milanese, from the Roman, where it is much less prominent. At the end of the consecration chrism is poured into the water in the form of a cross.

The Gallican renunciation is single; the interrogation of the faith is threefold as elsewhere. The baptismal formula added various clauses to the usual Western words, 'I baptize thee in the name of the Father, and of the Son, and of the Holy Ghost'; and ended, as in Spain, with the phrase 'that thou mayest have life eternal.' Baptism is followed by the chrismation, the washing of the feet, the giving of a white robe, and finally by communion. The *Missale Gothicum* furnishes a mass for the newly baptized and in the *Missale Gallicanum Vetus* the Easter masses have references to baptism.

In the *Missale Gothicum* the sections must be read in the following order: XXXIV., XXVII., XXXV. The first section is entitled, 'For making a Christian,' that is, the entry into the catechumenate. It consists of a signing of the eyes, ears, nose, tongue[2], and breast, together with appropriate prayers. The second section is the mass *in symboli traditione*; the

---

[1] German., *Ep.* II.

[2] Mabillon reads *linguam, conuersus* for the meaningless *conuersus*.

candidates for baptism are mentioned as present in
the prayer *post nomina*, that is, after the reading of
the diptychs, from which it would appear that the
catechumens were dismissed at Autun later than at
Paris, if they were dismissed at all[1]. The third
section contains the baptism itself. The water is
consecrated with five liturgical forms[2], a preface, or
invitation to prayer, a collect, a *contestatio*, an
exorcism of the water, and a formula accompanying
the pouring in of chrism[3]. The exorcism seems to
be out of place; it ought to precede the *contestatio*,
as it is absurd to exorcise the water after it has been
blessed. The baptismal formula is, 'I baptize thee
N. in the name of the Father and of the Son and of
the Holy Ghost, unto remission of sins, that thou
mayest have life eternal.' According to the rubric,
the interrogations are put during baptism; this is a
trace of the old custom of interrogating the candidate
in the water. The prayer which accompanies the
chrismation is corrupt. The rite ends with two
formulas of thanksgiving of an invitatory character,
resembling the Milanese[4]. Whatever may be the

---

[1] In St Germanus (*Ep.* 1.) the catechumens are dismissed before
the bringing in of the oblation; but the *post nomina* is later than
this.

[2] The following definitions should be kept in mind. *Praefatio*
in Gaul means an invitation to prayer; *Contestatio* in Gaul =
Illatio in Spain = *Praefatio* in Rome, that is a preface or eucharistic
prayer, beginning with *Sursum corda*.

[3] Infusio Chrismae salutaris Domini nostri Iesu Christi ut fiat
fons aquae salientis cunctis descendentibus in eo in uitam
aeternam. Amen. Cf. the modern Roman *Benedictio fontis* on
Easter Eve, where a somewhat similar phrase occurs.

[4] *Man. Ambros.* II. 209.

character of the rest of the *Missale Gothicum* the baptismal service is in no wise Roman, and may be taken as the purest form of Gallican rite.

In the *Missale Gallicanum Vetus* the preparation for baptism is contained in sections IX.—XVI., but these sections are in great confusion. Section IX. is a fragment of a prayer for candidates for baptism; the title and beginning are lost. Section X. is an exorcism, and section XIII. is *Praemissiones ad scrutamen* or 'Preliminaries for examination'; it consists of a 'preface' and collect and may have been used at a 'scrutiny,' though it is not clear when and how; it is the sole mention of 'scrutinies' in Gaul. Two forms of exposition of the creed are given in sections XI. and XVI., and sections XII. and XIV. contain the 'Exposition of the Gospels at the opening of the ears to the Elect' and an explanation of the Lord's Prayer, both from the Gelasian Roman forms. Possibly we have two rites, (i) IX.—XII., (ii) XIII.—XVI., either of which would be used on Palm Sunday. In any case there is a rather clumsy combination of Roman and Gallican forms.

This book is very eclectic in its sources. The "Exposition or tradition of the creed" in sec. XI. is a cento[1] of Rufinus and the ps.-Eusebius of Emesa; the section ends with a prayer *Exaudi* which also occurs in the *Manuale Ambrosianum* (II. p. 471). Sec. XII. is the same as *Sacr.*

---

[1] Neale and Forbes, *The ancient Liturgies of the Gallican Church*, pp. 163—165. The disorder of the *Missale Gall. Vetus* is easily explicable, since it is 'a volume containing fragments of two separate Sacramentaries which have nothing to do with one another.' See E. Bishop in *J.Th. St.* III. 491.

Gelas. I. xxxiv., and sec. XIV. corresponds fairly closely to *Sacr. Gelas.* I. xxxvi.; at the end of sec. XIV. there is an announcement that the Primicerius and Secundicerius will continue the instruction on the Lord's Prayer and creed, followed by the conclusion *Potens est* which also occurs in the *Gelasian Sacramentary.* From this it is clear that the original form of this section contained an Exposition of the creed after the Lord's Prayer. Section XVI. is found in the pseudo-Augustinian sermon CCXLII[1].

In this book the chrism appears to have been consecrated on Maundy Thursday[2]. The rite of baptism is contained in section XXV. The consecration of the font falls into two parts, (*a*) a preface, collect, and exorcism, (*b*) a preface, blessing, and *contestatio fontis* or solemn prayer of consecration; the hallowing of the font concludes with signing of the water with chrism and a prayer. The renunciation and interrogations follow; the latter are very peculiar and represent a protest against Arianism, made at the time when the Catholics lived under Arian rule in Gaul. They are as follows: 'Dost thou believe the Father, the Son, and the Holy Spirit to be of one virtue? Dost thou believe the Father, the Son, and the Holy Spirit to be of the same power? Dost thou believe the Father, the Son, and the Holy Spirit, of threefold verity, the substance remaining one, to be perfect God?' To each the candidate answers, 'I believe.' The baptismal formula is, 'I baptize thee believing in the name of the Father and of the Son and of the Holy Ghost, that thou mayest

---

[1] Migne, *P.L.* xxxix. 2191.
[2] Sec. XVII. Contestatio.

have life eternal for ever and ever.' The 'infusion of chrism' is performed with the Roman prayer for the unction of the head. The words used at the washing of the feet are similar in all these books. The service closes with a final collect.

The sources of sec. xxv. are even more various than those of the earlier sections. The prayer *Omnipotens sempiterne Deus adesto* is in *Sacr. Gelas.* i. xliv. at the beginning. The preface *Dominum immortalium munerum* is in the Spanish *Liber ordinum*, p. 219. The *contestatio fontis* is found in the Mozarabic Missal[1]. The prayer at the chrismation of the neophyte is found first in the *de Sacramentis*; it is found in all Western rites except the *Liber ordinum* and the *Missale Gothicum*.

In the *Bobbio Missal* the same disorder of parts occurs as in the *Missale Gothicum*; the reception into the catechumenate is placed before baptism on Easter Eve, whereas it is the initial ceremony of the whole rite of initiation. It consists of a signing and an insufflation; the latter is accompanied by the words, 'Receive the Holy Spirit and keep him in thy heart.'

The Exposition of the Gospels on Palm Sunday follows the Roman use with some abbreviation; the Exposition of the creed is based on a pseudo-Augustinian sermon[2].

The consecration of the water consists of an exorcism and a eucharistic prayer, between which is placed a much abbreviated form of the Roman

---

[1] In the consecration of the font on Easter Eve.
[2] *Serm.* in *Append.* ccxliii. (Migne, *P.L.* xxxix. 2193).

consecration of the font. The ceremonies which immediately precede baptism shew signs of a combination of various rites; they are: an exorcism of the candidate, the *Effeta* without oil or saliva, an unction, a touching of nose, ears, and breast, the renunciation (which is thrice repeated, by an approximation to Roman use), and the interrogations. The baptismal formula ends with the clause 'that thou mayest have life eternal.' After baptism follow the chrismation, the giving of a white robe, and the washing of the feet. Two invitatories to prayer, such as are found in the *Missale Gothicum* or the Milanese books, close the rite.

The rite of baptism in the *Stowe Missal*[1] is similar to the above, with the exception that the Expositions of the Gospels and creed are entirely omitted and salt is given as at Rome. Further than this it is not easy to go, as the book is in the most complete confusion; the forms have been thoroughly shuffled, so that the parts are inverted and related sections widely separated. The *Bobbio* and *Stowe Missals* are very closely connected and a brief discussion of the sources used and their mutual relations as regards baptismal services may help to throw light on the further question of the history of the two books as a whole.

The baptismal rite of the *Stowe Missal* contains four or five strata: 1. The Gelasian rite as contained in the *Gelasian Sacramentary* among the services for

[1] Ed. Warren; also published in facsimile by the Henry Bradshaw Society, vol. xxxi.

Lent and Easter Eve. 2. Some further Gelasian forms, attached to the Vigil of Pentecost. 3. The Gelasian order for visiting the sick. 4. One or two Gregorian forms. 5. A good deal of non-Roman matter common to the *Stowe* and *Bobbio Missals*. Besides these, there are small and not very important sections peculiar to either book.

The following is the analysis of the sources[1]:

			Gelas. Sacr.	*Stowe M.*	*Bobbio M.*
1.					
	i.	xxx.	O. s. d. P. D. n. I. C., respice	209	
				Rogamus	
		xxxi.	Exorcizo te	208	
		xxxiii.	Ergo maledicte[2]	207	
		xlii.	Nec te lateat	210	
			Abrenuntias	209	
				twice	
		xliv.	O. s. d. adesto magnae (to end of consecration of font)	213	323
			Credis	215	
			D. o. P. D. n. I. C. qui te regenerauit	216	325
2.		lxxi.	D. s. P. o. ae. D. qui es et eras	211	322
		lxxv.	Exorcizo te	213	323
3.	iii.	lxxv.	Deus qui ad salutem	207, 211	
		lxxvi.	Exaudi nos (beginning)	211	
			Gregor. Sacr.		
4.		229.	Benedic Domine	220	
		263.	Medelam.	209	

[1] Quotations are made from the sections of Wilson's *Sacr. Gelas.*, the pages of Warren's *Stowe Missal*, and Mabillon's *Sacr. Gallic.* (in *Mus. Italicum*, I. ii. ed. Paris, 1724); the *Gregorian Sacramentary* from the pages of Muratori's edition.

[2] For the word *designare* in this exorcism cf. *Lib. ord.* col. 74, 568.

5. *Bobbio Missal*   *Stowe Missal*

p. 324.	Exorcizo te	p. 220
	(cf. *Sacr. Gelas.* I. lxxvi. *Lib. ord.* col. 25,	
	Man. Ambros. II. 467)	
p. 324.	Effeta	p. 210
p. 324.	Ungo te	p. 209
p. 324.	Operare	p. 216
p. 325.	Accipe	p. 217
	(cf. *Missale Gothicum*, p. 249)	

From the above analysis it is clear that, though there is Roman matter in *Stowe* which is not in *Bobbio*, there is no Roman matter in *Bobbio* which is not in *Stowe*, except the Exposition of the Gospels. Again, an examination of the prayers shews that *Stowe* is generally nearer in language than *Bobbio* to the Roman forms. On the other hand, the disorder of *Stowe* makes it impossible to suppose that *Bobbio* was copied from it. It would, therefore, appear that neither is copied from the other, but that there is some common source now lost. This source was formed by combining Irish and Gelasian books, and from it *Bobbio* was not very accurately copied. The *Stowe Missal* represents a further stage; more Roman matter, often irrelevant, was added, and, by some means, the resultant book fell into utter confusion.

The *Stowe Missal* is certainly an Irish book; and the *Bobbio Missal*, apart from matter common to *Stowe*, has Irish touches of its own[1], though the book itself is assigned to North Italy. It would

---

[1] *E.g.* the ending of the interrogative creed on p. 324 is similar to that in the *Antiphonary of Bangor*, vol. I. fol. 19 *v.* (Henry Bradshaw Society, vol. IV.).

therefore appear that both these books are of Irish origin, and that the connecting link with North Italy is to be found in Irish monasticism.

The Irish rite appears to have borne a strong resemblance to the Gallican, as, for instance, in the matter of the washing of the feet of the neophytes[1]. The *Effeta* and the unction just before baptism, to judge from *Bobbio* and the fragments of *Stowe*, had some peculiarities[2].

The Gallican books were superseded by Roman books by the orders of Charlemagne[3]; nor did the Irish books succeed any better in maintaining their position against the aggression of the dominant Roman influence.

[1] Cf. the formulas of the four books; *Stowe* has a good deal of peculiar matter.

[2] *Sacr. Gallic.* p. 324; *Stowe Missal*, pp. 209, 212. The prayer in *Stowe*, p. 208, *Deus qui ad salutem hominis* is interesting as it connects the giving of salt and the renunciation. The connexion might seem to point to the older Roman rite as found in John the Deacon (III., IV.); is this prayer a legacy from the pre-Gelasian rite?

[3] *Mon. Germ. Hist., Capitularia Regum Francorum*, tom. I. p. 64, cap. 23; **Mansi**, *Concil.* XIV. 66, can. 4.

PART II

CHAPTER I

THE CONSECRATION OF WATER, OIL, AND CHRISM

THE consecration of the water used in baptism does not belong to the earliest tradition, for we cannot doubt that the baptisms mentioned in the New Testament were performed in any water that was at hand[1]. We may, perhaps, find evidence of the early practice in the *Clementine Homilies*[2], where we read how Mattidia is baptized in the sea. A parallel to this would appear to be furnished by the *Canons of Hippolytus*, where, according to one rendering, baptism in sea water is prescribed[3]. But the meaning is not certain and, perhaps, no more

---

[1] Acts viii. 38. So St Basil states that the blessing of the water is derived from a secret tradition, not from any written authority; *de Spir. S.* XXVII. 66.

[2] *Hom.* XIV. 1.

Can. Hipp. 112. Achelis has 'prope fluctuantem aquam maris puram paratam sacram.' Haneberg's rendering is 'prope undas piscinae aquae purae benedictione paratae.' Prof. Burkitt (*J. Th. St.* I. 279) thinks that the running water of a stream is meant.

than moving, 'living,' water is intended. This would agree with the tradition of the Church Orders, where great emphasis is laid upon the provision that the water shall be in motion. The words 'living water' occur in the *Didache*[1]; in the *Testament of our Lord*[2] the water is to be 'pure and flowing'; in the *Egyptian Church Order*[3] the water is to be drawn into the font or flowing into it. It is clear that there was a tradition that baptism ought to be performed in running water, though provision is made for cases where that could not be had by a permission to use other water in such circumstances. Tertullian[4] says that 'it makes no difference whether one is washed in the sea or a pond, a river or a spring, a cistern or a tub.' The provision was becoming obsolete.

The practice of consecrating the water used for baptizing must have grown up when the custom of using running water was dying out, and baptism began to be performed in water contained in a font of some kind. The earliest idea is that of the consecration of the element of water by the baptism of Christ[5]; the consecration of water specially for baptism is later. Probably the first mention of

---

[1] VII. 1, ἐν ὕδατι ζῶντι; but this is not made essential, and exceptions are allowed.

[2] II. 8.

[3] Horner, *The Statutes of the Apostles*, pp. 152, 253, 316.

[4] *de Bapt.* 4. Baptism was performed by Victor of Marseilles in the sea; Ruinart, *Acta Sincera*, 'S. Victor Massil.' XI. (p. 338).

[5] Ignat., *Ep. ad Eph.* 18; Tert., *adv. Iud.* 8.

consecration of the water is to be found in Tertullian[1]. So St Cyprian[2] speaks of the water as 'purified
and sanctified by the priest first, that he may be
able, by his baptism, to wash away the sins of the
man who is baptized.' About the same time, at
the Council of Carthage, held in the year 256 A.D.,
Sedatus of Tuburbo refers to 'the water sanctified
in the church by the prayer of the priest[3].' In the
East similar language is employed by St Cyril of
Jerusalem, who says that plain water obtains sanctity
by the invocation[4]. St Basil mentions the blessing
of water and chrism among the things which rest
on an unwritten tradition. The custom of blessing
the water made its way into all the rites. The
Apostolic Constitutions[5] contain a form of consecration
of a simple character: first, God is blessed for His
work in the incarnation and in redemption; then the
prayer proceeds to ask God to sanctify the water, that
he that is baptized may be crucified with Christ, die
with Him, be buried with Him, and may rise with
Him to the adoption which is in Him, by dying to
sin and living to righteousness. In all other rites the
main feature is a petition that God may send His
Holy Spirit upon the water; very commonly mention
is made of the expulsion of all evil influences from

---

[1] *de Bapt.* 4, igitur omnes aquae de pristina originis praero-
gatiua sacramentum sanctificationis consequuntur inuocato deo.
superuenit enim statin spiritus de caelis et aquis superest sancti-
ficans eas de semetipso, et ita sanctificatae uim sanctificandi
combibunt. [2] *Ep.* LXX. 1.

[3] Concil. Carth. VII. in Routh, *Rell. Sacr.* III. p. 120.

[4] *Cat.* III. 3. [5] *Const. Ap.* VII. 43.

the water, and of the results of baptism on the recipient. Various ceremonies accompany the prayer of consecration. The most general are, breathing upon the water, signing it, and pouring in chrism in the figure of a cross.

The blessing of the water is not mentioned in *The Testament of Our Lord*; it is implied in the *Canons of Hippolytus* and expressed in the *Egyptian* and *Ethiopic Church Orders*. A form of consecration is interpolated in the *Ethiopic Statutes*[1].

In the later Roman rite the consecration is cast in the form of a eucharistic prayer; in the course of the prayer, the 'Words of Institution' of baptism—'Go teach all nations, baptizing them in the name of the Father, and of the Son, and of the Holy Ghost'—are recited and the Holy Spirit is invoked. At the invocation of the Holy Spirit the Pope breathes on the water and the two dignitaries who attend him plunge their tapers into it. Finally chrism is poured into the water in the form of a cross and the water is stirred.

The dipping of the candles in the water is interesting, as it is analogous to the pagan rite of consecrating lustral water by dipping a torch taken from the altar in it. There is adduced in the note some ancient evidence of the pagan practice[2].

---

[1] Maclean, *The Ancient Church Orders*, p. 98.

[2] Eurip., *Hercules Furens*, 928; Aristophan., *Pax*, 884; Athen., *Deipn.* IX. 76, 409; Hesych., δαλίον· δαλόν, ἐν ταῖς ἱεροποιίαις εἰώθασι τὸν δαλὸν ἐμβάλλειν εἰς τὴν χέρνιβα καὶ περιρραίνειν τὸν βωμόν; *Notae Menardi in Librum Sacramentorum S. Gregorii*, 306 in the third vol. of the Benedictine ed. of the works of St Gregory.

The Gallican forms in the *Missale Gothicum*, the *Missale Gallicanum Vetus*, and the *Sacramentary of Bobbio* have come down to us in a somewhat disordered state[1]. The general form appears to have been a *Praefatio* (in Gallican rites, an address or invitatory) followed by a collect, an exorcism of the water, and a eucharistic prayer, with the usual ceremonies[2].

The Oriental rites in general display much similarity in the consecration of the font. The reason of this likeness is a common connexion with the Syrian form, which they have copied in their developement and elaboration. The following is the general form[3]:

1. Prayer of the priest for himself (Apologia).
   [In the Syrian rite this is at the beginning before the consignation and renunciation.]
2. Recital of the works of God.
3. Prayer that the water may be hallowed.
4. Exorcism of water with insufflation.

[1] Mabillon, *de Liturgia Gallicana*, reproduced in Migne, *P.L.* vol. LXXII.

[2] The *Missale Gothicum* xxxv. has some interesting language on the work of the Angel in the consecration, *e.g.* in the Collect, 'descendat super aquas has Angelus benedictionis tuae,' and in the *Contestatio*, ' ...qui Bethsaidas aquas, Angelo medicante, procuras .. Angelum pietatis tuae his sacris fontibus adesse digneris...desuper infunde Spiritum tuum, sanctum Paraclitum, Angelum ueritatis.' The last phrase appears to fix the reference to the Holy Spirit. The language (but not the thought) is somewhat reminiscent of Tertullian. Cf. *de Bapt.* 4, medicatis quodammodo aquis per angeli interuentum; 6, in aqua emundati sub angelo spiritu sancto praeparamur. For the liturgical office of the Angel cf. the Roman Canon of the Mass, 'per manus sancti angeli tui.'

[3] Dom Puniet in *D.A.C.L.* s.v. 'Bénédictions de l'eau.'

5. Consecration of water and effects of consecration.
   [Here the Syrian inserts an invocation of the Holy
   Spirit.]
6. Prayer for those to be baptized.
7. Signing of the water with chrism.   Alleluia[1].
   [The Greek and Armenian rites use oil.]

The Egyptian prayers for the consecration of the
water have borrowed the above form, but both in the
Coptic and Ethiopic rites[2] they have prefaced it by
other orders of consecration so that by accumula-
tion there are two, and in the Ethiopic three, sets
of prayers of a similar nature and function.   As
these prayers have already been analysed and discussed in connexion with the Egyptian rites, there
is no need to dwell further upon them here.

In the use of the ceremony of breathing two
meanings of the symbolic action are to be distinguished, which may be termed 'insufflation' and
'exsufflation' respectively.   'Insufflation' of the
water is used only in the Roman rite, and it sym-
bolizes the descent of the Holy Spirit into the water;
in other rites 'exsufflation' is used to express the
expulsion of malign spiritual influences.   With the
Roman 'insufflation' may be compared the use of
the same action in the Coptic rite of confirmation,

---

[1] This last ceremony is alluded to by the Areopagite; *de Eccles.
Hierarch.* II. 2, 7, καὶ τὸ ὕδωρ ταῖς ἱεραῖς ἐπικλήσεσι καθαγιάσας
καὶ τρίσι τοῦ παναγεστάτου μύρου σταυροειδέσι χύσεσι τελειώσας
αὐτὸ καὶ ταῖς τοῦ μύρου πανιέροις ἐπιβολαῖς ἰσαρίθμως τὸ ἱερὸν
τῆς τῶν θεολήπτων προφητῶν ἐπιπνοίας μελῴδημα συνεπι-
φθεγξάμενος κ.τ.λ.   The *Scholia* of St Maximus and the *Para-
phrase* of Pachymer refer the last clause to Ps. xxix and the *Alleluia.*

[2] *Rit. Or.* I. pp. 205, 218, 227.

and in the *Bobbio Missal*[1] in admission to the catechumenate; in either case with the words *accipe
Spiritum sanctum*[2]. On the other hand 'exsufflation' is used in the Roman rite at the beginning
of the catechumenate, with the same significance as
in other rites, as a ceremony of exorcism.

In all parts of the Church infant baptism has
long been the custom, and baptism is not, as is
presupposed by the early books and by many features
of later practice, a long and composite series of rites,
but a single action. In the West this has led to
compression, omission, and some adaptation. This
is also the case in the Byzantine rite. But in Syria
and Egypt the process has been carried much further
and the rites are re-arranged on the model of the
eucharistic Liturgy. Particularly is this the case
with the rites of the Coptic Jacobites and Syrian
Maronites[3]. In these cases the blessing of the water
occupies the position of the *Anaphora*.

On the effects of the consecration of the water
strong views were held in some parts of the Eastern
Church. St Cyril of Alexandria says that 'through
the operation of the Spirit, the sensible water is trans-
elemented to a kind of Divine, inexpressible power[4].'

---

[1] Mabillon's *Sacramentarium Gallicanum*, p. 323.

[2] *Rit. Or.* I. p. 209; Mabillon, *Musaeum Italicum*, vol. I. pt 2,
p. 323. In both 'insufflation' and 'exsufflation' the symbolism of
the action is derived from the double sense of πνεῦμα, *spiritus*,
i.e. breath and *spirit*. The breathing signifies the conveyance or
expulsion of spiritual influence.

[3] *Rit. Or.* I. 191 f., 329 f.

[4] *in Ioann.* II. 1 (Aubert, p. 147); the word used is ἀναστοι-
χειοῦται with a variant μεταστοιχειοῦται. Cf. Suicer, s.v.

In some quarters this teaching was developed extravagantly, for in one or two books we find expressions that directly teach a change of nature in the water, in prayers for the de-consecration of the water. The rite of the Coptic Jacobites has such a prayer[1], in which occur the words : 'We pray and beseech thee, O thou who art good and a lover of men, that thou wouldest change this water to its former nature....' A rubric follows: 'Here the priest shall put a little plain water in the font'—which is very like an ablution in the Liturgy. In the Nestorian rite a similar prayer is found, an addition, as it appears, made between the seventh and twelfth centuries[2]. It runs thus: 'This water was sanctified by the Amen, so may it by the same Amen be loosed from its sanctification and return to its former nature.' In both these cases the water is regarded not merely as hallowed and separated from all other water by consecration and sacred purpose, but as in itself undergoing a change.

In the preceding pages we have seen what an important part is played by the use of oil and chrism throughout the rites, in the admission to the catechumenate, in the consecration of the water, and, above all, in confirmation. A few words must now be said upon the consecration of the oil and chrism for these purposes.

μεταστοιχειόω, and Pusey, *The Doctrine of the Real Presence*, p. 207. For the Antiochene view cf. Theodoret, *Quaest. in Gen.* II. 26, οὐκ ἐπειδὴ φύσιν ἑτέραν ἔχει τοῦ βαπτίσματος ὕδωρ.

[1] *Rit. Or.* I. 208.

[2] Diettrich, *Die nestorianische Taufliturgie*, p. xviii.

In early times when baptisms were usually performed at Easter, it would be natural that the oil and chrism should be prepared shortly before that festival that they might be ready for use when occasion required.   And it is in accordance with what we should have expected that we find in most parts of the Church that the sacred oils are consecrated on Maundy Thursday.   That this custom, however, did not become a fixed rule at an early date is shewn by a canon of the First Council of Toledo[1], allowing a bishop to consecrate chrism at any time.   But in later times it became the practice to confine the consecration, at least as far as the chrism was concerned, to Maundy Thursday.   At Rome both oil and chrism are consecrated on that day.   In Byzantine, Egyptian, and Syrian[2] regions the chrism is hallowed on Maundy Thursday, the oils being blessed by the priest in the service at which they are used.   It is not known what day was assigned for this purpose in Gallican countries, but Mgr Duchesne suggests Palm Sunday, from the order of the exposition of baptism in St Germanus of Paris; with this idea the title of the Sunday, *dies unctionis*, well accords[3].   The separation of the consecration of chrism from that of the oils was due to the fact that the former was reserved to bishops or

[1] First Council of Toledo, can. 20, and the collection of Martin of Braga, can. 51 (Mansi, IX. 856).

[2] At least in the Maronite and Nestorian rites; in the Monophysite the oil is consecrated on Maundy Thursday by the bishop.

Christian Worship, Eng. trans. p. 320; St Germanus of Paris, *Ep.* II. (Migne, *P.L.* LXXII. 95).

even higher dignitaries, while the latter was a simple blessing which presbyters could perform. Accordingly the consecration of chrism became a separate service performed once a year, at which chrism was hallowed for the year ensuing and distributed as occasion demanded. The minister of the consecration of the chrism is the bishop. The above mentioned Council of Toledo censures those presbyters who presumed to make chrism for themselves. We do, indeed, find that in the troublous times of Hunneric the African presbyters consecrated chrism; but John the Deacon[1], our authority for the fact, asserts that it was done with the consent of the bishops, and alleges that it was justified by necessity, as all the Catholic bishops had been exiled by the Arian Hunneric. But this is an isolated exception. St Leo[2] laments among other mournful consequences of the murder of Proterius, bishop of Alexandria, at Easter 457 A.D., this in particular, that the hallowing of the chrism had failed; clearly it was not supposed that, the bishop being dead, there was any other means of securing a consecration of chrism. Even in Gallican countries, where presbyters were allowed to confirm, the consecration of chrism was confined to the bishops[3]. In the East the consecration of chrism has long been reserved to the patriarchs or, in default of them, the metropolitans. The patriarch

---

[1] Ioh. Diac., *Ep.* in Mabillon's *Mus. Italic.* vol. I. pt 2, p. 73.

[2] *Ep.* CLVI. 5.

[3] Council of Vaison, can. 3. Cf. Benedict. XIV, *De Syn. Dioec.* VII. 8.

of Alexandria consecrates not only for Egypt, but
also for Ethiopia. Similar customs prevail in regard
to the other patriarchates[1]. In the West, however,
any bishop might and must consecrate chrism for
the use of his diocese, and from him the priests
must obtain it. The Western practice is older than
the Eastern, as appears from the statements of early
Eastern writers; but the West did not follow the
East, perhaps because the hierarchical system of
patriarchs and metropolitans was less elaborately
developed, and as there was but one patriarch in
the West, the bishop of Rome, it was not practicable
to limit consecration of chrism to him.

At Rome, the blessings of the oils took place at
the mass on Maundy Thursday after the Pope had
communicated and before the communion of clergy
and people[2]. The Pope took from the archdeacon
the *ampulla* containing fragrant oil, breathed thrice
on it, and recited over it a eucharistic prayer in a
loud voice. Then he breathed on the *ampulla* containing pure oil, and a prayer, not eucharistic, was
said over it in a low voice. After this the mass
proceeded.

In the Coptic and Syriac rites the consecration
of chrism is of enormous length, being cast in the
form of a eucharistic Liturgy, and furnished with a
framework of lessons and prayers, so that its structure
is in all respects parallel to its model.

The Greek form, on the other hand, is admirably

[1] Denzinger, *Rit. Or.* i. p. 54.
[2] Einsiedeln MS. in Duchesne, *C.W.* Eng. trans. p. 482.

short, consisting of one prayer only, said in the liturgy of Thursday in Holy Week, after the inter-cessions[1] which are made at the close of the *Ana-phora* and after the consecration.

The wording of the prayers used in the con-secration of oil and chrism will be considered in connexion with the theological aspects of the rites. The prayers are occupied principally with the effects of the use of the chrism, but the essential and central feature is a petition for the descent of the Holy Spirit ; this may be termed the 'form' of the rite. The types of unction in the Old Testament are frequently alluded to. In the case of the oil there is not so much uniformity ; the hallowing is spoken of as effected by the operation of the Holy Spirit or, in still more general terms, supplication is made that certain effects may follow from its use.

Some Eastern writers, starting from the invoca-tion of the Holy Spirit in the consecration, have asserted a 'Real Presence' of the Third Person of the Trinity in the chrism. So St Cyril of Jerusalem says : 'But see that thou do not suppose that unguent to be mere unguent. For as the bread of the Eucharist, after the invocation of the Holy Spirit, is no longer mere bread, but the Body of Christ ; so also this holy unguent is no longer mere unguent, nor, as one might say, common, after invo-cation, but is a gracious gift of Christ, and, by the presence of the Holy Spirit, is made able to produce

---

[1] Brightman, *Liturgies Eastern and Western*, p. 390. The con-secration follows the blessing καὶ ἔσται τὰ ἐλέη.

the effect of His divinity[1].' Such was also the teaching
of the Armenian Vartanus ; others went further and
maintained a figurative Presence of Christ in the
Eucharist, a Real Presence of the Holy Spirit in the
chrism[2]. In fact there is discernible a tendency
to exaggerate the importance of chrism, so as to
make other sacraments dependent on it and therefore
inferior to it, on the ground that baptism, confirmation, ordination, and the consecration of altars
were all performed by, or at least with the use of,
chrism. This tendency is seen in the pseudo-
Dionysius[3] and in the sermon or exposition in the
Jacobite Syrian rite[4] of consecration.

This chapter may be concluded by a few remarks
about the composition of the chrism and the distinction in the uses of oil and chrism. The oil for
use in these rites is olive oil (*oleum oliuae*, ἔλαιον)
and the use of any other oil is esteemed irregular[5].
To form chrism, various substances are added to the
oil. At Rome the Pope poured balsam into it. In
the East, the pseudo-Dionysius says that the chrism
'is a collection of fragrant materials[6].' In the
fully developed Eastern rites the chrism is prepared
with great elaboration of composition. The Greek
Euchologion orders that olive oil, to which are added

[1] Cyr. Hier., *Cat. myst.* III. 3; Pusey, *Real Presence*, pp. 91, 92,
386 ff.
[2] Denzinger, *Rit. Or.* I. p. 58.
[3] Dion. Areop., *de Eccl. Hier.* IV. 3. 10 f.
[4] Denzinger, *op. cit.* II. p. 543.
[5] Denzinger, *op. cit.* I. p. 51 f.
[6] *de Eccl. Hier.* IV. 3, 4.

no less than thirty-six different substances, shall be boiled with wine, on which the oil rests to prevent it from burning. The Egyptian Monophysites also prepare the chrism in a complicated manner[1]. The Syrians, like the Romans, mix balsam with the oil.

The usual distinction in the use of these oils is that simple oil is employed for unctions before baptism and chrism for confirmation and for the consecration of the font, ordination, dedication of altars and churches, and other similar purposes. Exceptions are, that in the older form of the Armenian rite the chrism is not used in baptism and confirmation, but oil alone, and that the Greeks pour oil, not chrism, into the font during the consecration[2].

---

[1] Denzinger, *op. cit.* I. p. 51 f.

[2] The sources of this chapter are the forms of consecration of the water in the various rites; for the consecration of chrism, see the mass of Maundy Thursday in the *Gregorian* and *Gelasian Sacramentaries*, the Roman *Ordines* and Duchesne, *op. cit.* pp. 305—308; Denzinger, *op. cit.* I. pp. 51 f., 248 f., 361 f., II. pp. 526 f.; Dion. Areop., *de Eccl. Hier.* IV., particularly IV. 2; *Eucholog. Graec.* ἀκολουθία τοῦ ἁγίου μύρου.

CHAPTER II

THE AGE OF BAPTISM AND CONFIRMATION

It has for many centuries been the custom in the Church for infants to be baptized shortly after their birth. In the early ages naturally, as now in the mission field, the candidates for baptism were commonly converts from Judaism or heathenism, and were therefore adults. But as the progress of Christianity produced Christian families, infant baptism grew up immediately, or at least very rapidly and at an early date; when, finally, Christianity became the religion of the Empire, baptism of adults became a rare event and quite exceptional. The stages of the evolution from adult to infant baptism will be discussed in this chapter.

What was the practice of the Apostolic period cannot now be determined for lack of evidence. Presumptions are urged which shew that infant baptism was likely or unlikely, but the presumptions derived from the writings of the period are so faint and evenly balanced that it is difficult to establish even a probable conclusion[1]. It seems better, therefore, to proceed to the later practice.

The full discussion of the subject belongs properly to N.T. studies; the matter is dealt with at length in Hastings' *D.B.* s.v. 'Baptism.'

Dealing first with the age of baptism, we find early evidence of the reception into the Church of infants, or at least very young children. In the middle of the second century St Polycarp, pressed by the proconsul to swear by Caesar and revile Christ, replied : ' Eighty-six years have I been serving Him and He hath done me no wrong ; then how can I blaspheme my King who saved me ?[1]' This answer implies that he had been baptized at an early age, if not in infancy. Again St Justin Martyr, writing about the same time, speaks of those who from child-hood had been disciples of Christ[2]. By the end of the second century clear testimony to the baptism of infants is furnished by Tertullian, who by his objection to the practice proves that the thing objected to really existed. ' Why,' he asks, ' does the age of innocence hasten to the remission of sins?[3]' He wishes baptism delayed, not only in their case, but also in the case of others, whom he there-upon mentions—the unmarried in particular. The danger of sin after baptism was so great that it should not be incurred, since, as was then commonly taught, grave post-baptismal sin could only once be forgiven[4]. The fear of falling into grave sin after baptism was a powerful motive for delay, as we shall see later. St Irenaeus is also a witness to the practice

[1] *Ep. de Mart. S. Polyc.* c. 9.
[2] Justin, *Apol.* I. 15, οἳ ἐκ παίδων ἐμαθητεύθησαν τῷ Χριστῷ.
[3] *de Bapt.* 18.
[4] Dr Swete, *Penitential Discipline in the First Three Centuries* in *J.Th.St.* IV. (1903), 321.

of baptizing infants[1]. St Cyprian, Tertullian's disciple
and admirer, likewise furnishes evidence of the practice, but takes a different view from his master ; he
justifies it on the ground of original sin, and holds
that there was no necessity to postpone baptism till
the eighth day, as was then usual on the analogy
of circumcision, but that infants should be baptized
within two or three days of birth[2]. We have testimony to the practice also in Origen[3], in certain works
written at Caesarea[4].

Infant baptism is familiar to the writers of the
Church Orders, being mentioned in the *Canons of
Hippolytus*, the *Egyptian Church Order*[5], the
Testament of Our Lord[6], and the *Apostolic Consti-
tutions*[7].

Caution should be used in drawing conclusions from
the use of the word 'infants,' since the word may be
applied to adults, as being 'new born babes' in Christ.
This is certainly the case in several passages where the
persons addressed as 'infants' or children are instructed
in a manner that clearly shews them to be adults; in
other places it is stated that adults are 'infants' in virtue
of their baptism[8].

---

[1] Iren., II. c. xxiii. 4.

[2] Cypr., *Ep.* LXIV. 2, 5.

[3] *Hom.* VIII. *in Lev.* 3, *Hom.* XIV. *in Luc. Evang.*, *Ep. ad Rom.*
lib. v. 9 (Lommatzsch).

[4] For Alexandria, Clement, *Paed.* III. 289 (Potter) is frequently
quoted, but the word used ($\pi\alpha\iota\delta\iota\omega\nu$) does not necessarily mean
infants; cf. I. 127.

[5] *Texte u. Unter.* VI. 4 (1891), p. 94.

[6] II. 8.   [7] VI. 15.

[8] *Peregr. Ether.* in Duchesne's *Chr. Worship* (Eng. trans.),
p. 512; Zeno Veron., *Tract.* II. 43 and 45; Tert., *de Cor.* 3, *adv.*

Infant baptism was, therefore, well established at an early period in the history of the Church. Nevertheless, it did not at once become general, and up to the fifth century, and perhaps later, a great number of candidates for baptism were adults. Several causes retarded the growth of infant baptism. One reason was the late growth of the doctrine of original sin, in the East especially ; it was felt that infancy did not need baptism. Others thought that though infant baptism was right, yet, except in danger of death, the age of consciousness ought to be awaited. This latter is the view of St Gregory of Nazianzus[1], who held that the third year was a suitable age, since the child could then listen to the words of the rite and make the proper answers, receiving an impression, though not, of course, understanding perfectly. Another cause was that which was referred to in speaking of Tertullian, the belief that grave post-baptismal sin could not be remitted, or could be but once remitted. This motive must have been weakened in the course of the third century as the penitential discipline developed. Yet even when it was definitely determined that the Church had power to forgive all sins, before and after baptism, the system of penance was so onerous and humiliating that many shrank from the danger of incurring the discipline. Another cause for delay

Marc. I. 14; *Can. Hipp.* 144 in Duchesne, *op. cit.* p. 534; Clem. Alex., *Paed.* Lib. I. cap. v. 104 f. (Potter), to which may be added *Paed.* III. 289 quoted above.

[1] *Or.* XL. 28.

was a disinclination to enter upon the Christian life with its stricter duties and standards. From these last two causes principally, a practice grew up of deferring baptism till the latest possible moment. Accordingly, many were baptized on their deathbed by affusion, as it was called in antithesis to immersion ; this was termed ‘clinic’ *i.e.* sick-bed baptism. The authorities of the Church discouraged the practice, and if any man who had received ‘clinic’ baptism recovered, he was held to be disqualified for promotion to the priesthood[1]. The most famous example of the delay of baptism is the emperor Constantine, of whom Eusebius[2] writes : ‘When he realized that life was drawing to a close, he thought that this was the time for purging away all the faults that he had ever committed, trusting to wash from his soul by the power of mystic words and by the saving laver, all the offences that it had befallen him, a weak mortal, to commit.’ It must have occurred occasionally that a sudden death prevented baptism ; this happened to the younger Valentinian, for whom St Ambrose expresses the charitable hope that his intention to receive baptism might be taken for the deed[3].

The view of baptism and of Christianity which this postponement evinced was indeed low and debased ; it could not be justified by reason and it was

---

[1] Concil. Neocaesar. can. 12; see Routh, *Rell. Sacr.* iii. 66, iv. 200, and the notes of Beveridge and Justellus, *ib.* pp. 236—239.

[2] *de Vita Constant.* iv. 61.

[3] *de obitu Valent. consol.* 51—53.

condemned by its results. Grave as have been the
faults of baptized Christians, they cannot be put in
the same category as the patent folly and deliberate
cynicism of reserving the prime of life for paganism
and postponing the Christian life to old age and
a future existence.

We must next consider the age at which confirmation was bestowed. To deal first with the East,
the practice of the Greeks and Orientals is, and
always has been, as far as we can see, the same.
Confirmation has always followed immediately upon
baptism and the rites of initiation are concluded
by the first communion. In early days the bishop
took the leading part in baptism and 'sealed' the
neophytes. But with the progress of Christianity
conversions ceased because there were no heathen
remaining, and the practice of delaying baptism was
suppressed; none therefore but infant candidates
for baptism remained. With the spread of infant
baptism the restriction of baptism to Easter and
other solemn seasons fell into disuse, since the babes
were initiated at all times of the year, soon after
their birth[1]. But it was not possible for the bishop
to officiate in such cases; therefore the work was
delegated to the presbyters. In the East, the further
question whether a presbyter could confirm does not
appear to have been raised. The affirmative was

---

[1] Cypr., *Ep.* LXIV. 2, where the time of baptism is discussed
with one who said 'intra secundum uel tertium diem quam nati
sunt, constitutos [infantes] baptizari non oportere, et considerandam
esse legem circumcisionis antiquae.'

tacitly assumed; accordingly the whole service was relegated to presbyters and the unity of the rites of initiation was sedulously maintained. The consecration of the chrism, however, was strictly reserved to the bishop. The long series of exorcisms, instructions, baptism, confirmation, and communion, was compressed into a single rite, which could be performed at any time. The instructions were omitted as unnecessary for infants; the rest remained, and the child-candidate passed through all the stages from the entry into the catechumenate to the communion of a full Christian in the course of a single rite, with which the bishop had nothing to do, save that he alone might hallow the chrism. The Eastern practice is therefore quite simple. Infant baptism supervened, as in the West, but, in the absence of any doubt about the competence of presbyters to 'seal' or confirm, the whole of the rites of initiation was delegated without trouble or confusion.

In the West the course of events was far different. Infant baptism became there also the established custom by an inevitable developement, which was greatly furthered by the issue of the Pelagian controversy, and, in particular, by the gloomy views which were held by great theologians[1] on the future of unbaptized infants. But the question of confirmation and communion met with very varied treatment; the practice seems to have been different, not only in different places at the same time, but in

---

[1] *e.g.* St Augustine. Cf. *contra Iulian. Pelag.* v. 11. 44; *de Anima et eius orig.* III. 9. 12; 13. 19; *Sermo* CCXCIV.

the same place at different times.   The Greek custom
of presbyteral confirmation had a wide vogue.
St Augustine[1] relates how a woman took her child,
which was still an infant[2], to the presbyters ; 'it was
baptized, sanctified, anointed, received the imposition
of the hand.'   It appears from this that the presbyters
bestowed confirmation on the child.   Such also was
the use in Gaul up to the Carolingian era, from
which time Roman ideas largely prevailed and presbyteral confirmation died out; in Spain, it is clear
from the *Liber ordinum* that the practice lasted still
longer.   Nay, even in Italy, if we may judge from
the canonical enactments of the fifth and sixth
centuries, the practice was only with difficulty suppressed.   Of course, the cessation of presbyteral
confirmation does not necessarily carry with it the
cessation of infant confirmation.   We have, indeed,
a good deal of evidence that, even where confirmation
was reserved to bishops, it was, nevertheless, imparted
to infants[3] along with baptism.   But it was impossible
that bishops should continue to confirm infants,
except those who were baptized at Easter and
Whitsuntide.   The Church became more and more
closely connected with the State and, in consequence,
many bishops were deeply involved in secular affairs.
And, even had not this been so, the administration
of the large dioceses of the West made it impossible

[1] *Sermo* cccxxiv.

[2] 'filium catechumenum infantem lactentem.'

[3] *Notae Menardi in Librum Sacram. S. Greg.* 328.   In these
cases only the baptisms at solemn seasons can have been contemplated.

that bishops should attend the baptisms of more than
a portion of their flocks. To meet this difficulty
baptism and confirmation were separated. The
practice was of ancient standing in the West; from
the third century it had been sporadically in use.
For Rome we have the evidence of the work *de Rebaptismate*[1]. The Luciferian disputant in St Jerome
asserts the practice to be universal[2]. St Gregory
speaks of the Sicilian bishops going round to confirm[3]. But it was not so in Gaul[4]: there until the
introduction of Roman discipline in the Carolingian
era the usage was that of the East in this as in many
other matters.

The state of affairs in the West was confused,
and in two respects it offended the Roman sense of
order and authority. First, because there was an
unregulated diversity of practice, and secondly,
because an important sphere of action, the reception
of new members into the Church by the rites of
initiation, was withdrawn from the head of the
diocese. Accordingly the Roman bishops, from
Innocent the First[5] onwards, set their faces against
confirmation by presbyters, and fought energetically
for the privilege and prerogative of the episcopal

[1] Printed among the works of St Cyprian, see §§ 4, 5.

[2] Jerome, *Dial c. Lucifer*. 8.

[3] *Epp.* Lib. XIII. 18.   In Lib. X. 45 he assumes that a bishop of
Clusium in Etruria would confirm those who had been baptized.

[4] For Spain cf. Council of Elvira, can. 77; Ildephonsus, *de
Cognit. Bapt.* CVIII., CXXXI.

[5] See the letter of Innocent to Decentius, bishop of Eugubium,
Ep. XXV.

order. Their efforts were finally successful, and the result was the familiar Western mediaeval practice of bringing children to be confirmed, whenever a bishop visited the district. This was often scandalously rare, and it happened that confirmation was not infrequently performed by some passing prelate, officiating on horseback in the road. The general provision was made, that, if a bishop were available, children should be confirmed within their third year. Thus, though the two rites were separated, yet confirmation was administered at a very early age. The practice of instructing candidates for confirmation dates from the period of the Reformation[1].

In connexion with the separation of baptism and confirmation should be mentioned the custom of giving communion to those who had been baptized but not yet confirmed. The practice seems to have been prevalent in the Carolingian era, as it is taken as a matter of course by several divines of that period[2]. The custom became common, and at the present day in the Roman communion it is usual to make the first communion before confirmation. In England Archbishop Peckham[3] recognizes the existence of the usage, when he tries to check the neglect of confirmation, ordering that no one shall communicate who is not confirmed, unless he is at the point of death or can show reasonable cause for not

---

[1] Hall, *Confirmation*, p. 104.

[2] *e.g.* Alcuin, *Ep.* xc.; Raban. Maur., *de Cleric. Instit.* I. 29 (Migne, *P.L.* cvii. 313).

[3] Lyndewood, *Prov.* I. tit. 6, cap. 5.

having been confirmed. This provision was taken into the Sarum Manual[1] and passed thence into the Anglican Prayer Book, with the effect that in the English Church confirmation is practically always prior to the first communion.

The use of sponsors in baptism is of early date. In the time of Tertullian it was an established practice, and thenceforward it is frequently mentioned. In the case of adults the sponsors guaranteed the candidate's character, instructed him, accompanied him at the rite, and formed links of union between the new member and the Church. In the case of children the duty of making the answers at baptism devolved upon the sponsors, and their responsibilities were naturally much heavier than when they acted for adults. In ancient times one sponsor for each person was considered sufficient, but in the middle ages frequently several people stood god-parents to a child. St Augustine mentions that parents were usually sponsors for their children ; in the time of Charles the Great a synod at Mainz forbade the custom[2]. From the filial relation which subsisted between sponsors and those for whom they stood a theory of spiritual relationships was built up. Justinian first made the restriction a part of legislation ; the scope of the prohibitions was enlarged by the Trullan Council, and by the canonists spiritual relationships were treated similarly to the rest of the relationships acting as impediments to

---

[1] Maskell, *Mon. Rit.* I. 35.
[2] Augustine, *Ep.* xcviii.; Mansi, xiv. 75, can. 55 (813 A.D.).

marriage, and were extended even to the catechist and other ministers. Thus a wide field was provided for the activities of canon lawyers and for dispensations, until the Council of Trent limited considerably the extent to which these relationships[1] acted as a bar to marriage.

[1] For the question of sponsors cf. *Dict. of Christ. Ant.* s.v. 'Affinity,' 'Sponsors'; Stone, *Holy Baptism*, p. 103.

CHAPTER III

THE MINISTER OF BAPTISM AND CONFIRMATION

In dealing with the age of confirmation and the separation of baptism and confirmation we have touched upon several points relating to the minister of these rites. But it is convenient to treat the question of the minister with more fulness, and to trace the process by which the existing differences in practice were reached.

In the New Testament the function of baptizing is not confined to any particular class of Christians. In the Acts of the Apostles[1], Philip, one of the Seven, baptizes; again[2], apparently Ananias baptizes Saul. At a later date St Paul dissociates himself from the ministry of baptism[3]. In regard to the imposition of the hands, this action is twice in the Acts employed by Apostles to confer the Hóly Spirit after baptism[4]. The case of Ananias and Saul is ambiguous, and admits of two interpretations, according as we consider the Holy Spirit to have been given before or after

---

[1] viii. 38.   [2] ix. 18.   [3] 1 Cor. i. 17.
[4] viii. 17, xix. 6.   Dr Chase, *Confirmation in the Apostolic Age*, p. 35, adds 2 Tim. i. 6.

baptism[1]. But the evidence is too slender to justify a positive conclusion[2] on the point whether the ministry of this act was confined to any one class or order of Christians.

We now proceed to deal with the later practice of the Church and the manner in which she applied to her circumstances the material of traditional usage and the New Testament writings. Two opposite tendencies are discernible in the developement of practice, a centripetal and a centrifugal; the first arising from a desire to make the bishop the centre of the Church's life, as a precaution against fissiparous movements : the second springing from the necessity of extending the range of the ministry of the sacraments, on account of the increase in the work of bishops and the danger that candidates might die before they could be made members of the Church and receive the remission of sins.

The former tendency is strongly expressed by St Ignatius of Antioch, who says that ' it is not lawful, apart from the bishop, to baptize, or to hold an *agape* ; but what he approves, this is also wellpleasing to God, that all that is done may be safe and secure[3].' This text is illustrated by the great rites as they were performed in the early ages every year. In them the whole action of initiation, from

[1] Dr Chase, *op. cit.* p. 30, thinks that it preceded baptism.

[2] Simon (Acts viii. 19) thought that the Apostles could both give the Holy Spirit and transmit their power; but he did not understand what he saw, and perhaps regarded the act as a piece of magic.

[3] *Smyrn.* 8.

the beginning of the catechumenate to the first communion at Easter, is divided among the ministers of the Church, so that nothing is done 'apart from the bishop,' though only a few acts are performed by him in person.   To take a few instances : in the *Didascalia*[1] the decision whether a candidate is to be accepted or no rests with the bishop.   Further, the whole action of the baptism is ascribed to the bishop, though the various parts of the rite were carried out by subordinate ministers.   The preliminary unction in the case of women was, if possible, performed by a deaconess ; otherwise by the officiant.   Baptism could be administered by a deacon or a presbyter, but never by a woman.   The final instruction after baptism was imparted by deacons and deaconesses to men and women respectively.   In the *Canons of Hippolytus*[2], similarly, the acceptance or rejection of a candidate rests with the bishop, who also exorcizes the candidates on Easter Eve, and early on Easter morning consecrates the oils of exorcism and thanksgiving.   The catechumen is anointed with the oil of exorcism by a presbyter ; another presbyter takes him by the hand and baptizes him.   The latter presbyter is said to be taking the part of a deacon, but it is not quite clear whether this refers to the act of baptism or merely to the preceding profession of faith.   After baptism a presbyter anoints the neophytes with the oil of thanksgiving which is now termed 'chrism,' signing the brow and mouth and

[1] *Die syr. Didaskalia* in *Texte u. Untersuch.* N.F. x. 2, p. 29.
[2] *Canons of Hippolytus*, 91—139.

breast, and anointing the whole body. Finally, the bishop lays his hand on him and signs him. In the pseudo-Dionysius the bishop accepts the candidate and, after making him a catechumen by imposition of the hand and signing, gives him to the presbyter to instruct. The main portion of the rite of baptism is, in this case, assigned to the bishop. He begins the prior unction, leaving the presbyters to complete it; he baptizes, and he seals the neophyte with chrism. The presbyters are mere assistants, and the deacons perform menial tasks, such as helping the candidate to undress and dress.

In the West early descriptions of baptism are furnished by the *de Mysteriis* of St Ambrose and the cognate work *de Sacramentis*[1]. The latter work distinguishes the various ministers fairly clearly. The *Effeta* or 'opening' of the organs of sense was performed by the bishop. The first unction was the work of a presbyter, assisted by a deacon. The bishop exorcized and blessed the water, and a presbyter with the help of the deacons baptized. The unction after baptism was the act of the bishop, who also began the *lotio pedum*, or 'foot-washing,' which was completed by presbyters, and signed the neophytes. At Rome the work was divided as follows. The admission to the catechumenate was assigned to a presbyter. At the scrutinies, except the last, the exorcisms were made by exorcists, and a presbyter prayed over the catechumens; at the last scrutiny on Easter Eve the candidates were exorcized by a

[1] Printed among the works of St Ambrose.

presbyter. The Pope himself consecrated the oil and chrism on Maundy Thursday. The *Effeta* and renunciations fell to a presbyter. The actual baptism was begun by the Pope and completed by the inferior clergy. The unction of the head after baptism was performed by a presbyter, and the signing of the forehead with chrism by the Pope ended the rite.

We see that the liturgical tradition of the early Church was that the rite of confirmation, whatever form that rite took, and of consecration of chrism, belonged to the bishop, and that presbyters or deacons might baptize, but only as assistants of the bishop in a rite over which he presided. It must now be enquired what variation from the liturgical tradition was allowed in early times, and how modern practice arose from different combinations and inter-pretations of the two traditions, that of the solemn rite, and that of the rite as performed at any time and place.

In the Eastern Church great hesitation has been shewn about allowing any below the rank of presbyter to baptize. There are, however, in early times a few examples contrary to the general practice. The best known is the story, related by Rufinus[1], of the baptisms performed in sport by St Athanasius when a child, and subsequently accepted as valid by Alexander, bishop of Alexandria. The story is of little worth as history, but its acceptance by Sozomen

---

[1] Rufin., *H.E.* I. 14, whence Socrat., *H.E.* I. 15, Sozom., *H.E.* II. 17; it is repeated by many other historians and biographers of St Athanasius.

and Socrates seems to shew that lay-baptism had not yet come to be regarded as absolutely impossible; in fact, the latter says that it was not an isolated example. St Cyril of Jerusalem alludes to 'bishops or priests or deacons[1]' as ministers of baptism. Nevertheless the feeling of the Greek Church was adverse to baptism by any but priests or bishops. Particularly important in this connexion is the rule laid down in the *Apostolic Constitutions*[2], that baptism is to be regarded as sacerdotal and therefore on a level with offering sacrifice or blessing; it is, therefore, stringently forbidden to all below the presbyterate. Doubtless this prohibition had considerable influence, though the book in which it is found was not accepted as authoritative by the Church. On the other hand the patriarch Nicephorus, at the beginning of the ninth century, promulgated two canons, declaring that laymen might baptize in certain cases[3]. But subsequent Greek writers acrimoniously attacked these canons; also the above quoted story of St Athanasius was contradicted or treated as an isolated exception[4]. It does not appear that the Greek Church made up its mind on the subject; and the doubt is increased by a lack of a clear distinction in Greek writers between regularity

---

[1] *Cat.* XVII. 35.   [2] III. 10 and 11.

[3] Bingham, *A Scholastical History of...Baptism by Laymen*, pt I. ch. ii. par. 1, and Cotelerius' notes on *Const. Ap.*, *loc. cit.* An anonymous Greek homily (inter opp. Chrysostomi, ed. Montfaucon, x. 842) says that deacons may baptize in the absence of the presbyter.

[4] Bingham, *op. cit.* pt I. ch. i. par. 10.

and validity. In the rest of the East the general practice is to forbid the ministry of baptism to all but priests[1].

What has been said about baptism by laymen applies still more strongly to baptism by women. The practice is very stringently prohibited in the *Apostolic Constitutions*[2]. Here also occasional exceptions are found in later times, as in Metrophanes Critopulus and Gabriel Severus, patriarch of Philadelphia[3].

With regard to the baptisms of heretics the Eastern practice shews a similar vacillation. Two early councils, at Iconium and Synnada, decided that rebaptism should take place. This was the line taken by the African Church, and it was followed by Firmilian and Basil of Caesarea. The Council of Nicaea ordered that the followers of Paul of Samosata should be rebaptized, but accepted the Novatians[4]. In the middle of the fifth century we find that the practice of the Constantinopolitan Church was to rebaptize the Eunomians, Montanists, and Sabellians, and to confirm the Arians, Macedonians, Sabbatians, Novatians, Apollinarians, and Quartodecimans. This practice received conciliar sanction in the Trullan Council, with the addition that the Nestorians and Monophysites were to be received on renunciation of their heresy and profession of orthodoxy[5].

[1] Denzinger, *Rit. Or*. Proleg. p. 21.
[2] III. 9.
[3] Bingham, *op. cit.* pt I. ch. ii. par. 1.
[4] Euseb., *H.E.* VII. vii. 4, Council of Nicaea, can. 19.
[5] On the '7th canon' of the council of Constantinople in 381

In the West baptism by laymen was always deemed valid. From Tertullian[1] downwards we have evidence of this. Baptism by women was not allowed by Tertullian, and was forbidden by the Gallican canons current under the title of 'The Fourth Council of Carthage[2].' The baptisms of heretics were a subject of controversy between the Roman Church[3] under Stephen and the African Church under Cyprian. The dispute was not formally decided, but the view that prevailed was that the baptisms of heretics were to be accepted, that is, if they possessed valid 'form' and 'matter.' The question whether an unbaptized person could baptize was answered in the negative by St Jerome[4], and left doubtful by St Augustine[5], who confessed himself unable to determine the matter. The final decision of the mediaeval Western theologians on the question of the minister was that, in case of necessity, baptism could be performed by any person, 'whether clerk, or layman, even excommunicate, believer, or unbeliever, or catholic, or heretic, man or woman, provided that the form and intention of the Church be preserved[6].'

A.D. and the 95th canon of the Trullan Council in 692 A.D. see Bright, *The Canons of the First Four General Councils*, p. 119, and Hefele, *History of the Church Councils*, II. 366, v. 236.

[1] *de Bapt.* 17.

[2] Tertull., *loc. cit.*; 'IV. concil. Carthag.' can. 100.

[3] The Alexandrine Church sided with the Roman.

[4] *Dial. adv. Lucifer.* 12.

[5] *de Bapt. contr. Donat.* VII. 53. 101 f.; *contr. Ep. Parmen.* II. 13. 30.

[6] *Rituale Rom., de ministro baptismi*; cf. the *Decretum*, pt III. *de Consecr. dist.* IV. c. xxiii., xxiv.; Thom. Aquin., *Summa Theol.* pt III. quaest. lxvii. art. 5.

Thus, while the Eastern Church was grudging and hesitant in extending the ministry of baptism, the Western Church, while of course regarding the priest as the ordinary minister, allowed and urged the greatest freedom in imminent peril of death. To this end diligent care was taken that midwives and other people likely to be present at births should be instructed in the right manner of baptizing.

Concerning the rite of confirmation, the practice of the Church has always confined it to bishops and presbyters, but within these limits great variety of usage has been current. In the East, as soon as the bishop ceased to be the principal minister in the reception of new members into the Church, the presbyters took over the whole rite, baptism and confirmation, with the sole limitation that the unction after baptism must be performed with chrism that had previously been consecrated by the bishop[1]. Such was also the custom in Gaul. But in Italy and Spain the practice of separating baptism and confirmation had long been current. This must have grown up from an idea that confirmation belonged specially to the bishop, which was a natural conclusion to draw from the liturgical use and from the earliest tradition—for the references in the New Testament seemed to favour that view. We find the idea expressed by several authorities in different parts of the West. St Cyprian states that the

---

[1] For Egypt cf. Ambrosiaster, *Comment. in Ep. ad Ephes.* IV. 11, apud Aegyptum presbyteri consignant, si praesens non sit episcopus.

baptized received the imposition of the hand from the prelates[1]. The Council of Elvira, in the beginning of the fourth century, orders that, if a deacon baptize, the person baptized shall be afterwards confirmed by the bishop[2]. Similar provision is made in the case of baptism by a layman[3]. This appears to shew that ordinarily presbyters confirmed, but that also, in many cases, baptism and confirmation were separated, particularly in parishes 'ruled' by a deacon. Jerome assigns confirmation to the bishop, but as a matter of orderliness and dignity, not as fundamentally necessary[4]. His language is interesting : 'Thence it comes that, without the chrism and command of the bishop, neither presbyter nor deacon has the right of baptizing.' It almost appears that in the mind of Jerome the administration of chrism could be allowed to deacons, provided that it was consecrated by a bishop, and provided that the imposition of the hand was reserved to the episcopate.

However this may be, soon after Jerome's work appeared, Pope Innocent I definitely regulated the practice of confirmation. Regarding the unction

---

[1] *Ep.* LXXIII. 9, quod nunc quoque apud nos geritur, ut qui in Ecclesia baptizantur, praepositis Ecclesiae offerantur et per nostram orationem et manus impositionem Spiritum sanctum consequantur et signaculo Dominico consummentur.

[2] Can. 77. *perficere* is the word used for 'to confirm.'

[3] Can. 38.

[4] *adv. Lucif.* 9. This work was composed at Antioch, about 379 A.D., and is, therefore, uncertain authority for the West ; though the practices described are certainly Western, and Tertullian is the source of much of the actual language.

of the brow as the essential element of confirmation, he laid down that 'presbyters, whether they baptize in the absence of the bishop or in his presence, may anoint the baptized with chrism, but only with chrism that has been consecrated by a bishop; they may not, however, sign the brow with that same oil, because that is the right of bishops, when they deliver the Holy Spirit, the Comforter[1].' This direction, which Innocent gave to Decentius, bishop of Eugubium, was of great importance, and the sentence which has been quoted is frequently embodied in later treatises on baptism. The same line was taken by Pope Gregory in the case of Sardinia[2]; but the usage there established was for presbyters to sign with chrism the brow of the baptized after the Gallican manner, and the Pope was forced to give it his sanction.

The Roman rule did not, as we have seen, make its way at once or without difficulty in the West. In the meantime considerable uncertainty of practice existed, as is shewn by the prescription of the Council of Orange[3], forbidding two chrismations, one at baptism and another at confirmation. It seems that there had arisen a duplication, presbyters following their custom and anointing at baptism, and bishops repeating the act at confirmation in accordance with the new discipline. Accordingly the council lays down that the unction with chrism shall be performed once only.

---

[1] Innocent, *Ep.* xxv. [2] *Ep.* iv. 9, 26.

[3] Can. 2.

The rule laid down by Innocent referred only to the signing with chrism; the imposition of the hand is not mentioned, but is probably included and implied in the words 'when they deliver the Holy Spirit.' The imposition of the hand came to take a very subordinate position, and was frequently, as now, reduced to an extension of the hands or omitted entirely. Where it was used, it preceded the signing with chrism, and was performed by the bishop. The imposition of the hand was usually, but not always, confined to bishops[1].

The Roman bishops pursued the policy of Innocent and Gregory with persistency. When the Church in the Carolingian empire was reformed under Roman influence, the Roman rule which limited confirmation to bishops, was carried out with greater vigour. Also the imposition of the hand takes a more prominent position in the treatises on baptism and confirmation than had previously been the case.

The Carolingian era was the period at which the mediaeval practice was formed in this as in many other matters. Henceforth it was the rule of the Western Church that confirmation should be reserved for the ministry of a bishop. Thus the usage of the Western Church was sharply divided from that of the Eastern; on the one side we have a single rite of which the priest only is minister; on the other two rites, separated by a considerable period, of the first of which a priest ordinarily, in necessity anyone,

---

[1] In Egypt the presbyters laid on the hand; cf. also *Liber ordinum*, col. 33, and Aug., *Serm.* cccxxiv.

could be the minister, and the second of which can be administered only by a bishop.

In reference to Western usage, it should be noticed that it is only the signing of the brow which appertained to the bishop; the unction of the top of the head was left to the presbyter[1]. The distinction was, doubtless, a compromise, by which the presbyter retained his ancient right of anointing, yet a special signing with chrism was formally reserved to the bishop. In a distant part of the world, in Syria, there is evidence of exactly the opposite practice. It has been mentioned, in an earlier chapter of this book[2], that in the *Didascalia* the only unction is that before baptism. The writer of the *Apostolic Constitutions* in his adaptation of this part of the *Didascalia* and its prescriptions for the baptism of women, says: 'The deacon shall anoint their brow only with holy oil and after him the deaconess shall anoint them.... But only in the imposition of the hand shall the bishop anoint her head[3].'

With regard to confirmations by schismatics and heretics, it was generally held that they were invalid. The discussion of this question is connected with the reconciliation of penitents which is considered in a subsequent chapter[4].

---

[1] *unctio in fronte* in distinction from *unctio in uertice*. In the *Egyptian Church Order* and some of its cognates there are also two unctions but without the distinction.

[2] pp. 12—14.

[3] III. 15. χρίειν is used of the deacon and bishop, ἀλείφειν of the deaconess.

[4] pp. 229—232.

CHAPTER IV

SUBMERSION, IMMERSION, AND AFFUSION[1]

THE older writers on Christian antiquities assumed
that baptism was normally performed by submersion
of the whole body ; such, for instance, is the view of
Bingham[2] and Wall[3]. And from a survey of the
literary evidence alone such would be a natural de-
duction. But in modern times we are compelled to
take a wider view than the merely literary. In all
subjects of ancient practice and custom a revolution
has been worked by the addition of archaeology to
our sources of information ; and by the employment
of archaeological testimony the interpretation of
literature has been changed. This is especially the
case with the subject of this chapter. The archaeological evidence all points to immersion, not submersion, as the method of baptism current in the
Church throughout the early period.

The fonts which have survived from the first six

---

[1] In this chapter, for the sake of clearness, *submersion* is used
for total immersion, including the head, *immersion* for an immersion
which does not imply that the whole body is at any one time under
water, and *affusion* for pouring water on the body or 'sprinkling.'

[2] *Christian Antiquities*, bk xi. ch. xi. sec. 4.

[3] *Infant Baptism*, pt ii. ch. ix.

centuries of the Christian era are all shallow in depth, usually between two and four feet. The deepest is that of St Sophia at Constantinople which reaches to four feet six inches; but few are over four feet. Baptism by submersion could be performed in such fonts only if the person baptized lay down. But in the majority of cases even this is impossible from the insufficient diameter of the basin, not to mention the absurd appearance of such an action. Moreover, such a manner of baptizing is unsupported in literature or pictorial representations, of which a considerable number have survived. The method of baptism in these fonts was analogous to the practice of the ancients in the baths, just as the fonts themselves were modelled on the baths. In the *frigidaria* of the Romans the water is of no great depth and the bathers stood in the bath, pouring water over themselves or letting it flow over them from a projecting spout. The baths at Pompeii are an instance; the cold bath was about three feet nine inches deep and thirteen feet eight inches in diameter. Such baths were called *baptisteria, piscinae,* λουτρά, titles which recall to our minds the Christian fonts[1]. Baths of this kind, or the smaller type used in private houses, served as models for fonts, or were converted into fonts at a later time.

In the light of the above evidence let us now consider some expressions in literature. The word used for baptism by Tertullian, *tinctio*, with its verb *tinguere*, is quite in accordance with the archaeology

[1] Plin., *Ep.* II. 17, v. 6.

of the subject, since the primary meaning of *tinguere* is to 'wet' or 'dip' part of an object. In Cyprian's epistles[1] there is a discussion about the validity of baptisms of the sick, who were said to be *perfusi* or *aspersi*, as opposed to *loti* of the regularly baptized. This might mean that there was a distinction between sprinkling and submersion in the writer's mind. But it is not necessary to suppose more than a comparison of a sprinkling on the one hand, and a baptism, involving a wetting of the whole body, on the other hand; in fact the distinction is not so much between affusion and submersion, as between a private baptism and one performed in public with all the accompanying formalities at a sacred season. For the use of *lotus* in this connexion the 'Passion of Perpetua' can be cited[2]; the spectators in the amphitheatre, seeing Saturus covered with blood from the bite of a leopard, cry out mockingly, *Saluum lotum, saluum lotum*, that is, 'well bathed,' bearing testimony, according to the writer, to his second baptism.

On the other hand, the comparison of baptism to burial, frequent in Christian writers from St Paul downwards[3], points to the method of submersion, and has been generally taken so by writers on the subject of baptismal customs. To us, to whom burial means the placing of the body in a deep grave and covering it with earth, the consideration appears conclusive. But regarding this simile in the light of ancient

---

[1] *Ep.* LXIX. 12 f.

[2] *Texts and Studies*, vol. I. cc. 18 and 21; Introd. p. 8.

[3] Rom. vi. 4; Col. ii. 12.

burial rites, we are compelled to admit that it is less conclusive than at first sight appears. In the case of burial in the earth the essential feature was the casting of earth on the corpse; this is the theme of the *Antigone*[1] of Sophocles, and Aelian[2] refers to the practice. In the circle of ideas such as these the casting of water on the candidate would appear to fulfil the essentials of the comparison to burial.

But burial in earth was not the only method practised in the early Church. The corpse, or the ashes, were frequently placed in a tomb above ground or in the catacombs; the descent into the font would resemble such a burial. St Cyril of Jerusalem says: 'You were led to the holy font of the divine baptism, as Christ from the cross to the appointed tomb[3].' But the rest of the passage is difficult to reconcile with anything but submersion. It runs: 'And you confessed the saving confession, and descended thrice into the water, and again ascended, there also symbolically representing the three days' burial of Christ. For as our Saviour spent three days and three nights in the belly of the earth, so also you in the first ascent imitated Christ's first day in the earth, and by the descent, the night. For as he who is in night no longer seeth, but he who is in day liveth in light, so also in the descent, as in night, you saw nothing, but, on the other hand, in the ascent, you were as in day.'

It would, therefore, appear that submersion was not

---

[1] vv. 246, 256.   [2] *Var. Hist.* Lib. v. c. 14.
[3] *Cat. myst.* II. 4.

the general practice of the early Church, but came to be thought the right mode at a later age when infant baptism was the prevalent custom. The Council of Chelsea orders submersion in the ninth century[1]. So also Walafrid Strabo, in the same century, implies that submersion was the correct method, but only possible, as fonts were then made, in the case of infants[2]. The schoolmen held that submersion was the safer way[3]. It was not, however, held to be necessary, and in actual practice affusion was accepted as perfectly valid, both in the East and in the West.

Why did submersion come to be regarded as the ideal method of baptizing? Probably the reason is etymological. When Latin, and to some extent Greek, ceased to be the popular speech, and were interpreted by grammarians rather than by living use, a tendency arose to give to the words βαπτίζειν, *baptizare*, *mergere*, etc., their full, original sense, and to regard them as implying and requiring submersion. But it has been seen that the evidence as a whole, including that of archaeology, does not support the etymological sense of the words, but rather justifies the action of the Church in considering the essence of baptism to be the ritual application of water, not literal submersion.

Out of this question arises a further point,

[1] Council of Chelsea, can. 11 (816 A.D.).

[2] *de Eccl. Reb.* XXVI.

[3] Thom. Aq., *Summa Theol.* pt III. quaest. lxvi. art 7. In the East submersion is ordered by the synod of Tvin (527 A.D.) for the Armenian Church. *D.A.C.L.* tom. 2, pt I. col. 297.

namely, the number of immersions, sometimes three, sometimes one being used. In general, it may be said, trine immersion was the practice of the Church. The Greeks lay particular emphasis on this, and the *Euchologion* cites, in support of the practice, among other authorities, the fiftieth of the Apostolic Canons and the 'seventh canon' of the Council of Constantinople[1]. The latter 'canon' condemned the baptisms of the Eunomians, who were extreme Arians, because they practised single immersion. At the present day, however, the Greeks accept baptisms performed with one immersion. We have in the *Didache*[2] still earlier evidence; 'pour water thrice upon the head in the name of Father, Son, and Holy Ghost,' is the method enjoined in that book.

In the West trine immersion was usual, except in Spain, where a single immersion was adopted to symbolize the unity of the Godhead in opposition to Arianism, though actually their practice agreed with that of the Eunomians mentioned above[3]. Although the Spanish custom had the support of Pope Gregory, it was vigorously attacked by Alcuin[4] who did not scruple to charge the Spaniards with forgery.

The *Canons of Hippolytus* preserve an ancient practice[5] of connecting the three parts of the creed

---

[1] On this so-called canon see note on p. 193.

[2] Ch. vii.

[3] Fourth Council of Toledo, can. 6 (633 A.D.); Gregory the Great, *Ep.* I. 43; and the letter of Licinianus, *ib.* II. 54; Isidore of Seville, *de Viris Illustr.* XL.

[4] *Epp.* xc. cxiii.

[5] Tertull., *adv. Prax.* 26, alludes to it.

with three immersions, the baptismal formula being repeated at each immersion[1]. With this agree the *Testament of our Lord*[2] and several other Church Orders, except that the baptismal formula is not mentioned; the same phenomenon is found in the pseudo-Ambrosian *de Sacramentis*[3]. Later the triple interrogation in the actual baptism was prefixed to baptism, as we see in various rites, for example, the Roman, or merged in the profession of faith which followed the renunciation, as in the Syrian and Coptic rites.

A peculiarity of the Syrian rites is the splitting up of the baptismal formula by the insertion of *Amen* after the name of each Person of the Trinity. The Copts have a separate formula for each Person. The Armenians repeat the formula at each immersion[4].

[1] 124—133.   [2] II. 8.

[3] II. 7, 20.

[4] Denzinger, *Rit. Or.* I. p. 387. On the subject of this chapter see C. F. Rogers, *Baptism and Christian Archaeology* in *Studia Biblica et Ecclesiastica*, vol. v. pt iv.; on Jewish baptisms *J. Th. St.* XII. (1911), 437—445 and 609—612.

CHAPTER V

THEOLOGICAL ASPECTS OF THE RITES

WE now proceed to consider the theological ideas
expressed in the baptismal rites, and particularly
the benefits which were associated with the reception
of baptism. In spite of the great length of many of
the rites, we shall find that the conceptions of their
effect and nature are by no means so complicated as
we might have supposed. The various actions of
baptism and confirmation are accompanied by prayers,
built up mainly of a few scriptural phrases, which are
repeated again and again. It is commonly the case
with liturgies that the ideas contained are simple in
character and not numerous; difficulty and com-
plexity begin with the construction of a theology to
harmonize and explain the ideas. The most per-
plexing question is that of confirmation; the liturgies
do not speak with a harmonious voice on the subject,
and it is a matter of some labour and doubt to determine what is the exact effect of the rite which
follows baptism.

The institution of Christian baptism has always
been referred to the occasion recorded in the Gospel
according to St Matthew (xxviii. 19), on which our

Lord says : 'Go then and make disciples of all the nations, baptizing them in the name of the Father, and of the Son, and of the Holy Ghost.' In regard to this passage three questions arise : (*a*) Are the words 'baptizing them in the name of the Father and of the Son and of the Holy Ghost' genuine ? (*b*) What is their meaning ? (*c*) Do they prescribe a formula of baptism, or merely give a description of its nature ?

(*a*)　The words in question have been vigorously attacked, on the ground that they are an interpolation for dogmatic reasons, and did not attain an assured position in the text until after the Council of Nicaea ; on this view the words would merely be a reflection of a later developement of the formula, not evidence for an early occurrence of the formula. The attack evoked a vigorous defence, which has made it appear that critically there is no cause to doubt that the words are an authentic portion of the Gospel.

It is urged against the words that they were absent from the text used by Eusebius of Caesarea, and that the silence of the New Testament and of early Christian literature prior to Tertullian shews that they belong neither to the synoptic nor to the early ecclesiastical tradition. But the manuscripts and versions are unanimous in supporting the authenticity of the current text of the passage ; the treatment of the quotation in Eusebius is due to the special circumstances of his writings and finds parallels in other ancient writers, who certainly had the text as we have it[1]. Moreover the Trinitarian formula

[1] For the discussion of this matter see Mr F. C. Conybeare in

of baptism occurs earlier than Tertullian, in the *Didache* and Justin, as will be shewn later.

(b) The words 'in the name of the Father and of the Son and of the Holy Ghost' have received a twofold interpretation. On the one view, the Greek words are interpreted strictly in their literal sense; it is contended that we should translate rather than transliterate the word βαπτίζειν, and that we should render the word εἰς by 'into,' not 'in.' The meaning would then be 'to immerse into the name,' and the connotation that of incorporation into, and union with, the three divine Persons. In support of this significance St Paul's language in the Epistle to the Romans and elsewhere is cited[1]. According to the other view, we ought not to press the literal meaning of the words βαπτίζειν and εἰς, since the former had, in the language of the New Testament, lost its original sense, and acquired a new religious signification of 'ceremonially cleansing by water[2]'; in regard to the preposition, the frequent interchange of εἰς and ἐν, without any change of meaning, is well known[3] to students of the New Testament. Thus the words 'baptizing them in the name' would be a commission 'to invoke the Name and to bring

the *Hibbert Journal*, Oct. 1902; Professor Kirsopp Lake in the *Encyclopedia of Religion and Ethics*, vol. II. p. 380. On the other side, Dr Chase in *J.Th.St.* VI. (1905), 481, and VIII. (1907), 161.

[1] Rom. vi. 3 f.; Gal. iii. 26 f.; 1 Cor. x. 1.

[2] Cf. Mark vii. 4, βαπτισμοὺς ποτηρίων καὶ ξεστῶν καὶ χαλκίων, and in the same verse the variant reading βαπτίσωνται for ῥαντίσωνται; also Luke xi. 38.

[3] Blass, *Grammar of New Testament Greek*, E.T. § 39. 3, § 41. 1.

into play the power which accompanied the naming of the Name'; the person baptized confessed his faith in the Name, and the baptizer acted authoritatively in the Threefold Name. This view is supported by the use of 'in the name' and 'into the name' without any difference of meaning, and by the Syriac and Latin versions, which both shew 'in the name[1].'

(c) The third point arising out of the passage in St Matthew's Gospel is the formula of baptism. If we start at the other end and work backwards, we find that the baptismal formula in use in the Church in later times was always in the words of this passage, with the difference that the East used the passive, 'N. is baptized,' the West and Egypt the active, 'I baptize thee.' The use of the Threefold Name can be traced back to Tertullian[2], Justin Martyr[3], and the *Didache*[4]. If the last named work may be placed before 160 A.D., we bring back the practice to the middle of the second century. The sole earlier evidence is the passage in the Gospel; the threefold formula does not occur elsewhere in the New Testament. In the allusions to baptism in the Acts of the Apostles and the Epistles, the phrase 'in the name of Jesus Christ' in various forms[5] always occurs. These latter passages have caused much

---

[1] Tertullian, however, has 'in nomen'; but this is an individual eccentricity. For this view see Dr Armitage Robinson in *Encyclopedia Biblica*, I. 473, and *J.Th.St.* VII. (1906), 186.

[2] *adv. Prax.* 26. [3] 1 *Apol.* 61. [4] Ch. VII.

[5] εἰς τὸ ὄ. τοῦ κυρίου 'Ι., Acts viii. 16, xix. 5; ἐν τῷ ὀ. τοῦ κ. 'Ι. Χ., 1 Cor. vi. 11; ἐν τῷ ὀ. 'Ι. Χ., Acts ii. 38 (v.l. ἐπί), x. 48.

perplexity to theologians[1]. Without entering upon
the history of their interpretation, we may say that
they can be dealt with in two ways : either they
preserve the earliest formula which was soon displaced by the Trinitarian formula ; or they give
a description of the baptism, characterizing it as
Christian baptism, without stating the actual formula
used. Which of these two ways is right, is difficult
to say ; the matter must be left to theologians and
students of the New Testament. But in the liturgical
history of baptism there is but one form, namely, that
which employs the Threefold Name.

The following summary of the language used
about baptism in the New Testament does not profess to be an account of the doctrine of baptism, nor
is it claimed that the passages quoted are all definite
references to the rite ; the object is rather to give
the starting point of the ideas expressed in the
liturgies, and the models to which liturgical language
was conformed. For that purpose the following heads
will suffice :

(a) Cleansing from sin ; remission of sins[2].

(b) Union with Christ and His Church ; to the
former may be referred the interpretation of the act of
baptism as death, burial, and rising again with Christ,
to both the idea that Christians are members of Christ[3].

---

[1] See Ambros., *de Spir. Sanct.* I. 3, 42 (Migne, *P.L.* XVI. 713,
and the note of the editor which gives the various references to
the history of the patristic and scholastic exegesis of the subject).
Cf. Cyprian, *Ep.* LXXIII. 17.

[2] Acts ii. 38, xxii. 16 ; 1 Cor. vi. 11 ; Eph. v. 26 ; Heb. x. 22.

[3] Rom. vi. 3—11 ; Col. ii. 12 ; 1 Cor. xii. 12 f., 27.

(c) Sonship attained by putting on Christ in baptism[1].

(d) New birth or regeneration[2].

(e) Enlightenment[3].

(f) Salvation[4].

The relation of the Holy Spirit to baptism in the New Testament[5] is better deferred till we come to deal with confirmation.

In the Epistle to the Ephesians[6] we have possibly a fragment of a baptismal hymn; this however is conjectural.

All these ideas and the language in which Scripture conveys them are applied to baptism in the liturgies. We give a few instances.

In the *Canons of Hippolytus* the bishop prays at the imposition of the hand, saying: ‘We bless thee, Lord God Almighty, for that thou hast made these worthy to be born again, even these upon whom thou pourest thy Holy Spirit, so that they are now united to the body of the Church, never to be separated by alien works. Grant rather to them to whom thou hast already given remission of sins, also a pledge of thy kingdom, through Jesus Christ our Lord[7].’

In *Bishop Sarapion's Prayer Book*, the following petitions occur: ‘Form all that are being regenerated after thy divine and ineffable form, in order that

---

[1] Gal. iii. 26 f.

[2] Tit. iii. 5. Cf. 1 Pet. i. 23; Jn iii. 5; 1 Jn iii. 9; Jas. i. 18.

[3] Heb. vi. 4; cf. Suicer, *Thesaurus*, s.v. φώτισμα.

[4] [Mk] xvi. 16; Tit. iii. 5; 1 Pet. iii. 21.

[5] Acts ii. 38.   [6] v. 14.

[7] *Can. Hipp.* 137—8.

having been formed and regenerated they may be able to be saved and counted worthy of thy kingdom. And as thy only-begotten Word coming down upon the waters of the Jordan rendered them holy, so now also may he descend on these and make them holy and spiritual to the end that those who are being baptized may be no longer flesh and blood, but spiritual and able to worship thee the uncreated Father through Jesus Christ in Holy Spirit.' 'Count [this thy servant] worthy of the divine mystery and of thy ineffable regeneration.' 'Guide him to the regeneration with thy right hand : let thy only-begotten Word guide him to the washing : let his regeneration be honoured, let it not be empty of thy grace : let thy holy Word accompany him, let thy holy Spirit be with him scaring away and driving off every temptation.' 'Render him clean in the regeneration, make him to have fellowship with thy angelic powers, that he may be named no longer flesh but spiritual, by partaking of thy divine and profitable gift. May he be preserved up to the end to thee the Maker of the world[1].'

The prayers of the fully developed liturgies are too long to quote ; the following is a summary of the main ideas.

Roman Rite : Adoption. Regeneration. Renovation (*gentibus innouandis*[2]). Purification. Remission of sins.

---

[1] Translation by the late Bishop of Salisbury (S.P.C.K.).

[2] Tit. III. 5 (Vulgate), per lauacrum regenerationis et renouationis spiritus sancti.

Missale Gothicum: Remission of sins. Regeneration. Eternal life.

Missale Gallicanum Vetus: Regeneration. Remission of sins. Putting on of Christ.

The Greek *Euchologion:* Redemption. Incorruptibility. Sanctification. Remission of sins. Defence against diseases and evil spirits. Purification. Enlightenment. Regeneration. Renewal. Adoption. Life. Remaking (μεταποιηθῆναι) for the putting off of the old man and the putting on of the new. Imitation of Christ's death and resurrection.

These expressions, derived almost entirely from Scripture, are repeated in other rites, and cause no difficulty. Very different is the case of the relation of the gift of the Holy Spirit to baptism and confirmation respectively. To discuss the question is beyond the province of this chapter, and a short account of the different types of doctrine must suffice.

Two views have been taken in this controversy, one, that the Holy Spirit is given in confirmation, the other, that the Holy Spirit is given in baptism and that confirmation adds special graces of the Holy Spirit, for strength and support. For the arguments on both sides the reader is referred to the works in the notes[1].

In the New Testament the gift of the Holy Spirit is once expressly connected with baptism. 'Let each of you be baptized,' says St Peter, 'in the name of

---

[1] On the subject of confirmation and the grace conferred by it see *Church Quarterly Review*, xxxiv. (1892), 1 f., xlv. (1898), 357 f.; **Mason**, *The Relation of Confirmation to Baptism*; Wirgman, *The Doctrine of Confirmation*.

Jesus Christ, unto remission of sins, and you shall receive the gift of the Holy Spirit[1].' It is not stated whether the Spirit was received in baptism itself, or in some accompanying act, which would be included under the title of baptism, as being a part of the rite of initiation. The gift of the Spirit is associated with the laying on of hands twice in the Acts of the Apostles[2]; it may, however, be said that since the results of the laying on of the hand in these cases was followed by visible results—speaking with tongues and prophesying—it is different from confirmation in the later Church, which has no such results, and it is, therefore, rather charismatic than sacramental. In the Epistle to the Hebrews[3] the imposition of the hand is reckoned among the fundamentals of Christianity. More than this cannot be said without entering on to disputable ground[4].

There is no certain mention of unction in the New Testament, but certain passages which might be thus interpreted and would certainly refer to unction if we had other evidence to prove that it was in use, are of interest on account of their influence on liturgical language. Such are the employment of the words 'sealing' (σφραγίζειν) and 'chrism' (χρῖσμα, χρίειν) in connexion with the Holy Spirit[5]. In the absence of any

<hr>

[1] Acts ii. 38; cf. ix. 17, 18.

[2] viii. 17, xix. 6; 2 Tim. i. 6 is interpreted in this sense by Dr Chase in *Confirmation in the Apostolic Age*, pp. 35 f.

[3] vi. 2.

[4] For a discussion of all passages which may refer to confirmation in the New Testament see Dr Chase, *op. cit.*

[5] 2 Cor. i. 22, χρίσας...σφραγισάμενος...δοὺς τὸν ἀρραβῶνα; Eph. i. 13, 14, iv. 30; 1 Jn ii. 20, 27.

confirmatory evidence the texts cited cannot certainly be attributed to confirmation, and the references are given merely as originals of later prayers at confirmation.

In *Sarapion's Prayer Book* the prayer which comes 'after the acceptance[1],' contains the phrase, 'let thy Holy Spirit be with him scaring away and driving off every temptation.' As this mention of the indwelling Spirit follows an allusion to baptism, we look for a connexion of the Holy Spirit with confirmation. Turning then to the ' prayer in regard to the chrism with which those who have been baptized are being anointed,' we find that the baptized are anointed with chrism in the sign of the cross and become thereby 'partakers of the gift of the Holy Spirit.'

In the *Canons of Hippolytus* an imposition of the hand is connected with a prayer for those 'on whom thou pourest thy Holy Spirit that they may be united to the body of the Church,' that they may be granted 'a pledge of thy kingdom[2].'

The Roman books contain the prayer for the descent of the sevenfold Spirit, which is familiar to us from its use in the English Prayer Book in a form but slightly altered from the Latin. The Spanish writers also refer to the gift of the sevenfold Spirit and the *Liber ordinum* has a prayer of a similar tenor to, but in different language from the Roman.

In the Coptic rite the priest prays at the unction that God would 'bestow the Holy Spirit by the

---

[1] μετὰ τὴν ἀνάληψιν = συνταγήν, σύνταξιν (Wordsworth) ; but ἄλειψιν may be the correct reading (Brightman in *J.Th.St.* I. (1900), 252).

[2] For 'pledge' cf. 2 Cor. i. 22, v. 5, ἀρραβῶνα.

unction of holy chrism, that it may be a seal and
strength'; it is an 'unction of the grace of the Holy
Spirit, of a pledge of the kingdom of heaven, of
participation in eternal life and immortality,' 'the
perfecting of the grace of the Holy Spirit and the
shield of faith and righteousness.' A shorter Coptic
rite[1], which, though without authority and not in
actual use, still may express ideas current in Egypt
at the time of its composition, agrees with the longer
rite, and, in the prayer at the imposition of hands,
speaks definitely of a sending of the Holy Spirit,
referring to the descent of the Holy Spirit on our
Lord at His baptism and connecting the two actions,
baptism and the imposition of hands, with our Lord's
language about birth 'of water and the Spirit.'

In all these quotations the gift of the Holy Spirit
is clearly connected with the rite that follows baptism.
Let us now consider a number of prayers where the
teaching is less clear and unmistakable.

In the Greek *Euchologion* the words used at the
signing with chrism are, 'The seal of the gift of
the Holy Spirit[2].' With these should be connected
another passage in the same rite, where, in consecrating the water, the priest prays for the candidate
'that being planted together in the likeness of thy
death through baptism, he may be a sharer of thy
resurrection; and guarding the gift of the Spirit and
increasing the deposit of grace he may receive the
prize of the high calling and may be numbered with

---

[1] Denzinger, *Rit. Or.* i. p. 233.
[2] σφραγὶς δωρεᾶς πνεύματος ἁγίου.

the first-born which are written in heaven.' There
is not in this prayer any implication that the gift of
the Spirit is received in baptism; rather a description
is furnished of the ensuing rites and their effects, so
that the phrase 'gift of the Spirit' alludes to the
formula of confirmation, 'the seal of the gift of the
holy Spirit.'

In the Armenian rite, on the other hand, the gift
of the Holy Spirit is clearly associated with baptism.
The prayer for catechumens entreats that the candidate may 'receive in due time the Holy Spirit in
the baptism of regeneration.' Also the baptismal
formula runs : 'N. is baptized in the name of the
Father and of the Son and of the Holy Ghost. Redeemed by the blood of Christ from the slavery of
sins, he wins the liberty of the adoption of sons of
the heavenly Father, that he may be co-heir with
Christ and a temple of the Holy Spirit.' This might
mean that he becomes a temple for a subsequent
indwelling of the Holy Spirit; but the former prayer
is against this and we must conclude that the rite
speaks of the Holy Spirit as given in baptism. The
signing with chrism contains no mention of the Holy
Spirit; it is called a 'seal' and associated with a
multitude of spiritual gifts and blessings.

The other Eastern rites are very confused in their
teaching of the bestowal of the Holy Spirit. The
Jacobite rite has a prayer at the unction before
baptism that those who are to be baptized may receive
the Holy Spirit. The consecration of the water is
for 'renewal of the Holy Spirit'; a still stronger

expression occurs in the same prayer, when supplication is made 'that thy Holy Spirit may dwell upon
these thy servants who are baptized,' and God is
asked to 'perfect them,' and this by the 'holy
laver.' Here we have the indwelling of the Spirit
and the word 'perfect,' which means 'confirm,' attributed to baptism. The final rite is described as
signing with 'holy chrism, the seal of true faith, the
fulness of the gift of the Holy Spirit.' Similarly in
the Maronite rite the indwelling of the Holy Spirit is
very definitely asserted to be an effect of baptism.
In the Nestorian rite the grace of the Holy Spirit is
ascribed to 'the mysteries of spiritual baptism.'

Turning to a very different part of the world, the
countries where the Gallican rite prevailed, we find a
number of liturgical books in which the Holy Spirit
is very sparingly mentioned in this connexion. In
the Sacramentary which is called the *Missale Gothicum* the form of consecration of the font contains
a petition 'that those who descend into this font, in
the name of the Father, and of the Son, and of the
Holy Ghost, may obtain pardon of sins, and also
infusion of the Holy Ghost.' Whether this 'infusion
of the Holy Spirit' belongs to baptism or the subsequent chrismation is not clear; the prayer attached
to the latter is mutilated, and therefore does not
help us. The *Missale Gallicanum Vetus* has, at the
'infusion of chrism,' the Roman prayer for the unction
of the head by the presbyter. The same Sacramentary, in the *immolatio*, or 'preface' of Maundy
Thursday, has a prayer over the chrism, to the effect

'that when we anoint thee a new family, a breath
of heavenly grace may be wafted, coming upon them
by the co-operation of the Holy Spirit, that they also,
truly thy Christs and thy sons, may be made ever
co-heirs of this name by the illapse of the Holy
Spirit.' This seems to make it clear that the gift
of the Holy Spirit is referred to the chrism, but it
is curious that the confirmation prayer does not
express the thought.

The rites which have been examined do not, as a
whole, give a definite testimony about the moment
when the Holy Spirit was supposed to be given. The
Roman, Greek, and Egyptian rites connect it with
confirmation ; so also probably the Western rites
generally. But the Eastern rites seem to contain
no clear idea when or whereby the Holy Spirit is
bestowed. Many attribute it to baptism ; one even
to the first unction. They may be said indeed to
regard the Holy Spirit as operative throughout the
rite, as dwelling in the oil and water and chrism,
which were consecrated by His operation and power,
and thereby acting continuously upon the candidate.
This haziness of thought is increased by the complete
absence of any idea of separating confirmation from
baptism. What we regard as two rites, they consider
only as one rite, so that what has happened is not
so much a transference of the effects of one rite to
another, as a shifting of moments within a single
rite. But we may suspect that in Syrian countries
this confusion was of long standing and took its
origin from a period when there was nothing

corresponding exactly to confirmation. It has been
shewn[1] that the *Didascalia,* along with many other
Syrian works, witnesses to a tradition of baptism
without any following rite but with an unction preceding the actual baptism. In the *Apostolic Constitutions* also we have an example of the high value
attributed to the first unction; it is 'a type of
spiritual baptism,' it 'stands for the Holy Ghost,' it
is 'for the remission of sins and the first preparation
for baptism[2].' The *Apostolic Constitutions* do, indeed, possess an unction after baptism and set such
a high estimate on it that without it baptism is
considered absolutely inefficacious[3]. Yet the idea
associated with this latter unction is very vague; the
prayer accompanying it asks that 'the sweet odour
of Thy Anointed[4] may continue upon him [the can-
didate] firm and fixed; and that, now he has died
with Him, he may arise and live with Him.' The
effect of the latter unction is that it completes or
'perfects' the rite of initiation and gives it validity;
it is, in fact, the 'seal' of the rite. Now whatever
may be the origin of the works on which the *Apostolic
Constitutions* are based, we know that the compilation
was made in Syria. May we not see, both in the
Apostolic Constitutions and in the liturgical tradition,
a similar uncertainty about the effects of the two
unctions in baptism and the moment when the Holy
Spirit is given? If we adopt this view, we are able
to divide our liturgical authorities into two classes.

[1] pp. 11 f.   [2] III. 15, 16, 17, VII. 42, 44.
[3] VII. 44.   [4] τοῦ Χριστοῦ σου.

In the one, which comprises the Roman, Greek, Gallican, and Egyptian rites, the gift of the Holy Spirit is connected with the post-baptismal unction. In the other which consists of the Syrian rites[1] (with the Armenian) the bestowal of the Holy Spirit is associated with baptism or the prior unction rather than with the sealing with chrism.

The signing with chrism in confirmation is frequently called the 'seal' and 'perfection,' because by it the rite of initiation is made 'perfect' and complete and, so to speak, 'sealed.' Illumination and salvation are also attributed to it. Before the unction in the Armenian rite the priest prays to God : 'Sanctify [the neophyte] with thy truth and the light of the graces of thy Holy Spirit, that he may be a temple and dwelling place of thy divinity, and may be able boldly to stand before the altar of thy Only-begotten, our Lord Jesus Christ.'

Confirmation has, in modern times, often been considered as a species of ordination to the priesthood which the whole body of the Christian Church possesses. This idea is not without patristic authority ; St Ambrose[2] says that by the unction of confirmation 'we are anointed to the kingdom of

---

[1] A further piece of evidence is the form for the consecration of chrism, given at the end of the second volume of Denzinger's *Rit. Or.* But it speaks with an uncertain voice ; sometimes it appears to connect the gift of the Holy Spirit with chrism, but in the enumeration of the effects of the chrism in the actual prayer of consecration all mention of the Holy Spirit is omitted, and this omission is significant.

[2] *de Myst.* vi. 30 ; cf. Jerome, *contra Lucifer.* 4, sacerdotium laici id est baptisma.

God and the priesthood.' And in the ancient rites
the chrism with which the priests under the old
Covenant were anointed is often alluded to in connexion with the unction after baptism, and the Old
Testament is cited for types of unction to kingship
and priesthood[1].

'Confirmation,' the Western name for the rite,
is not found until the fifth century. Pope Leo
the First uses the word in a letter to Nicetas of
Aquileia[2]; it is also found in several homilies which
recent scholars have attributed to Faustus of Riez,
who flourished in the same century as Pope Leo[3].
Probably the origin of the term is to be sought in
the Latin version of 2 Cor. i. 21[4], but the growth of
its use coincides with a tendency to speak of the
rite as conferring strength and increase of grace
(*robur et augmentum gratiae*), and to abandon the
older language by which confirmation was associated
with the gift of the Holy Spirit. The corresponding
Greek words are βεβαίωσις and στερέωσις; but the
first occurs only in the *Apostolic Constitutions*[5], and
the second is late and possibly a translation of the
Latin word. The ordinary Greek word is σφραγίς;
other terms are χρῖσμα and μύρον. Before *confirmatio*
came into use the Latins employed the terms

---

[1] Tertull., *de Bapt.* 7; *Const. Apost.* III. 15.

[2] *Ep.* CLIX. 7.

[3] Mason, *op. cit.* pp. 191, 192.

[4] qui autem confirmat nos uobiscum in Christum et qui unxit
nos Deus. Cf. Ambrose, *de Myst.* VII. 42, signauit te Deus Pater,
confirmauit te Christus Dominus.

[5] III. 17; cf. VII. 44, βεβαίαν.

signaculum, *chrisma*[1], and *perfectio*. The corresponding verbs were also used. In the Eastern rites 'seal' and 'perfection' were favourite terms; among the Nestorians the latter word is employed in the formula which accompanies the signing after baptism. For the imposition of the hand *manus impositio* and *manum imponere* are used; the word *manus* is always in the singular.

The unction which precedes baptism is most commonly regarded as a defence against all evil influences, fleshly or spiritual, in preparation for baptism. It is a purification and preparation of the candidate for participation in the great rites which are to follow. We have seen how high a value is placed on it by the author of the *Apostolic Constitutions*, and in the rite of the Syrian Jacobites. The latter has a prayer before this unction, which runs[2]: 'Holy Father, who through the hands of thy holy Apostles didst give the Holy Spirit to those who were baptized: now also, using the shadow of my hands, send thy Holy Spirit upon those who are to be baptized, that filled with him and his divine gifts, they may bear thee fruit, thirtyfold, sixtyfold, and a hundredfold....*N.* is signed with the oil of gladness, against all working of the adversary, that he may be grafted into the good olive-tree in the holy, catholic, and apostolic Church, in the name of the Father, and of the Son, and of the Holy Ghost, unto life for ever and ever. Amen.' Probably this prayer, which is used in all the Jacobite rites, comes down from a time when there was no rite after baptism, and is the original prayer which was used at the anointing immediately before baptism.

[1] Either feminine or neuter with the genitives *chrismae*, *chrismatis*.

[2] Denzinger, I. 273. For the association of the gift of the Holy Spirit with unction before baptism cf. Theodoret, *in Cant.* I. 2.

Whether confirmation is a sacrament was much disputed between Protestant and Roman divines at the Reformation period. The decision of the point depends upon the definition of the word 'sacrament'; for our purpose it is enough to observe that it was so termed in the Church from early times. Baptism and confirmation are called *utrumque sacramentum* in Cyprian[1] and at the council held at Carthage in the year 256 A.D.[2] Here, as elsewhere, the Africans formed the terminology of ecclesiastical Latin. In later times the scholastic enumerations of the sacraments include confirmation[3]. Similarly in the East, from the pseudo-Dionysius downwards, chrism is reckoned among the mysteries[4].

It was at all times held by the Church that the sacraments of baptism and confirmation cannot be repeated, if validly performed. Of course, if the rites were not validly administered, their valid performance is not a repetition but merely a fresh beginning. Furthermore, an invalid baptism annuls an otherwise valid confirmation. But what constitutes a valid rite? We have, in a previous chapter spoken of the various opinions held in regard to the

---

[1] *Ep.* LXXII. 1.

[2] Routh, *Rell. Sacr.* III. 117.

[3] Rabanus Maurus, *de Cleric. Instit.* I. xxiv.; Greg. Bergam., *de Euch.* XIII. xiv. (Hurter, *SS. Patrum, Opusc. Select.* vol. XXXIX.); Peter Lombard, *Sentent.* IV. dist. ii. 1; Thom. Aq., *Summa,* III. quaest. lxv.; and the Council of Trent, Sess. VII. can. 1, De sacram.

[4] So Gabriel Severus in Simon's *Fides Eccl. Orient.* Paris 1671, p. 39; cf. Winer, *Confessions of Christendom,* p. 240.

T. 15

minister. The proper matter of baptism is water; the form is, ' *N*. I baptize thee '—or ' The servant of God *N*. is baptized—in the name of the Father, and of the Son, and of the Holy Ghost,' the former being Western and Egyptian, the latter Eastern. The Greek Church lays great emphasis upon threefold immersion ; but, as it does not now, at any rate, re-baptize those who have received baptism by single immersion or affusion, it may be said that it considers baptism by affusion to be irregular, but not absolutely invalid. With regard to confirmation the greatest difficulty exists in determining either the form or the matter, since there is no consistent tradition on which to rest. It is quite clear from a study of the rites that the form of words was different in each of the great liturgical areas. Two acts can claim to be regarded as the matter, unction and imposition of the hand. The latter action has the clear evidence of the New Testament[1] to support it; for the former definite testimony begins at a later period. The ecclesiastical writers do not enable us to draw a certain conclusion. In the East unction alone is known. The few exceptions hardly affect the universality of the statement. Firmilian, bishop of Caesarea in Cappadocia, writing to Cyprian[2], uses the words *manus impositio*. The *Apostolic Constitutions* speak of a χειροθεσία whereby the Holy Spirit is given[3]; but the word appears to be due to the

---

[1] For the evidence see the passages quoted pp. 1, 215.

[2] Cypr., *Ep.* LXXV. 8.

[3] II. 32; cf. III. 15, VII. 44.

compiler, except in one case ; nor is it certain that
it means anything more than unction. In later Greek
authors allusions to the laying on of hands occur,
but usually in connexion with one of the passages
in Scripture where the action is mentioned ; hence
they may be regarded as archaisms, due to accom-
modation to the matter of the exegesis. The extant
liturgies are in accord with the patristic evidence.
In all Eastern rites the matter of confirmation is
unction. In the Nestorian and Egyptian rites a
laying on of the hand occurs, but only as a blessing.
The sole exception is a curious composition of Egyptian origin, in which confirmation is performed by
an imposition of the hand alone, without any unction;
this rite, however, is without any authority and is not
used[1].

The Western Fathers speak in this matter with
an uncertain voice, and attribute the gift of the Holy
Spirit to either action, or both. The latter tendency
is especially noticeable among the Carolingian divines,
who were perhaps conscious of the strong support
that either could claim, on the one hand from Scripture, on the other from tradition, and who desired
to maintain both as a measure of caution. The
Roman liturgical books have an imposition of the
hand accompanying the prayer for the descent of the
sevenfold Spirit, followed by a signing with chrism.
The former action had, however, an insecure position
and tended to disappear. It was first reduced to an
extension of the hands over the candidates, and then

[1] Denzinger, *Rit. Or.* I. p. 233.

dropped[1] entirely. In a similar way the imposition
of the hand received little attention, either in the
theological discussions of the schoolmen, or in the
legislation of the Western Church[2]. Eugenius the
Fourth, following Innocent the Third, distinctly
states that unction takes the place of imposition of
the hand. The emphasis laid on chrismation may,
to some degree, have originated from the Gallican
custom, for in the Gallican books there is no imposition of the hand, but unction only ; in fact, in some
books there is merely a 'pouring on' of chrism, so
that there appears to be no contact, and therefore
no common feature between confirmation as thus
performed and an imposition of the hand[3].

It is clear that the differences in practice are
great, and we cannot say that the Church has a prescribed rite of confirmation. It would indeed appear
that she took over from older custom two actions
signifying dedication or consecration, and that of the
two unction with chrism (generally with the sign of the
cross) had a firmer place. But both actions appear
in Tertullian[4], the imposition of the hand being there
associated with the gift of the Holy Spirit. Both

[1] In the Sarum rite unction alone is used (Maskell, *Mon. Rit.
Eccl. Angl.* 2nd ed. vol. I. p. 39).

[2] Pet. Lomb., *Sentent.* IV. dist. vii. ; Thom. Aq., *Summa Theol.*
pt III. quaest. lxxii. art. 2 ; Duns Scotus, *in libr. sentent.* Lib. IV.
dist. vii. quaest. 1 ; Eugen. IV., *Decret. ad Armen.* in Mansi, *Sacr.
Concil. Collect.* XXXI. 1055.

[3] *Missale Gothicum,* chrisma eum tangis; *Missale Gallicanum
Vetus,* infusio chrismae; *Sacramentarium Gallicanum,* suffundis
chrisma in fronte eius.

[4] *de Bapt.* 7, 8.

actions are found in use among the Gnostics[1] in connexion with baptism, and it is possible that they found both already firmly established; if this is so, the dual practice belongs to an early stage in the history of the Church, if not to the earliest. It is surprising that the difference of custom excited so little interest; where it is mentioned, it is glossed over in a very unconvincing manner[2].

The reconciliation of heretics stands in close connexion with the rites of baptism and confirmation. In early times we find two methods of receiving heretics into the Church. At Rome and Alexandria, and also in Palestine, the custom was to put them to penance, and then to admit them by laying on the hand (*manum imponere in paenitentiam*). In the rest of the East they were treated as heathen, and baptized and confirmed afresh; this was also the custom in Africa, at least from the time of Agrippinus[3], bishop of Carthage. The difference in the method of dealing with heretics led to a controversy between Cyprian of Carthage and Stephen of Rome[4]. The Roman bishop maintained the traditional practice of his see, namely, to reconcile heretics by imposition of the hand after penance had been done.

---

[1] Clement of Alexandria, *Excerpt. ex Theodot.* 22; Iren., *adv. Haeres.* I. 14. 2, 3 (Harvey).

[2] Innocent III., *Regest.* VII. 3 (Migne, *P.L.* CCXV. 285); Symeon Thessal., *Dial.* cap. 70 (Migne, *P.G.* CLV. 237).

[3] Cypr., *Ep.* LXXI. 4.

[4] Cyprian's *Epp.* LXIX.—LXXV., and the anonymous tract *de Rebaptismate* in the appendix to the works of Cyprian, furnish the material for the history of the controversy.

The African bishop allowed this practice in the case of those who, baptized in the Church, had gone over to the heretics, and afterwards, recognizing their fault, had returned. But he protested energetically against the application of the same method to those who had begun their life as Christians in an heretical sect. He attacked the practice on the ground that it was illogical and inadequate to lay the hand on heretics without baptizing them also. Cyprian's argument is based on the assumption that such a laying on of the hand implied a *first* imparting of the Holy Spirit and so was equivalent to the laying on of the hand after baptism. It seemed, therefore, to him that the Roman Church was supplying confirmation to the converted heretic, when she ought to have supplied baptism also.

The arguments of Cyprian were strongly supported by Firmilian, bishop of Caesarea in Cappadocia. Nevertheless the Roman bishop stood firm. In support of Stephen's position the tract *de Rebaptismate* was drawn up, the author of which attempts to furnish a theological basis for the practice of reconciling heretics merely by imposition of the hand. Thus he distinguishes water-baptism from the baptism of the Spirit, and maintains that each is valid, in its own sphere, without the other. In the case of heretics baptism avails because of the Invocation of the Name of Jesus Christ, and only needs to be supplemented by the baptism of the Spirit, which is given by the laying on of the hand. Here again, as in Cyprian, the laying on of the hand in the reconciliation of heretics seems to be identified with the rite which followed baptism. The Roman practice of recognizing heretical baptism eventually prevailed, but it appears to have been so far modified by the controversy that the imposition of the hand on those baptized and confirmed in an heretical sect was considered to confer on them the Holy Spirit[1]. The African Church finally accepted the Roman practice at the Council of Carthage in 348 A.D. (canon 1). It may be added that where confirmation was performed by signing with chrism, the method of reconciling heretics took the same form[2].

In the East a good deal of confusion still remained in the treatment of converted heretics. Different customs were in use in adjacent districts[3]. A new system grew up, probably in the Church of Constantinople, according to which each several heresy was treated on the basis of a careful consideration of its dogmatic position and liturgical practice. According to the result of this examination, the heretic was either baptized and confirmed, or merely confirmed, or simply required to abjure his heresy and make an orthodox profession. The method of treating the following sects is interesting. The Eunomians, Montanists, Sabellians, Manichees, and Gnostics were baptized and confirmed; they did not believe in a Trinity of Persons, or they employed extravagant

---

[1] Siricius, *Ep.* I. 1 (*P.L.* XIII. 1133); Innocent, *Ep.* XXIV. 4.

[2] First Council of Orange (441 A.D.), can. 1; Council of Epaon (517 A.D.), can. 16.

[3] Basil, *Epp.* CLXXXVIII. can. 1; CXCIX. can. 47.

and inadmissible rites. The Arians, Macedonians, and Novatians were sealed with chrism, according to the Greek rite of confirmation; the fault here was defective belief in the Holy Spirit. The Nestorians and Monophysites were accepted on abjuring their heresy and making an orthodox profession; hence it was admitted that they had valid orders and sacraments.

This system was built up in various stages, of which the first is the statement of fifth-century practice at Constantinople, known as the "seventh canon of the Second Oecumenical Council," and the last is the ninety-fifth canon of the Trullan Council[1]. Even in the West this practice had some currency, and was regarded as authoritative by Gregory the Great[2]. But it is probable that the earlier practice of confirming converted heretics sufficed for the simpler and fewer heresies of Western Christendom.

[1] Council of Constantinople (382 A.D.) in Hefele, *History of Christian Councils*, II. 366; Trullan Council (692 A.D.), *ib.* v. 235. Cf. Timothy of Constantinople in *P.G.* LXXXVI. 10–74.

[2] *Ep.* XI. 67. Cf. *Moral.* Praef. 17, where the language seems to imply the other custom of laying the hand on heretics to bestow the sevenfold Spirit.

THE EASTERN RITES.

TABLE I. *Early forms of the Syrian Rite.*

St Cyril of Jerusalem.	"St Dionysius the Areopagite." (*De eccl. hier.* II. 2.)	James of Edessa. (Denzinger, *Rit. Or.* I. 279.)
During Lent		Part I.
	Hymn.	
	Instruction.	
Enrolling of names.	Examination.	Prayer over catechumens.
Exorcism with insufflation.	Imposition of the hand and signing.	*Apologia sacerdotis*[1].
Instruction.		Prayer of incense.
	Enrolling of names.	Enrolling of names.
In the vestibule of baptistery.	Prayer.	Signing of brow.
Partial undressing.	Partial undressing.	Prayer and exorcism.
Renunciation.	Renunciation with insufflation.	Renunciation.
Profession of faith.	Profession of faith.	Profession of faith.
	Blessing and imposition of the hand.	Prayer of thanksgiving.
In the baptistery.		Part II. *In the baptistery.*
		Creed.
Complete undressing.	Complete undressing.	Prayer of unction.
Unction with oil.	Signing and unction with oil.	Signing with oil.
	Consecration of water. Threefold pouring in of chrism crosswise; threefold Alleluia.	Consecration of water. Insufflation; *conteratur caput draconis*; threefold pouring in of chrism crosswise.
Baptism. White robes.	Baptism. White robes.	Baptism.
Unction of brow, ears, nose, and breast with chrism.	Signing with chrism.	Signing with chrism; *et hoc signaculum in nomine tuo accipiant.*
		Thanksgiving.
Communion.	Communion.	Communion.

[1] That is a prayer of the priest for himself and his ministry.

TABLE II.   *The fully developed Syrian Rite.*
(Denz. *Rit. Or.* I. p. 280.)

PART I.   Introductory prayer.
              Psalm *Miserere* with "farced" matter.
          Prayer over catechumens.
              Psalm *Afferte Domino* with Alleluia.
              Bidding, *Prooemium*, and *Ordo*.
              Quqaya.
              Prayer of incense.
              Psalm.
              Lections (Rom. vi. 1—8.   John iii. 1—8).
          Apologia sacerdotis.
          Prayer of incense.
          Threefold signing of brow without oil.
          Undressing.
          Prayer and exorcism.
          Renunciation.
          Profession of faith and prayer of thanksgiving.

PART II. (in the baptistery).
          Creed.
              Pouring in of water into the font with a prayer.
          Prayer of unction (*Pater sancte*).
          Signing of brow with oil.
              Bidding, *Prooemium*, and *Ordo*.
              Quqaya.
              Prayer of incense.
          Consecration of water (see separate table).
          Unction of body with oil.
              Hymn.
          Baptism.
              Hymn.
          Prayer (*Hoc quoque signaculum*).
          Unction of body with chrism.   White robes.
          Thanksgiving.
              Crowning and girding.
          Communion.
              Hymn.   Final blessing.

TABLE III. *The derived Rites.*

Greek, *Rit. Arm.* p. 389.	Armenian, *ib.* p. 86.
ON THE EIGHTH DAY.	ON THE EIGHTH DAY
Signing of brow, breast, and mouth. **Prayer.**	**Prayer.**
ON THE FORTIETH DAY.	ON THE FORTIETH DAY.
Prayer.	**Prayer.** Prayer. **Prayer.**
OFFICE FOR MAKING A CATECHUMEN.	OFFICE OF CATECHUMENS.
Partial undressing. Insufflation, signing of brow, mouth, and breast. **Prayer.** Three exorcisms.	Imposition of the hand. Prayer.
	ON THE DAY OF BAPTISM.
Prayer. Insufflation, signing of brow, mouth, and breast. Exorcism. Complete undressing. Renunciation. Profession of faith. [Creed.] Prayer.	Prayer. Exorcism. Renunciation. Profession of faith. Creed.
OFFICE OF BAPTISM.	OFFICE OF BAPTISM.
Litany. **Apologia sacerdotis.** Consecration of water (see separate table). Consecration of oil. Signing and unction with oil. Baptism. **Thanksgiving.** Signing of brow, eyes, nose, mouth, and ears with chrism. Communion.	Consecration of oil. Psalm; lections; *litany.* Consecration of water. Pouring in of oil. *Alleluia.* Undressing. **Prayer.** Baptism. Two prayers (the second is Syrian). Unction of parts of the body with oil. Thanksgiving. Prayer. Communion. Thanksgiving. Prayer.

TABLE IV. *The consecration of water* (*DACL*. II. i. 697, s. v. 'Bénédictions de l'eau.')

The Syrian rite. (Denzinger, *Rit. Or.* i. p. 275.)	The Greek rite. (Conybeare, *Rit. Arm.* p. 399.)
1. *Domine Deus omnipotens, creator omnis creaturae.* 2. *Tu respice in has aquas.*	Replaced by a section from the Epiphany blessing of the waters Μέγας εἶ Κύριε; cf. *ib.* p. 418.
3. *Procul recedant ab eis.*	Φυγέτωσαν ἀπ᾽ αὐτοῦ.
4. Insufflation of the water.	Insufflation of the water.
5. *Conteratur, Domine, caput draconis.*	Συντριβήτωσαν.
6. *Sed tu Domine uniuersorum* with threefold signing.	Ἀλλὰ σὺ Δέσποτα τῶν ἁπάντων.
7. Invocation of the Holy Spirit. *Miserere nobis.*	
8. *Reuelare Domine.*	Ἐπιφάνηθι Κύριε.
9. *Alleluia* with threefold pouring in of chrism in the form of a cross.	Ἀλληλούια with threefold pouring in of oil in the form of a cross.

The Ethiopic rite. (*Rit. Or.* p. 227.)	The Coptic and Ethiopic rites. (*Ib.* pp. 205, 228.)
1. *Domine..factor omnium creaturarum.*	1. *Domine...qui caelum et terram...condidisti.*
2. *Aspice, Domine, super hanc...aquam.*	2. *Nunc etiam...respice...et ...hanc aquam...intuere.*
3. *Ut ab ea fugiant.*	6. *Da illi robur ut fiat aqua uiuifica.*
4. Already performed.	
5. *Et dissipentur coram signo crucis.*	5. *Concedeutnecineaexistat.* 3. *per sanctum nomen tuum.*
6. *Imo rogamus te.*	8. *ut omnes baptizandi in ea.*
7. Lacking.	9. *Alleluia* with threefold
8. *Appare Domine.*	pouring in of chrism in form of a cross.

Table I. displays the developement of the rite from the fourth to the seventh century. Table II. shews the method of fitting the rite, in the form which it had then acquired, into a liturgical framework. In Table III. the Greek and Armenian rites are set forth. The parts printed in clarendon type are derived, in the Greek from the Syrian, in the Armenian from the Greek; this, however, only applies to prayers; the connexions of the rites themselves can be seen by comparison of the Tables. Table IV. explains the relationships of forms for consecration of water; in the case of the Greek and Ethiopic the connexion is one of translation, but in the case of the fourth form, the Coptic, the connexion is one of general resemblance.

THE EGYPTIAN RITE.

(Denzinger, *Rit. Or.* i. pp. 192—232. Cf. Brightman, *Liturgies Eastern and Western*, pp. 144—244.)

The rite of baptism.

Prayer over the mother.
 Beginning of baptism.
Asking of names.
Prayer over oil of catechumens.
Unction with oil.
Asking of names.
Exorcism. Imposition of the hand.
Renunciation.
Profession. Short creed.
Signing with oil. **Ungo te oleo laetitiae.**
Imposition of the hand.
Exorcism. *En Dominator Domine.*
 Entry into baptistery.
Mixing of oil and water in the font.
Prayer. *Voca.*

The liturgical framework.

MASS OF THE CATECHUMENS.

THE LECTIONS.

Tit. ii. 11—iii. 7, 1 John v. 5—13, Acts viii. 26—39, John iii. 1—21, with the liturgical accompaniments of prayers, etc., as in the Liturgy.
 Prayer. Longanimis, multae misericordiae. Eight prayers (from the Anaphora) to which is added a special one for catechumens.

MASS OF THE FAITHFUL.

Prayer over baptistery. =
Prayer of imposition of the hand on the faithful.
Prayer of the priest i.e. apologia sacerdotis.

THE PRAYER OF THE VEIL.

THE PRAYERS.

Three prayers.

THE EGYPTIAN RITE—(*continued*).

THE CREED.

Pouring of oil into the font.
First consecration of the water.

THE KISS OF PEACE.

ANAPHORA.

[**Syrian consecration of the water.**]
Syrian consecration of the water.

Signing of water.   =   THE CONSIGNATION.

THE LORD'S PRAYER.

THE INCLINATION.

Pouring of chrism into the =   THE COMMIXTURE.
water.

Unus Pater sanctus, unus Filius sanctus, unus Spiritus sanctus.

Baptism.   =   THE COMMUNION.
Deconsecration of water.
Unction with chrism.
Imposition of the hand.
Insufflation.
White robes.
Girding and crowning.
Communion.
[Milk and honey.]
Blessing.   =   DISMISSAL.

Items in brackets [ ] are found only in the Ethiopic. Forms printed in clarendon type are Syrian, and those printed in italics are Greek. By subtracting from the first column all portions thus marked, a fair idea of the Egyptian baptismal rite is obtained.

THE WESTERN RITES.

TABLE I. *Rome.*

Ioannes Diac., Ep. ad Senarium; cf. older parts of the *Gelasian Sacramentary.*	The *Gelasian Sacramentary* and the *Ordo Romanus VII.*
Ad catechumenum faciendum.	*Ad catechumenum faciendum.*
Enrolling of names.	Enrolling of names.
Exsufflation, exorcism.	Signing of brow and imposition of the hand by priest.
Giving of salt.	Giving of salt.
Renunciation.	
Tradition of the creed.	*The first and second scrutinies.*
	Exorcisms by acolytes with signing and imposition of the hand.
The three scrutinies.	*The third scrutiny.*
Examination on the faith.	Exorcisms by acolytes as above.
	Exposition of the Gospels.
	Tradition of the creed.
	Tradition of the Lord's Prayer.
	Fourth, fifth, and sixth scrutinies.
	As the first.
After the third scrutiny.	*Seventh scrutiny on Easter Eve.*
	Exorcism by priest.
	Effeta with saliva.
Touching of ears and nose with oil.	
Unction of breast.	Unction of back and breast with oil.
	Threefold renunciation.
	Repetition of the creed.
	The baptism.
	Consecration of the water.
	Pouring in of chrism.
	Interrogation at the font.
Baptism.	Baptism.
White robes.	Signing of head with chrism by priest.
Unction of head with chrism.	Imposition of the hand.
	Signing of brow with chrism by Pope.
Communion.	Communion.
Milk and honey.	

TABLE II. *Roman Consecration of Font.*

(See *Dictionnaire d'archéol. chrét. et de lit.* II. i. 690, s.v.
'Bénédictions de l'eau ').

Modern Roman Missal	Gelasian Texts				Gregorian		Bobbio
	Wilson	O. R. I.	O. R. VII.	St Am.	Mén.	Mur.	
1. *O. s. d. adesto*	—	—	—	—	—	—	—
2. *Sursum corda*					—	—	
3. *Deus qui inuisibili*	—	—	—	—	—	—	—
4. *Deus cuius spiritus*	—	—	—	—	—	—	
5. *Deus qui nocentis*	—				—	—	O
6. *Respice Domine*	—						
7. *Qui hanc aquam*	—	—					
The water is divided crosswise			—				
8. *Sit haec sancta*	—						
The water is touched							
9. *Unde benedico te*	—	—			—	—	
Signing of water	—				—	—	—
10. *Qui te de paradiso*	O				—	—	O
The water is divided							
11. *Haec nobis praecepta*	—		—		—	—	
12. *Descendat in hanc*			—		—		
Dipping of candles					—	—	
Insufflation					—	—	
13. *Sanctificetur*							
Pouring in of oil							
14. *Infusio chrismatis*							O
Pouring in of chrism		—	—	—	—		
15. *Commixtio*							
Pouring in of both							

The documents referred to are Wilson's *Gelasian Sacramentary, Ordo
Romanus I.* and *VII.*, the *Ordo* of St Amand in Duchesne's *Christian
Worship*, p. 469, the *Gregorian Sacramentary* in Ménard and Muratori, and
the *Bobbio Missal*. The sign — means that the sections correspond, O that
the correspondence is partial. The core of the prayer is nos. 1—12. Of
these sections 2 is found only in Gregorian texts. Nos. 13 and 15 are
late, 14 is a Gallican addition which was early adopted but is not found in
the oldest Gelasian forms or the *Ordo* of Einsiedeln (Duchesne, *op. cit.*
p. 483).

TABLE III.   *Milan.*

The *de Mysteriis* and the *de Sacramentis*.	The *Manuale Ambros.* and *Ordo* of Beroldus.
	First week in Lent.
Enrolling of names.	Enrolling of names.
	Three Scrutinies.
	Twofold renunciation.
Signing.	"Exorcism of St Ambrose" with signings.
	Before the third scrutiny.
	Unction of the breast.
Palm Sunday.	*Saturday before Palm Sunday.*
Tradition of the creed.	Tradition of the creed.
Easter Eve.	*Easter Eve.*
Effeta.	
Unction of the body[1].	
Renunciation (twofold).	
Consecration of water.	Consecration of the water.
Exorcism[1].	Exorcism. Insufflation.
Invocation[1].	Pouring in of chrism.
Baptism with profession of faith.	Interrogations and baptism.
Unction of the head.	Signing of brow with chrism.
Washing of feet.	Washing of the feet.
White robes.	
Signing.	
Communion.	Communion[2].

[1] In the *de Sacr.* only.

[2] In some books.

Table IV. *Spain.*

The *Liber Ordinum* and St Ildephonsus.

At the scrutinies.

Exorcism.   Recordare Satanas.
Three capitula (read by bishop).
Exorcism.   Deprehensae sunt insidiae tuae.

Palm Sunday, in the morning.

Exorcisms (as above).
Ephphetatio (touching of ears and mouth with oil).

Palm Sunday, at mass.

Tradition of the creed.

Maundy Thursday.

Repetition of the creed.

Easter Eve.

Consecration of the water.
      Exsufflation and exorcism.
      Pouring in of oil.
Threefold renunciation.
Threefold profession of faith.
Baptism by single immersion.
Signing of the brow with chrism.
Imposition of the hand.
White robes.
Communion.

TABLE V. *Gaul and Ireland.*

Missale Gothicum.	*Missale Gallicanum Vetus.*	*Sacramentarium Gallicanum.* (Bobbio Missal.)
Ad christianum faciendum.		*Ad christianum faciendum.*
Signing of eyes, ears, nose, [mouth,] breast.		Signing and saying of creed. Insufflation. Accipe Spiritum sanctum.
On Palm Sunday.	†Exorcism. †Exposition of the creed.	*On Palm Sunday.*
Tradition of the creed.	†Exposition of the Gospels. †Exposition of the Lord's Prayer. †Exposition of the creed[1].	Exposition of the creed.
Baptism.	*Baptism.*	*Baptism.*
Consecration of the font.	Consecration of the font.	Consecration of the font.
Eucharistic prayer.	Exorcism.	Exorcism. Shortened Roman form.
Exorcism with insufflation. Pouring in of chrism.	Eucharistic prayer. Pouring in of chrism.	Eucharistic prayer. Pouring in of chrism. Exorcism of the candidate. Effeta. Touching of nose. Unction with oil. Touching of nose, ears, and breast.
	Single renunciation.	Threefold renunciation.
	Threefold profession.	Threefold profession.
Baptism with profession of faith.	Baptism.	Baptism.
Chrismation.	Chrismation.	Unction of brow with chrism. White robe.
Washing of feet. White robe.	Washing of feet.	Washing of feet.

[1] The parts marked † are in great confusion.

BIBLIOGRAPHY

A. GENERAL

AUGUSTI, J. C. W. *Denkwürdigkeiten aus der christlichen Archäologie.* Leipzig, 1817—31.

BINGHAM, J. *Origines Ecclesiasticae; or, The Antiquities of the Christian Church.* A good edition is that of Pitman (J. R.), London, 1840, 9 vols.

CABROL, F. *Dictionnaire d'archéologie chrétienne et de liturgie.* Paris. [Still appearing.] An invaluable work, especially useful for the vast store of materials there collected. The specially pertinent articles are Apertio Aurium ; Baptême ; Bénédictions de l'eau ; Bobbio, Missel de ; Catéchèse ; Catéchuménat.

CHASE, F. H. *Confirmation in the Apostolic Age.* London, 1909.

—— *The Lord's Command to Baptize, J. Th. St.* VI. (1905), 480 ; VIII. (1907), 161.

Church Quarterly Review, The. Articles on Confirmation appeared in XXXIV. (1892), 1—20, and XLV. (1898), 357—382.

CONYBEARE, F. C. *Three Early Doctrinal Modifications of the Text of the Gospels*, in *The Hibbert Journal*, I. (1902), 102.

DANIEL, H. A. *Codex Liturgicus Ecclesiae Vniuersae*, 4 vols. Lipsiae, 1853. A collection of various rites, including baptism and confirmation.

Dictionary of Christian Antiquities, edd. Smith and Cheetham. London, 1908. Articles on Baptism, Confirmation, etc.

DUCHESNE, L. *Christian Worship*. 3rd ed. London, 1910. Translation of *Origines du culte chrétien*.

HAHN, G. L. *Bibliothek der Symbole und Glaubensregeln der alten Kirche*. 3rd ed. Breslau, 1897.

HARNACK, A. *History of Dogma*. London, 1894—99. English translation of the original.

—— *The Apostles' Creed*. English translation. London, 1901.

HASTINGS, J. *Dictionary of the Bible*. Arts.: Baptism, Anointing, Laying on of hands.

—— *Encyclopædia of Religion and Ethics*. Arts.: Baptism, Confirmation.

HÖFLING, J. W. F. *Das Sakrament der Taufe*, 2 vols. Erlangen, 1846—48.

Journal of Theological Studies, The. See articles by Bernard, Bishop, Brightman, Burkitt, Chase, Robinson, referred to in text.

MASON, A. J. *The Relation of Confirmation to Baptism*. London, 1893. A most valuable collection of patristic passages on the subject.

ROBINSON, J. A. '*In the Name*,' *J.Th.St.* VII. (1906), 186—202.

ROGERS, C. F. *Baptism and Christian Archaeology* (*Studia Biblica et Ecclesiastica*, vol. v. pt iv.). Oxford, 1903.

STONE, D. *Holy Baptism*. London, 1899.

SUICER, J. C. *Thesaurus Ecclesiasticus*, 2nd ed. 2 vols. Amstelaedami, 1728. A collection of Greek ecclesiastical and theological terms with explanations and illustrative quotations.

SWETE, H. B. *The Holy Spirit in the New Testament*. London, 1909.

SWETE, H. B. *The Holy Spirit in the Ancient Church.* London, 1912.

WALL, W. *The History of Infant Baptism*, 4 vols. Oxford, 1836.

WIRGMAN, A. T. *The Doctrine of Confirmation.* London, 1897.

WORDSWORTH, J. *The Ministry of Grace*, 2nd ed. London, 1903.

B. DOCUMENTS AND SPECIAL TREATISES

1. *The early history and the Church Orders*

ACHELIS, H. *Die Canones Hippolyti (Texte und Unter-suchungen*, VI. 4). Leipzig, 1891.

BERNARD, J. H. *The Odes of Solomon*, in *J. Th. St.* XII. (1910), 1. Also in *Texts and Studies*, VIII. 3. Cambridge, 1912.

BICKELL, J. W. *Geschichte des Kirchenrechts.* Giessen, 1843—9. Only one volume ever appeared.

BURKITT, F. C. *On the Baptismal Rite in the Canons of Hippolytus*, in the *J.Th.St.* I. (1900), 279.

COOPER, J. and MACLEAN, A. J. *The Testament of our Lord.* Edinburgh, 1902.

FUNK, F. X. *Didascalia et Constitutiones Apostolorum*, 2 vols. Paderborn, 1905.

—— *Das Testament unseres Herrn und die verwandten Schriften.* Mainz, 1901.

GIBSON, M. D. *Didascalia Apostolorum*, 2 vols. in English and Syriac. (*Horae Semiticae*, nos. 1 and 2.) London, 1903.

HANEBERG, D. B.   *Canones S. Hippolyti.*   Monachii, 1870.

HARNACK, A.   *Die Lehre der zwölf Apostel (Texte und Untersuchungen, II. 1 and 2).*   Leipzig, 1884.

—— *Sources of the Apostolic Canons,* English translation. London, 1895.

HARRIS, J. R.   *The Odes and Psalms of Solomon.* Cambridge, 1909 ; 2nd ed. 1911.

HAULER, E.   *Didascaliae Apostolorum Fragmenta Veronensia Latina,* vol I.   Leipzig, 1900.

HORNER, G.   *The Statutes of the Apostles or Canones Ecclesiastici.*   London, 1904.

LAGARDE, A. P. DE, (BÖTTICHER).   *Reliquiae Iuris Ecclesiastici Antiquissimae.*   Leipzig, 1856.

MACLEAN, A. J.   *The Ancient Church Orders.*   Cambridge, 1910.

PLATT, T. P.   *The Ethiopic Didascalia.*   (Oriental Translation Fund.)   London, 1834.

TATTAM, H.   *The Apostolical Constitutions in Coptic.* (Oriental Translation Fund.)   London, 1848.

2.   *Eastern Rites*

1. **Syrian.**   CONNOLLY, R. H.   *The Liturgical Homilies of Narsai. (Texts and Studies,* VIII. 1).   Cambridge, 1909.

   DENZINGER, H.   *Ritus Orientalium,* 2 vols.   Wirceburgi, 1863.

   DIETTRICH, G.   *Die nestorianische Taufliturgie.* Giessen, 1903.

2. **Greek.**   CONYBEARE, F. C.   *Rituale Armenorum.* Oxford, 1905.

   GOAR, J.   ΕΥΧΟΛΟΓΙΟΝ *siue rituale Graecorum.* Paris, 1647.

3. **Armenian.**   CONYBEARE and DENZINGER as above.

3. *The Egyptian Rite*

BRIGHTMAN, F. E. *The Sacramentary of Serapion of Thmuis,* in the *J.Th.St.* I. (1899), 88—113, and (1900), 247—277.

DENZINGER, as above.

EVETTS, B. T. A. *The Rites of the Coptic Church.* London, 1888.

PITRA, I. B. *Iuris Ecclesiastici Graecorum Historia et Monumenta.* Romae, 1864.

WORDSWORTH, J. *Bishop Sarapion's Prayer Book.* 2nd ed. London, 1910.

On the Eastern. rites generally Denzinger's *Ritus Orientalium* is very valuable, both for its introductions and for its texts ; compare also ASSEMANI, J. A., *Codex liturgicus ecclesiae uniuersae in xv. libros distributus,* Romae, 1749—71, vols. 1—3.

4. *The Western Rites*

1. **Africa.** BISHOP, W. C. *The African Rite* in the *J.Th.St.* XIII. (1912), 250. The African writers are the sole source.

2. **Rome.** FELTOE, C. L. *Sacramentarium Leonianum.* Cambridge, 1896.

   Liber Sacramentorum S. Gregorii Papae, ex editione D. Hugonis Menardi in vol. III part i of the Benedictine edition of the works of St Gregory. Venice, 1744. Contains the *Gregorian Sacramentary* with copious notes.

   MURATORI, L. A. *Liturgia Romana Vetus.* Venice, 1748. Contains the Leonian, Gelasian, and Gregorian books.

   WILSON, H. A. *The Gelasian Sacramentary.* Oxford, 1894.

3. **Milan.** *Codex Sacramentorum Bergomensis (Ad utramque I. P. Migne Patrologiam Supplementum siue Auctarium Solesmense,* tom. I. vol. i. fasc. 1). Solesmis, 1900.

MAGISTRETTI, M. *Beroldus.* Milan, 1894.

—— *Monumenta Veteris Liturgiae Ambrosianae,* I. *Pontificale,* Milan, 1897 ; II., III. *Manuale Ambrosianum,* Milan, 1905.

4. **Spain.** FÉROTIN, M. *Liber ordinum (Monumenta Ecclesiae Liturgica,* vol. V.). Paris, 1904.

5. **Gaul and Ireland.** MABILLON, J. *De Liturgia Gallicana.* Paris, 1685. *Museum Italicum,* 2 vols. Paris, 1687—89. The latter work contains John the Deacon's *Epistle to Senarius* and the *Bobbio Missal.*

MURATORI, L. A. *Liturgia Romana Vetus,* in spite of its name, contains the Gallican books, the *Missale Gothicum, Missale Gallicanum Vetus,* and the *Sacramentarium Gallicanum.*

NEALE, J. M. and FORBES, G. H. *The Ancient Liturgies of the Gallican Church.* Burntisland, 1855. Contains the rites, together with valuable notes and references.

WARNER, G. F. *The Stowe Missal* (vol. XXXI. of the publications of the Henry Bradshaw Society). London, 1906. Vol. I., containing the facsimile, has alone appeared.

WARREN, F. E. *The Liturgy and Ritual of the Celtic Church.* Oxford, 1881.

And on Western rites in general see DUCHESNE'S *Christian Worship* and MARTÈNE, E., *De antiquis ecclesiae ritibus.* (4 vols. Antwerp, 1763—4.)

INDEX OF SUBJECTS

[See also Table of Contents, p. ix]